# Mint.com

## FOR

## DUMMIES®

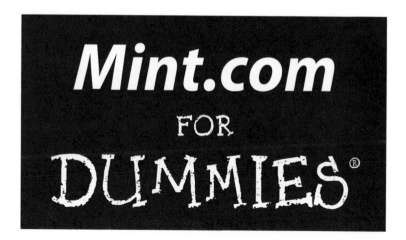

# Mint.com FOR DUMMIES®

by Gail A. Perry, CPA, and Matt Krantz

**Foreword by Aaron Patzer**
Founder, Mint.com

WILEY

Wiley Publishing, Inc.

**Mint.com For Dummies®**

Published by
**Wiley Publishing, Inc.**
111 River Street
Hoboken, NJ 07030-5774

www.wiley.com

For general information on our other products and services, please contact our Customer Care Department within the U.S. at 877-762-2974, outside the U.S. at 317-572-3993, or fax 317-572-4002.

For technical support, please visit www.wiley.com/techsupport.

Wiley also publishes its books in a variety of electronic formats. Some content that appears in print may not be available in electronic books.

Library of Congress Control Number: 2010939502

ISBN: 978-0-470-88318-1

Manufactured in the United States of America

10  9  8  7  6  5  4  3  2  1

WILEY

# About the Authors

**Gail A. Perry** is a licensed CPA, financial journalist, author, speaker, instructor, and the managing editor of *AccountingWEB,* a daily online news source for members of the accounting profession. Gail is a former senior tax accountant with Deloitte, the Big Four accounting firm, where she provided tax-planning services and financial advice to individuals and small businesses. An accomplished freelance writer, Gail is the author of 30 books on various aspects of personal finance, taxation, and financial software. Some of her titles include *Quicken All-in-One Desk Reference For Dummies*, *QuickBooks on Demand*, and *Surviving Financial Downsizing: A Practical Guide to Living Well on Less Income*. Gail has a bachelor's degree in Journalism and English from Indiana University.

**Matt Krantz** is a nationally known financial journalist who specializes in investing and personal finance topics. Krantz has been a reporter and writer for *USA TODAY* since 1999. He covers financial markets and Wall Street, concentrating on developments affecting individual investors and their portfolios. Matt also writes USATODAY.com's daily online investing column, "Ask Matt." Matt is the author of the best-selling investment books *Investing Online For Dummies* and *Fundamental Analysis For Dummies* and has appeared on Fox Business and Nightly Business Report.

# Dedication

This book is dedicated to my daughters, Katherine and Georgia, who make every day worthwhile. —Gail Perry

I dedicate this book to Aaron Patzer, whose invention is the reason I wrote this book and the reason you're reading it. —Matt Krantz

# Authors' Acknowledgments

Two of us get to have our names on the cover, but the behind-the-scenes team is no less important to the creation of this book. I would like to thank Kyle Looper, Matt Wagner, and Bob Woerner for reaching out to us in the first place and making this project possible. Thanks to Susan Pink and David Ringstrom for their editing skills and for pulling together all the loose ends and making sure everything works the way we say it does. Thank you also to the hard-working people in Composition Services, Graphics, and Indexing, who are responsible for designing the finished product. I would like to offer special thanks to my husband, Rick, who tolerates the weird schedule, diet, and attitude that accompany my forays into the book world, and to my boss, Rob Nance, who provided encouragement throughout the project.
—Gail Perry

Thanks to my wife, Nancy, for being the ultimate second set of eyes and reason. Thanks to my daughter, Leilani, for putting up with Dad during deadline days. All the effort by project editor Susan Pink, acquisitions editor Kyle Looper, and technical editor David Ringstom are much appreciated because they offered valuable guidance as well as suggestions and ways to improve the book. Aaron Patzer, founder of Mint.com, was a big help in sharing his deep expertise of the product. Mint.com spokeswoman Martha Shaughnessy was always available to provide materials and resources. Thanks to agent Matt Wagner for thinking of me for this project. And thanks to the editors at *USA TODAY* for supporting my growth as a writer and an author.
—Matt Krantz

## Publisher's Acknowledgments

We're proud of this book; please send us your comments at http://dummies.custhelp.com. For other comments, please contact our Customer Care Department within the U.S. at 877-762-2974, outside the U.S. at 317-572-3993, or fax 317-572-4002.

Some of the people who helped bring this book to market include the following:

*Acquisitions and Editorial*

**Project Editor:** Susan Pink

**Acquisitions Editor:** Kyle Looper

**Copy Editor:** Susan Pink

**Technical Editor:** David Ringstrom

**Editorial Manager:** Jodi Jensen

**Editorial Assistant:** Amanda Foxworth

**Sr. Editorial Assistant:** Cherie Case

**Cartoons:** Rich Tennant
(www.the5thwave.com)

*Composition Services*

**Project Coordinator:** Sheree Montgomery

**Layout and Graphics:** Samantha K. Cherolis, Joyce Haughey

**Proofreaders:** ConText Editorial Services, Inc., Lauren Mandelbaum

**Indexer:** Ty Koontz

---

**Publishing and Editorial for Technology Dummies**

    **Richard Swadley,** Vice President and Executive Group Publisher

    **Andy Cummings,** Vice President and Publisher

    **Mary Bednarek,** Executive Acquisitions Director

    **Mary C. Corder,** Editorial Director

**Publishing for Consumer Dummies**

    **Diane Graves Steele,** Vice President and Publisher

**Composition Services**

    **Debbie Stailey,** Director of Composition Services

# Contents at a Glance

# Table of Contents

# Foreword

· · · · · · · · · · · · · · · · · · · · · · · · · · · · · · · · · · · · · · · · · · · ·

*B*uilding a product that I wanted to use every day has been the ride of my life. In early 2006, I had the idea for Mint.com — an online, always up-to-date, free, easy-to-use, Web application to manage my finances.

In just four years, and working with a world-class team of developers, we built the product and saw millions of users sign up to manage their financial lives. Three years after my initial idea, we had grown so much that we were acquired by Intuit, makers of Quicken, QuickBooks, and TurboTax.

During this wild ride, our mission has remained the same: to help every individual worldwide understand and do more with his or her money. To that end, Mint.com has found people billions of dollars in savings. Mint.com is a free product; we make our money when we find you better prices on the things you buy most or better rates on your financial products. If you sign up for a savings account that will pay you more interest, that bank pays us a referral fee: truly a win for all three parties.

Mint.com is now the leading personal finance Web tool. It can link to all your bank accounts, credit cards, investments, and loans. It categorizes your spending automatically to show you how much you spend on gas or groceries, and gives you bill reminders and low-balance alerts via text messages or e-mail. Most importantly, Mint.com will give you control over your financial life so you can start saving for your children's education, your retirement, a car, a house, or any other goal.

When I began, I had the perhaps naïve idea that Mint could change our national savings rate. Today, 90 percent of Mint users report that they have altered their spending habits and are saving more because of the insights Mint.com provides. It's a start.

*Mint.com For Dummies* provides an easy step-by-step guide to getting the most out of Mint.com, both online and through our mobile applications. Beyond the basics, you'll find powerful tips for managing your personal, household, and small business finances; setting budgets; gaining insight into your investments; achieving financial goals; avoiding fees; and maximizing your savings. *Mint.com For Dummies* is the most thorough guide to using Mint.com that has been written.

Aaron Patzer
Founder and CEO, Mint.com
October 2010

# Introduction

M int.com is winning over millions of users for a reason. Several reasons, actually. More people are discovering that if they use Mint. com, the personal finance site can put them on the financial fast track. Mint. com can find ways for you to save more money, create a budget and stick to it, and shed oppressive debt. The site can also help you prepare for long-term goals such as buying a home or paying for college. And it's free.

If you're struggling to pay down debt, get a better credit card, or plan financial goals, Mint.com is ready to lend a hand. However, Mint.com can help you only as much as you help the site. It might sound strange to say that a Web site needs your help to work better, but it's true. Mint.com needs you to assist it in gathering your financial information and getting all your online accounts into your Mint.com account.

Although Mint.com is designed to be easy to use, you still need to understand a bit about personal finances to put the site to its best use. If you're uncertain of the meaning of terms such as *net worth*, *principal*, and *assets*, you might not be getting the most that Mint.com has to offer. That's where *Mint.com For Dummies* comes in. This book is your guide through the morass of personal financial planning jargon and a handbook for putting Mint.com to work for you. We help you confront your financial problems and move forward with confidence using Mint.com.

*Mint.com For Dummies* isn't just a user manual for Mint.com. Certainly, you'll find easy-to-follow, step-by-step guidance on using key features of the program. But think of this book as your guide to getting control of your money. You discover how to avoid financial pitfalls that routinely trip people up and how Mint.com can help keep you on the right path.

## About This Book

*Mint.com For Dummies* contains loads of information about what's entailed in running a tight financial ship. Every chapter is packed with information about the essentials you need to know about financial topics ranging from credit cards to budgets to health care to retirement, coupled with tips on how to set prudent financial goals.

*Mint.com For Dummies* is different from most financial planning books because after you understand how to manage your money, we show you how to use Mint.com to put your financial plan into action.

# Conventions Used in This Book

To help you get the information you need from this book as quickly as possible, we use the following conventions:

- ✔ Monofont is used to designate a Web address that you type in your Web browser.

- ✔ *Italics* signal a word we're defining that's an important term for Mint.com users.

- ✔ **Boldfaced** words make the key terms and phrases in bulleted and numbered lists jump out and grab your attention. We also use bold for user entry.

- ✔ Sidebars, which consist of text separated from the rest of the type in gray boxes, provide interesting and more in-depth commentary about a topic.

# What You're Not To Read

Personal financial planning is, well, personal. Your financial situation is as unique to you as your taste in music or food. For that reason, not every section in *Mint.com For Dummies* will apply to you. For instance, if you're debt free, feel free to skip the sections about reducing debt. Following are other elements that might not apply to every reader:

- ✔ **Passages marked with a Technical Stuff icon:** Mint.com isn't difficult to use, but some aspects of it might be more complicated than what you want to deal with. These sections of the book are clearly marked with a Technical Stuff icon. Read (or don't read) accordingly.

- ✔ **Text in gray boxes:** These areas, called sidebars, are tidbits of information we thought were interesting or fun. But we understand that you're busy and may not like to have as much fun with Mint.com as we do. You can skip these sidebars and not miss out on anything you need to know to use Mint.com.

- ✔ **The stuff in the front of the book:** All sorts of things to make lawyers happy are in the front of the book, including details about the book's copyrights. We've also dedicated this book and given details about ourselves in the front pages. You don't have to read any of this stuff to understand Mint.com, and you won't hurt our feelings if you don't want to find out more about the authors but instead want to jump right into the meat of the book.

# Foolish Assumptions

We assume that you know some things about your computer. We trust you're familiar with navigating the Internet, clicking links, using e-mail, and other basic tasks. We tried to make our directions as clear as possible, going as far as describing where various links are located, and we present screenshots when appropriate.

We cut you some slack regarding what you know about money and financial matters. If you're just starting out managing your financial affairs, *Mint.com For Dummies* has you covered. Even if you recently signed up for your first bank account, this book will show you how to add that account to Mint.com and start tracking your income and your spending and creating a budget. If you've been working and saving money for a few years and are hoping to move forward with some financial planning for your family and your current goals, you'll find loads of information about paying off debts and starting to plan. And if you're nearing retirement or already enjoying your golden years, you'll see how Mint.com helps manage retirement and investment accounts and make sure you don't use up your nest egg.

# How This Book Is Organized

The chapters are self-contained and can be read just like short stories. Feel free to flip the pages, skip from chapter to chapter, or just dive into the part with the best cartoon. Whatever works for you.

If you're already a Mint.com user, you might start with the last chapter, which contains ten tricks and tips to using the site you perhaps don't know about. If you've been wondering what your financial value is, dive into Chapter 12, which is about how Mint.com measures your net worth. If the taxman keeps you up at night, use the index to find all the pages that help you manage your tax hit.

## Part I: Getting Started

To be successful with Mint.com, you need to get off to a good start. In Part I, you find out how to create your Mint.com account and make sure everything is set up just right so you don't run into issues later. Because much of Mint. com's power lies in tracking the way you use your credit cards and manage your cash, we discuss those topics, too. And this part addresses computer security, and the advantages and risks of trusting a site such as Mint.com to monitor your sensitive financial information.

# Part II: Budgeting

Budgets have the reputation of being difficult to create and even more painful to stick with. Mint.com makes creating a budget practically automatic. But as anyone with automatic seat belts in their cars in the 1980s learned, automatic doesn't always mean better. Part II shows you how to make sure Mint.com is giving you realistic budget goals based on prudent assumptions. The part also deals with typical budget-busting items, such as infrequent expenses and periodic splurges.

# Part III: Planning and Saving

Some statistics about retirement are downright frightening. Of the oldest Americans, nearly half are at risk of not having enough money to pay for basic expenses in retirement, according to a 2010 report by the Employee Benefit Research Institute. And you whippersnappers should stop snickering. The study also found that 44 percent of younger Baby Boomers and 45 percent of Generation Xers are at risk of not having enough to retire. That means about half of Americans are facing a big-time problem in retirement.

But looking at those statistics another way means that more than half of Americans are prepared for retirement. Part III helps you be among the haves, not the have-nots. You find out how to monitor your net worth, how to make sure that big expenses don't derail your financial future, how to plan for big-ticket costs such as college and retirement, and how to navigate the costly health care jungle.

# Part IV: Borrowing and Investing

After you understand the basics of financial planning, it's time to tackle more complicated topics. And for many, figuring out how to manage debt is one of the more tricky financial situations to handle. While prudently using debt can be helpful or even wise, falling behind can unravel an otherwise well-thought-out financial plan. Similarly, not having a solid investment plan can mean that your money doesn't grow as quickly as the prices of things you need, eroding decades of hard work and savings. Part IV shows you how Mint.com helps you turn your financial picture into a masterpiece.

## Part V: The Part of Tens

We have so much great stuff to tell you about Mint.com that we couldn't possibly squeeze it all in four parts. In this last part, you find three well-organized sets of ten items that will make your experience using Mint.com that much better. You find ten ways to prepare for your taxes and ten methods to boost your credit score. Finally, you read about ten hidden tricks and tips that you can show off to your friends.

# Icons Used in This Book

While reading *Mint.com For Dummies*, you might see several cool-looking icons that catch your attention. If you've read a *For Dummies* book before, you know the drill when it comes to these icons. These icons signal parts of the book that are significant.

The Remember icon saves you the trouble of digging out your yellow highlighter. Here you'll find sections that are so important, you might want to move aside some space in your brain to hold them. Usually, these sections describe issues with Mint.com that you need to be aware of for the site to make sense.

The Tip sections contain nuggets of know-how that you can quickly pick up and put to use. Some consist of things we discovered by probing every nook and cranny of Mint.com for you. Tips help you work smarter and faster.

These pieces of techno information tell you why Mint.com is doing what it's doing or what the accountants talk about when they're filling out tax returns. Drop one of these bits of financial or technical jargon on the floor, come back in the middle of the night and turn on the light, and watch the computer geeks and accounting nerds scatter in all directions.

Money matters are rife with dangers. Part of creating a solid financial plan with Mint.com is knowing which mistakes to avoid making with your money. In addition, Mint.com has some quirks that you need to be aware of so that you don't make a bad decision based on a misunderstanding. These sections lay out these perils.

# *Where to Go from Here*

Enough with the introductory information. It's time to dig in and have a good time with Mint.com. Turn the page, get started, and head down the path of financial serenity, knowing that your questions about tracking and managing your finances with Mint.com can be answered with a quick look at this book.

# Part I
# Getting Started

"Don't be silly - of course my passwords are safe. I keep them written on my window, but then I pull the shade if anyone walks in the room."

# In this part . . .

*I*t's easy to put off managing your money. Tomorrow always seems like the perfect day to finally get your financial matters in order. But in this part, you find out how quickly you can be up and running and watching over your money with Mint.com. Unlike other ways of tracking your money, which you might have tried and struggled with before, Mint.com can tame your debts and track what you own right now. This part shows you how.

And if you want to know whether Mint.com is worth your time, you've come to the right place. You gain an appreciation of what Mint.com can do for you and find out how easily Mint.com can pull in all your financial information so you can get a bird's-eye view of how you're doing.

Mint.com is constantly telling you that it can save you money, and in this part you find out what that claim means. We also address the all-important topic of credit cards as well as Mint.com's great skill at alerting you to important changes in your accounts. Also, many people are concerned with security. In this part, you read about the security issues with managing your money online and how you can use Mint.com wisely to keep your private financial information private.

# Chapter 1

# Welcome to Mint.com

Doctor, scientist, academic, author, and all-around Renaissance man Louis Agassiz is quoted as saying, "I cannot afford to waste my time making money." Mr. Agassiz's time was well spent on various realms of scientific inquiry, such as the discovery that the Earth was once subjected to an ice age, and countless students were rewarded for his choice in allocating his time.

For most of us, however, managing and tracking finances and making money are closely related to reducing stress and living a comfortable life. If your financial records are scattered around your home, stuffed in drawers, stashed in pockets, filed in file folders buried under stacks of papers, or just stuck in your head, the chaos of your finances can carry over into your daily life.

Ready to come to your rescue is the Mint.com Web site. Fans claim that you can begin benefiting from the use of Mint.com within the first five minutes that you spend on the site. Going beyond that first five minutes is what this book is all about.

Within these pages, you will find advice and tips for utilizing the information in Mint.com to manage your finances, set realizable goals, oversee your short- and long-term investments, assemble your annual income tax information, prepare for your retirement, and live within a workable budget.

In these tough economic times, having a handle on your personal finances is not a luxury — it's a requirement. Using Mint.com is a giant step toward keeping control of your finances.

# Introducing Mint.com

Mint.com was started in 2005 by Aaron Patzer, a computer scientist and engineer who was frustrated in his attempts to manage his finances using programs such as Microsoft Money and Intuit's Quicken. Patzer complained that those programs required too much time to enter receipts and balance accounts. Wanting to save time by streamlining the money management process and gain some additional benefit from the use of the Internet, Patzer came up with the idea for Mint.com, went public with the site in 2007, and signed up fifty thousand users in the first month. The site now provides tools for more than three million users to manage and track their finances.

Although most people agree with the concept that it makes sense to take an active part in managing personal finances, that doesn't mean they actually do anything about their finances. Working with most personal finance software programs takes time, and you have to keep all those pesky little receipts from the grocery store and Taco Bell. Everyone knows what a pain that can be.

A nice solution is to sign up for a free service that not only takes the work out of keeping track of every little expense but also tells you when you've spent too much at the video store, when your bank is about to assess an unwelcome finance charge, and when it's time to pay your kids' allowance.

You can use Mint.com to help you keep an eagle eye on your every financial move, or you can check in occasionally just to say hello and look over your bank transactions. You can ask Mint.com to e-mail you friendly reminders, or you can skip the mail service and oversee your accounts yourself.

Mint.com users who take advantage of all that the program offers can save money in a variety of ways. Because Mint.com has partnered with nearly all the nation's banks that have Internet banking capability, the site can provide instant analysis of your accounts, your finance charges, and your normal banking activity; compare that information with its stores of data; and offer cool deals to save money.

You are not charged for these services, but Mint.com gets a referral fee from the bank if you switch to a new account. However, Mint.com looks for the best banking opportunities for you, whether or not there is a referral fee.

Mint.com not only tells you about good deals at banks and other financial institutions and helps you keep track of your hard earned cash but also designs a budget for you and tells you when you're misbehaving. That's right — you don't have to devise a budget and then try to stick to it. Mint.com creates the budget based on your financial history and then gently harasses you when you step over the line.

# *What about Clouds?*

"Your head is in the clouds." "Hey! You! Get off of my cloud." "I've looked at clouds from both sides now." You're no doubt humming along at this point. Look up and you see clouds all around you. So where is all the cloud computing hiding? Mint.com, like so many recently developed programs, lives entirely in the cloud (see Figure 1-1). That's a fancy way of saying that the program doesn't reside on your computer. But, you're using your computer right now and there it is — Mint.com, right on your computer. So what's the deal with clouds?

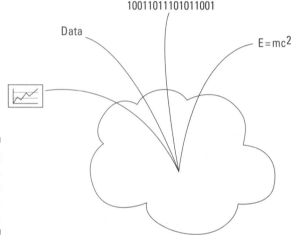

10011011101011001

Data

$E = mc^2$

**Figure 1-1:**
These days, the clouds are bursting with data.

Here's how data is stored in the cloud. Turn off your computer. Walk over to your neighbor's house, stroll down the hall at work to a coworker's office, or get on a plane and travel halfway around the world. Sit down at someone else's computer, get on the Internet, type www.mint.com, and enter your user name and password. There's your financial data, just as you left it.

Mint.com, and all the information it analyzes, is available only in cyberspace. You don't need any software on your computer or anyone else's to go to the Mint.com Web site and examine your money.

Having your Mint.com data in the cloud has the following advantages:

✔ You don't need to purchase or own any software.

✔ You don't even have to own a computer. You must have access to a computer, but it doesn't have to be your computer.

✔ If Mint.com decides it's time for an update, the program updates itself; you don't have to do anything.

✔ You don't have to worry if your computer crashes. Well, okay, you do have to worry if your computer crashes, but you don't have to worry about the safety of your Mint.com data.

✔ You don't have to worry about the security of your data. Your personal financial information is at least as safe on the cloud as it is on your personal computer or stuffed under your mattress. (For more on how Mint. com keeps your data safe, see Chapter 7.)

We like to think about secure Web sites and sensitive data as being tucked away in a hole in the ground instead of floating around in the sky. The data does reside in a physical place called a server farm, and in the case of Mint. com, that server farm resides underground. But "cold and dark" isn't nearly as fun-sounding as "light and fluffy," so the cloud concept is the one we use to describe information accessible only through the Internet.

# Changing Your Life with Mint.com

If you are a skeptic, you probably need to see Mint.com in action before you will believe that this program can change your life. We were in that camp before we started using Mint.com, so we know what you're thinking:

✔ First, you're worried about the safety of trusting all your financial information to an unknown source. See Chapter 7 to put your mind at rest.

✔ If you've used a different personal finance program, such as Quicken or Microsoft Money, you're thinking that this is just another program where you have to gather all your receipts, deposit slips, and check stubs, and then schedule time away from the family or the television or your favorite book or whatever you'd rather be doing every Sunday night so that you can keep your finances up to date. Nope. You don't have to do anything. Mint.com takes care of the staying-up-to-date part for you.

✔ Now you are really getting worried about security issues and are thinking there's no way you're going to let some unknown group of computer geeks who run a Web site keep track of your very personal finances. Back to Chapter 7.

✔ You think that it might be nice to see some reports about your spending habits, but you're not convinced of the usefulness of a budget or another analysis prepared entirely by a computer program. Part II is waiting to change your mind on this issue.

✔ You don't trust computers. You want your financial information stored in your desk or your file drawer. Wait. You're not that person, at least not anymore. You wouldn't have picked up this book if you weren't ready to give Mint.com a whirl.

# Finding where you've been

When you start using Mint.com, you'll soon discover that you have at your fingertips a quick history of your financial behavior. Just try deluding yourself about your frugality when you look at a report that shows you blew $300 last month on video games. Don't try to convince yourself that you cook all your meals at home when the report shows that you dined out 16 times in April.

But the spending news is not all bad. Look at how your medical expenses have decreased since last year. Check out the small amount spent at department and clothing stores, and pat yourself on the back for taking a pass on new additions to your wardrobe.

Mint.com tells you how much you've dropped in various spending categories and provides pretty graphs that illustrate all the places where your money has gone.

With a quick click, you can see how your current spending compares to previous time periods. But that feature is just the tip of the reporting iceberg. You can also see how your spending compares to that of other people who live in your city or in a city where you might like to live. You can even view comparisons of your spending versus the spending of the entire country.

You can track different types of spending. For example, how does your Starbucks spending compare to that of coffee drinkers in Des Moines or New Orleans?

Spending isn't the only type of financial activity that qualifies for these comparisons. Mint.com lets you compare your income, assets, debts, and net worth to that of others.

# Finding where you are

On the opening page of Mint.com, your spending for the month appears right before your eyes, along with a comparison to your budget. What? You have a budget? Yep. You didn't have to do a thing; Mint.com sets up a budget for you. The budget is a starting point — you can customize and work with the numbers so that they are appropriate for you.

If one budget isn't enough of a challenge for you, you can set up multiple budgets with different scenarios. We describe these options in Part II.

Mint.com also provides a detailed analysis of your recent financial activity and lets you identify how various spending and income items should be categorized. In this way, you can fine-tune your budget and the reports that Mint.com prepares for you.

## Finding where you're going

You don't really need a computer program to tell you how much you spent at the vet for your puppy's checkup. But a little help from Mint.com comes in handy when you want to read into the future to help plan your retirement and long-term goals.

Mint.com can also help you plan for big expenses, such as a college education, a wedding, or a vacation, and not-so-big expenses, such as carpeting, a new television, or repairs. Instead of worrying about how to set aside money, use the tools in Mint.com to prepare for these purchases and make them work within your budget.

# Gathering Information

To get the most out of the Mint.com experience, you should connect all your financial accounts to your Mint.com profile. Otherwise, you'll end up with a partial financial picture, hampering your ability to know your spending habits, make accurate plans, and take advantage of all Mint.com has to offer.

To get the full Mint.com experience, you need information from the following types of accounts:

- **Bank accounts:** If you have more than one account at the same bank, all the accounts will be pulled into Mint.com at once, so one login name is all you need. If you haven't signed up to access your bank account information online, do that now. You can't get much benefit from Mint.com if you don't connect your bank account. If you have accounts at more than one bank, gather login information from each bank.

- **Credit card accounts:** If your credit card accounts aren't set up with the same bank as your bank accounts, you need your login information. If you don't have online access to these accounts, now is the time to get it. Credit card accounts include bank credit cards, gas company cards, department store credit cards, and any other credit cards that you have and use. If you have, say, an old Sears card that you haven't used in ages, don't worry about setting up an account for it in Mint.com.

- **Investment accounts:** Do you have one or more investment accounts with a broker or a mutual fund? Find the login password and user name.

- **Mortgage:** Even if you don't access your mortgage online, you need to collect login information for the account. If necessary, set up your mortgage for online access so you can include your mortgage with your Mint.com profile.

When you enter the name of your bank or financial institution, Mint.com tells you whether that bank can be accessed online. If your financial institution isn't accessible online, see whether it has plans for online access.

While you're thinking about your house, list all the home improvements you've made, including the cost and the date. *Improvements* are purchases you make that add to the value of the house. Buying a throw rug doesn't count, but installing wall-to-wall carpeting does. Repairing a nick in the wall doesn't count, but painting the entire room does. You'll use this information to help in valuing your house in Mint.com.

✔ **Bank and car loans:** Again, set up online access for any loan accounts that you want to include in your Mint.com profile.

✔ **Cash spending:** Start thinking about how much of your spending is in cash instead of writing checks or swiping credit and debit cards. Tracking your cash gives you a complete picture of your spending habits. (For more information, see Chapter 5.)

After you gather the preceding information, you're ready to get started in Mint.com. If it's Saturday night and the banks are closed and you can't find or remember all your login information, you can still start using Mint.com — just make sure that you add the accounts as you get the information.

# Chapter 2

# Setting Up Shop

. . . . . . . . . . . . . . . . . . . . . . . . . . . . . . . . . . . . . . . . . . . .

## In This Chapter

▶ Getting started

▶ Setting up your bank accounts in Mint.com

▶ Entering credit card information

▶ Adding your investment accounts to the mix

▶ Entering info about your home

▶ Adding information about your vehicles

▶ Leaving and returning to your Mint.com account

. . . . . . . . . . . . . . . . . . . . . . . . . . . . . . . . . . . . . . . . . . . .

Since September 2007, more than three million users have signed onto Mint.com and started tracking their income and expenses and other finances through this financial Web site. Whether you're a newbie or a Mint. com regular, the information we present can make your Mint.com experience more robust and efficient. In this chapter, we describe how to get started in Mint.com and how to add the information that will make your Mint.com experience complete and worthwhile.

Mint.com is an online personal bookkeeper and financial advisor that can help you clean up your financial messes as well as give you tips and tools to improve your overall financial picture and save money. Mint.com is today's answer to the paper checkbook register and time-consuming paper budgets.

## Ready, Aim, Blast-off

Using "Blast-off" in the title of this section might make you think that we're talking about rocket science. You'll be pleased to know that Mint.com, although nestled in the clouds, is about as far from rocket science as you can get, at least for the user. As long as your technical knowledge includes using a mouse and reading information on a computer screen, you're going to do fine.

Turn on your computer, climb onboard the Internet, and go to www.mint.com. The site appears, a lovely, um, minty green.

Poke around if you like, exploring the menus, and then come back here when you're ready to get started. On the home page, shown in Figure 2-1, click the orange oval that reads: Free! Get Started Here.

**Figure 2-1:** The Mint. com home page.

You don't need to provide much information to get started in Mint.com, as you can see in Figure 2-2.

**Figure 2-2:** Enter your e-mail, zip, and password to begin your Mint.com experience.

Here's what you are asked to enter:

- ✔ **Your Email:** Enter your e-mail address so you can receive e-mail alerts when an important change occurs in your personal finances. Expect an alert if your bank account balance gets too low, a bill is due, or you've spent too much on a budget item. You can change your e-mail address, if necessary. If you tire of the alerts, you can turn them off. Chapter 6 discusses the ins and outs of Mint.com alerts.

- ✔ **Confirm Email:** One more time please — reenter your e-mail address to let Mint.com know that you know how to spell.

- ✔ **Zip Code:** If you think your zip code isn't an important part of your personal financial tracking, you're wrong. Mint.com asks for your zip code so that it can identify the stores where you shop, provide comparisons to other people in your area, and know your time zone so it can send messages when you're not sleeping.

- ✔ **Password:** Enter a password that is only for you and the folks at Mint.com to know. Actually, the people at Mint.com don't know your password because it is encrypted as you enter it. (See Chapter 7 for more information on the security of your password.) Your password must be at least 6 characters and no more than 16 characters. Spaces and the characters that appear above the number keys on your keyboard are allowed. When you enter a password, Mint.com rates it okay or strong. Shoot for a strong rating by using a combination of letters, numbers, spaces, and characters. The less your password looks like a recognizable word, the more likely you'll earn a strong rating.

- ✔ **Confirm Password:** Just to make sure you didn't make a mistake typing your password, enter the same password again. While you're at it, save the password — sticky notes attached to your computer screen are not recommended.

You're almost finished. Note the check box that reads Yes, I Agree to the Mint.com Terms of Use. "Terms of Use" is a link; click that link to read all about how Mint.com won't share your personal information with anyone unless you want them to. And even then, they'll give up only your e-mail address in case you want to find out about some offers that might save you money. You can also find out how Mint.com protects their servers by using biometrics (such as retinal scans and fingerprint identification and bodily odors), and how you'll be out of luck if you want to sue Mint.com. When you're ready, click to select the check box.

Now that you've completed entering this setup information, click the Sign Up button. Just like the horses at the Kentucky Derby, you're off and running. You are logged into Mint.com and can start using the program. When you return to Mint.com later, just enter your e-mail address and password to log in.

# Adding Bank Accounts

After you log in, the next step is to add an account. Without your accounts, Mint.com just stares at you and wonders what you're doing here. In this section, you start by adding your checking account.

Before you can add an account, it must be accessible online. If you haven't worked with your bank to set up your account for online access, leave Mint.com, do not pass go, and do not collect $200. Go directly to your bank's Web site and jump through whatever hoops are necessary to establish online account access. Remember the user name and password you use to log in to your online bank account because you'll need them when you get back to Mint.com.

## Adding your first account

You are entering your bank login information in Mint.com, but you are not transferring any banking powers to the site. In Mint.com, you can view and analyze your account activity, but you can't move your money around.

Follow these steps to add a bank account to Mint.com:

1. **Click the Add Account button.**

2. **Enter the name or Web site address for your bank, and then click Search.**

   A list of financial institutions containing the search words appears, as shown in Figure 2-3.

**Figure 2-3:**
A list of banks matching the name you typed.

3. **In the list, click your bank's name.**

   Mint.com reproduces the bank's logo, as shown in Figure 2-4.

**Figure 2-4:**
Enter your user name and password to see your banking transactions.

If the bank logo that appears isn't the same as the one you see on your bank account, you might have chosen the wrong bank. Click the Go Back button and look at the bank list. If you want to set up your bank account at another time, click Close.

4. **Type the user ID and password that you use on your bank's Web site.**

   Don't type your Mint.com user ID and password. Your user name is shown as you enter it, but your password is encrypted.

   If you have more than one account at a bank, you need to enter the bank information only once. Note that Mint.com doesn't ask you to enter a bank account number. No account numbers are recorded with Mint.com — one of the many ways the site keeps your bank account information safe.

5. **To add the bank to your Mint.com account, click the Add It! button.**

   Mint.com churns away for a moment or two (or longer, depending on the length of the login process at your bank) and then adds your bank to your list of accounts.

6. **Click Start.**

   Mint.com authenticates your login information with your bank.

7. **To add another bank account, repeat Steps 1–6.**

8. **When you've finished adding accounts, click Close.**

## I swear, I did everything right

Sometimes Mint.com encounters problem accessing information from banks and other financial institutions. When this happens, you see a *Sign in problem!* message and a Fix It! button to the right of your bank logo, as shown in Figure 2-5. Click the Fix It! button and follow the instructions to solve the problem.

**Figure 2-5:**
Uh-oh.

A typical problem with setting up a new account is a mistyped user name or password. Also remember that you should enter the user name and password for your bank account, not the ones you entered to set up your Mint.com account.

## The more accounts, the merrier

One of the key elements of Mint.com's success is the program's capability to help you look at all your accounts: accounts from multiple banks, credit cards, loans, investment accounts, and even assets, such as your car and home. The more financial information you enter, the more tools Mint.com has to help you manage your finances.

For now, enter any additional bank accounts that you have by repeating the steps shown in the "Adding your first account" section.

If you are married and want to analyze your finances jointly, enter any accounts owned by your spouse in addition to your own accounts. If you and your spouse are happy keeping your finances separate, each of you can set up a separate Mint.com account and work independently.

# Navigating the Credit Crunch

If you own a bank credit card and have an account at that bank, the credit card information automatically appears in Mint.com when you enter your bank account information. But if you have other credit cards, such as a department store card, you have to enter them separately.

The credit card setup process is the same as the process for setting up a bank account. First, make sure you already have an online account established with the credit card company. Then follow these steps:

1. **Log into Mint.com.**

   The Overview page appears.

2. **Click the yellow Add Account button, or click Your Accounts at the top of the screen.**

3. **Click the Add button.**

4. **Enter the name of your credit card company and then click Search.**

5. **In the list that appears, select the name of your credit card company.**

   The screen shown in Figure 2-6 appears so that you can enter your online login information.

**Figure 2-6:** Setting up a credit card is quick and easy.

6. **Enter the user name and password that you use on the credit card company's Web site and then click the Add It! button.**

   As with all the accounts in Mint.com, enter your login user name and password, not your name or account number.

7. **Click Start.**

   Mint.com finds your credit card provider and adds your account to your account list.

If you're setting up your credit card for online access for the first time, be sure to read the fine print on your credit card's Web site. Sometimes when you sign up to use online tools for accessing your credit card account, the company automatically sends your monthly statement via e-mail instead of sending a paper statement. If you want to continue getting paper statements, read the instructions carefully to make sure you can retain this option.

It's not the end of the world if you don't set up your individual credit cards. Mint.com tracks your credit card payments through your banking records, so you can monitor your credit card spending through your bank account. The advantage to entering your credit cards in Mint.com is that you have the added ability to track balances, finance charges, and detailed expenditures.

# Tracking Stocks, Bonds, and Mutual Funds

If you don't have an account at a brokerage company or an investment in a mutual fund, you can skip this section.

Investment accounts are a lot like savings accounts, in that you put money aside in these investments and hope to earn a bit on your savings. By adding your investments in Mint.com, you can see at a glance how all your investments are faring and use that information to make investment decisions.

The setup process is like the setup for your bank account. First, make sure you have online access to the account. Then follow these quick steps:

1. **On the Overview page, click Add Account.**

   Or click Your Accounts at the top of the Mint.com screen. Your existing accounts are displayed.

2. **Click the Add button that appears above your account listings.**

3. **Enter the name of the investment company and then click the Search button.**

4. **Select the correct name from the list provided.**

   If you are selecting a mutual fund from a company that offers several funds, only the company name appears, as you can see in Figure 2-7. Select the company name; Mint.com will collect all the information about investments you have within this fund family.

5. **Enter your login name and your password or PIN, depending on which options are presented to you.**

6. **Click Add It!**

**Figure 2-7:** Select your mutual fund family.

Now you can use Mint.com to view the performance of your investments, watch changes in the market, see at a glance where your money is invested, and compare your investments to the Standard & Poor's 500 indicator. If you have investments in more than one account, you can analyze them all on one screen.

# Home, Sweet Home

*Home* means the place where you live. Most people pay to live somewhere, although some lucky readers don't pay rent or a mortgage. They might live with parents, have already paid off their mortgage, or be bunking on a friend's couch. But if you make a rent or mortgage payment, you'll want to include that information in your Mint.com analysis.

## *Tracking your rent*

Homeowners need to enter their mortgage and the value of their home in Mint.com, topics covered later in this section. If you're a renter, getting Mint. com to track your rent is easy. Just do the following:

1. **Click the bank account you use to pay rent.**

   You can find your bank account by clicking the Overview tab at the top of the screen and then looking at the accounts listed under Cash on the left, as shown in Figure 2-8. If no accounts are listed under Cash, either you haven't entered a bank account yet (see "Adding Bank Accounts," previously in this chapter) or you need to click the little arrow to the left of Cash to display a drop-down list of your bank accounts.

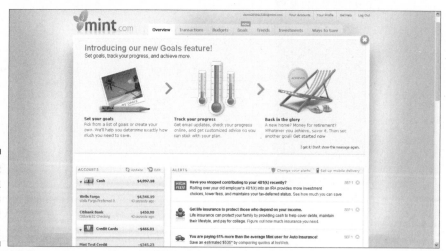

**Figure 2-8:** Your bank accounts are listed on the left.

2. **Find your last rent payment in the list of payments and deposits.**

3. **Note the category that Mint.com has assigned to your rent payment.**

   Mint.com may have already assigned the payment to Mortgage & Rent.

4. **If Mint.com doesn't have the correct category for your rent payment, click the arrow to the right of the Category field, on the same line as your rent payment, and choose Home⇨Mortgage & Rent.**

   You have to assign the category to this payee only once. From now on, Mint.com remembers that your payments to Joe the Landlord should be categorized as Mortgage & Rent.

# Tracking your mortgage

Entering your mortgage in Mint.com is slightly more complicated than entering a rent expense. The best way to track your mortgage is not by recording the monthly payment the way you do a rent payment but by recording the entire mortgage loan so that you (and Mint.com) know how much you owe, how much interest you're paying, and how much longer you have to endure those payments.

You should record your mortgage loan in Mint.com for other reasons, too. Mint.com stays on the lookout for better deals. If you're considering refinancing but don't know the going rates or where to shop for a new mortgage, Mint.com can do the legwork. See Chapter 17 for more information on how Mint.com can help lower the cost of your mortgage loan.

If someone asked you how much you still owe on your mortgage, would you have to admit that you have no idea? Those days are about to be over because Mint.com will remind you of your mortgage balance.

We understand that you might not want frequent reminders of your debts. You might want to remain blissfully ignorant of big honking debts such as how much you owe on your house or your student loans, or the amount you borrowed from your father-in-law, which you secretly hope he has forgotten about.

For now, however, we're going to assume that you'd like to take full advantage of all that Mint.com has to offer, so that means you have to take the bad with the good and fess up about how much debt you're carrying.

When entering mortgage information, Mint.com requires your login information for online access to your mortgage. If you haven't set up an online connection with your mortgage lender, establish that relationship first.

Get out your mortgage payment book, and do the following:

1. **Log in to Mint.com and click the Overview tab, which is at the top of the screen.**

2. **Click the Add It Now! link.**

   The link is next to the question: Do You Have a Mortgage, Student Loan, or Auto Loan? This area is below Loans, which is below Cash and Credit Cards. If you don't see the message, click the arrow to the left of Loans so that it's pointing downward. Alternatively, click the Add Account button on the left side of the screen.

3. **Click the Add a Loan link on the left side of the screen.**

   Or click the Add button below Financial at the top of the screen.

4. **In the Enter Your Bank's Name or URL field, type your mortgage company name. Then click the Search button.**

5. **Select your mortgage company in the list provided.**

   The screen shown in Figure 2-9 appears.

6. **Enter the user ID and password that you use for online access to your mortgage loan, and then click the Add It! button.**

   If your sign in information is incorrect, Mint.com displays a *Sign in problem!* warning with a Fix It! link alongside the name of the mortgage lender. Click Fix It! and read about the problem. You also see a phone number to call to get square with the lender.

7. **Click Start.**

   Mint.com pays a virtual visit to your mortgage company and makes a connection.

8. **If you have a second mortgage, go back to Step 3 and enter your additional mortgage loan.**

9. **When you're finished, click the I'm Done button.**

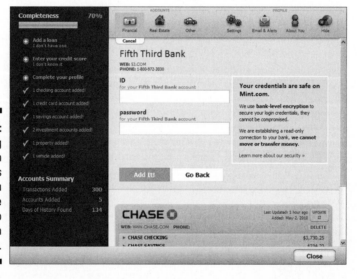

**Figure 2-9:** Entering a loan requires that you have online access to your loan information.

Now that your mortgage is recorded, read the next section so you can enter the value of your home.

## *Entering your home's value*

It's time for an interactive part of the Mint.com setup process. We like this part because we get to display an estimate of our home's value. Unlike stodgy accountants, who typically refer to the value of your house in terms of the purchase price when making financial statements, Mint.com lets you record the house at its true value, or at least a rough estimate.

You don't have to dig through any papers or try to remember passwords you haven't used in a while. All you need for this part of the setup is your address:

1. **On the Overview page, scroll down to the Property section on the left.**

2. **Click the Add It Now! button below Do You Have a House, Car, or Other Property?**

   If you don't see Do You Have a House, Car, or Other Property?, click the Add Account button.

3. **On the left side of the screen, click Add Real Estate.**

   Or click the little Real Estate icon at the top of the screen, as shown in Figure 2-10.

4. **Enter your street address, your suite or apartment number, and your zip code in the spaces provided, and then click Search.**

5. **Select your address in the list that appears.**

   If the correct address doesn't appear, click Search Again and enter the address again.

**Figure 2-10:** Click the little house.

6. **Make a selection in the drop-down list that appears.**

   Select whether this is your primary residence, an investment property, a vacation home, or other. Changing the property from Primary Residence to another choice changes the property's classification, not its value.

7. **Enter how you want the name of this property to appear in your Mint. com records.**

   The default name is the address. If you have homes in multiple states, you might want to distinguish them by calling them, say, Wyoming House and Florida House. Or you can get creative and give the home a nickname, such as Shangri-La, My Sanctuary, Home Sweet Hovel, or The Albatross.

8. **Examine the estimated value of your home and then click the Add It! button.**

   You've saved the home value to your assets.

Home prices are calculated based on information provided by Cyberhomes, which determines the price based on the sales prices of comparable homes in your zip code. You can view the details of your home assessment by going to www.cyberhomes.com and entering your address. You're allowed to make changes to this assessment, so examine the information carefully, note any additions or improvements you've made to your home, and view comparable homes to see if your home is being analyzed properly. Any changes you make on the Cyberhomes site should be carried over to your information in Mint.com. (Note, however, that our changes weren't updated and we read other complaints on the Mint.com site about update failures.)

## Changing your home's value

You can accept the Cyberhomes assessment or you can do your own valuation. If you're confidant that the information provided by Cyberhomes is not current, go ahead and change the value. You can alter the amount as often as you want:

1. **If your accounts are not already visible onscreen, click the Your Accounts option at the top of the Mint.com screen.**

   The Your Accounts screen appears.

2. **Click Real Estate, which is at the top of the screen.**

   You see all the real estate you've entered.

3. **Click the address of the home whose value you want to change.**

4. **In the Value field, enter your revised estimate.**

5. **Click Close.**

   The Overview page lists the revised value of your property.

## Describing your vehicle

Who knew there were so many kinds of vehicles? You might think the term *vehicles* would be divided into categories such as compact, luxury, SUV, sports car, and pickup, but Mint.com has something else in mind. Here are the categories from which you can choose:

✔ Automobile: This is self-explanatory. If you climb in it and drive it on the road, it's an automobile.

✔ Boat: If you can put it in the water, it's a boat.

✔ Motorcycle: Harley, Some Other Brand, dirt bike; you get the picture.

✔ Snowmobile: People in the Upper Peninsula know what this is.

✔ Bicycle: It turns out that the term *vehicles* means much more than cars. No motorized rolling modes of transportation such as one-, two-, three-, and four-wheel bikes are in the Bicycle category.

✔ Other: This category is for types of transportation such as wheelchairs, hot-air balloons, airplanes, wheelbarrows, Segways, and motorized scooters.

TIP

If you plan to update the value of your home, on Mint.com or www.cyber-homes.com, consider the prices at which other homes in your neighborhood have sold in recent months.

# Adding Your Car

If you own a car, that car is an asset with value. Okay, maybe the 1969 Rambler station wagon on cement blocks in your backyard is better valued as a big flower pot than a collectible classic. For purposes of this section, if you have a vehicle that is drivable, you have something of value, and that value should be included in your Mint.com records.

Ignore for the moment that you might owe money on the vehicle. If you're still paying off a loan, you enter that information separately. First enter the type of vehicle and find out how much it's worth.

From the minute you drive your car off the showroom floor, the car is losing value. (A car increases in value when it's considered a classic, but even that car lost value before it became collectible.) It's time to get busy and let Mint.com tell you just how much, or how little, your car is worth:

1. **At the top of the Mint.com screen, click Your Accounts.**

2. **Click Add a Vehicle, which is on the left side of the screen.**

3. **Select the type of vehicle.**

    See the "Describing your vehicle" sidebar for information on identifying the type of vehicle you own.

4. **Enter the name you want to use to distinguish this vehicle from any other vehicle you enter.**

5. **Enter a value for the vehicle, as shown in Figure 2-11.**

    Use your best estimate of the current market value of the vehicle, which means how much you think you could get for this vehicle in a fair deal.

    Mint.com has teamed with Kelley Blue Book to help you value your vehicle. To check out a tool to help you estimate the cost of your car, click Goals and then click Buy a Car.

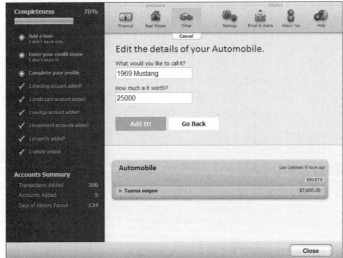

**Figure 2-11:** Enter what you believe you can get if you sell the car.

6. **Click Close.**

    Your vehicle information is officially part of your Mint.com financial picture.

# Shutting Down

You may have noticed that Mint.com doesn't wait around. If you ignore it for too long, the Web site goes to sleep. Maybe you skipped over to another screen for a few minutes, or perhaps you ran out to the kitchen for a snack. Before you know it, Mint.com has returned to the login screen that you see in Figure 2-12, and you need to enter your user name and password to get back in.

Furthermore, when Mint.com reverts to its login screen, any transactions you were in the middle of entering are removed, and you have to start over again. For example, if you start to enter your car in Mint.com and then bop over to the Kelly Blue Book page to investigate the car's current market value, Mint.com shuts down. You have to log in again and start over entering the vehicle information.

Mint.com shuts you out for a good reason: It doesn't want you to walk away from your computer and let some casual observer gain access to your financial records. However, go ahead and close the program if you plan on leaving your desk; don't rely on Mint.com to do it for you.

# Chapter 3

# Saving $1,000

· · · · · · · · · · · · · · · · · · · · · · · · · · · · · · · · · · · · · · · · · · · · · · · ·

## In This Chapter

▶ Cutting costs on your credit cards

▶ Checking out your checking account

▶ Saving money on your savings account

▶ Saving on bank CDs

▶ Getting the best deal on your investments

▶ Making smart 401(k) rollovers

▶ Finding good deals on automobile insurance

· · · · · · · · · · · · · · · · · · · · · · · · · · · · · · · · · · · · · · · · · · · · · · · ·

*P*romotional documentation about Mint.com states that, "Mint.com typically finds users $1,000 in savings opportunities in their first session —
minutes after registering." Having read that, you might already have the travel
agent on the phone, getting ready to book a vacation with your $1,000 windfall.

The good news is that Mint.com is not kidding when it says you'll find ways
to save money when you use the program. The bad news is that the savings
don't happen all at once, and it's up to you to make money-saving decisions
based on Mint.com's suggestions.

So before you spend that $1,000, read this chapter for insights into where
those savings can occur and what you can do to take advantage of the tips
you get from Mint.com.

## Saving with Credit Cards

We usually associate *spending* with credit cards, so it's a refreshing twist to
think of credit cards and saving in the same breath. Obviously, the best way
to save with credit cards is to stop using them. But for many of us, swiping
cards is a way of life, and people waiting in line at the store get upset when
the person at the front of the line fiddles with cash or, worse yet, takes out
a checkbook and starts writing. We're all in a hurry, and charging helps us
hurry along.

The next best way to save while still using your credit cards is to be aware of the charges and costs involved with using your cards and to get the best deal possible. That's where Mint.com comes in.

You can save money on the credit cards you use in several ways:

✔ **Get a lower rate on the monthly finance charge.** If you pay off your card in full each month, the monthly finance charge is of no consequence to you. But if you carry over amounts to the next month, getting a lower monthly finance charge rate means that you keep the fee to a minimum.

✔ **Find a card with a low rate for balance transfers.** Then transfer the amounts on existing cards with high interest rates to the new card.

✔ **Get premiums for charging.** These premiums are in the form of cash, discounts at restaurants and stores, bargains on hotels, frequent flyer miles, and more.

✔ **Explore introductory offers.** Some new cards give you little or no interest for a fixed amount of time.

Mint.com checks the offerings of various credit card suppliers, compares those offerings with the credit cards you own, and makes suggestions for cards that will save you money.

To get these suggestions from Mint.com, you first have to let the program know about your credit card spending. If you haven't entered any credit cards yet in Mint.com, follow the instructions in Chapter 2 and then come back here. If you don't have any credit cards, Mint.com simply suggests cards that offer the best deal for new users.

Saving with credit cards represents a big chunk of the $1,000 you were told you would save. But wait! Upon close examination, the savings amounts are displayed as three-year savings. So now you begin to see that you're not going to save that $1,000 all at once. This savings program requires a time commitment.

By default, Mint.com shows you how much you might save over a three-year period if you sign up for one of the suggested credit cards and use it for three years with an amount of charge activity similar to your current spending. However, you can change that time period to two years or one year using the option above the credit card suggestions (see Figure 3-1). If you think your charging activity might change over the next three years, use a one- or two-year estimate instead.

Criteria for credit card suggestions

Change timeframe

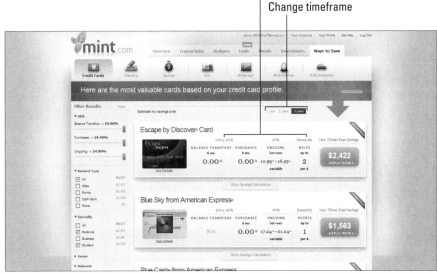

**Figure 3-1:**
You can change the estimate from three years to one.

# Choosing a credit card

How do you know which credit card to choose when there are so many? Banks, airlines, alumni associations, and many other organizations offer credit cards. Mint.com helps you sift through all these offers to figure out which ones suit your financial situation.

Click the Ways to Save tab at the top of the Mint.com page and then click the Credit Cards button. Mint.com shows you several options for credit cards that offer savings over what you use currently.

If you're considering choosing one of the suggested credit card offers that Mint.com describes, first decide on your priorities. You can see in Figure 3-2 that Mint.com has several criteria for making its card suggestions:

✓ **Intro APR:** The introductory *annual percentage rate*, or APR, is the finance charge you pay on a monthly basis, presented as an annual percentage. This amount is divided into two criteria:

**Balance transfers:** The *balance transfers rate* is the amount of interest you would pay if you transfer your charge balance from an existing credit card. The rate shown might or might not be the rate you would actually receive. This rate and all other interest rates are described using words such as *variable* and *as low as*. You won't find the actual balance transfer rate for which you qualify until you apply for the card.

- **Purchases:** The *purchases interest rate* is the amount of interest you pay on ongoing purchases when you carry over your balance from one month to the next instead of paying the entire balance each month. This rate relates to a certain introductory period, so you might pay a low rate of interest for six months or so, and then pay the ongoing interest rate (see the next bullet item).

✔ **APR:** The APR, or annual percentage rate, also called the *ongoing interest rate,* is the rate of interest that applies to purchases made after the introductory period has ended. The ongoing APR rate is higher than the purchases interest rate.

✔ **Rewards:** Credit card rewards are prizes you get for using the credit card. The more you charge, the more benefits you earn. These benefits can be in the form of cash, frequent flyer miles, amounts you can use to purchase gifts from catalogs, and so on.

Note that a little Sponsored banner appears in the upper-right corner of the descriptions of many suggested credit cards, banks, brokers, and so on (refer to Figure 3-2). That banner means Mint.com receives a benefit if you apply for the service. (Mint.com makes its money through these sponsorships.) There is no additional cost to you if you sign up for a sponsored service.

**Figure 3-2:**
Credit card solutions cover all the bases.

# Applying for a credit card

When you find a credit card whose description looks appealing, click the Apply Now button to find details about what the card offers, including actual interest rates, fees, rewards, and all the fine print about what happens to your rates if you miss a payment.

If you're still interested in applying for the credit card, fill out the requested information and then click the Submit Application button. Your application is forwarded to the credit card company's computer and processed immediately.

Your credit score is affected by credit card applications. Ten percent of your credit score is based on credit inquiries. More inquiries, lower score. Making lots of credit card applications is a red flag that you're getting turned down for credit, so choose one card that appeals to you and apply. If you get turned down, wait six months and work on improving your credit score (see Chapter 22) and then apply again.

# Saving with Checking Accounts

Many banks pay interest to account holders. Some banks require that you maintain a minimum balance to get that interest; others do not. We recommend that you consider keeping your cash in your own bank because longevity and familiarity have their benefits. Keeping accounts at one bank and making the acquaintance of the people who work at your bank's branch office can make a difference when you need extra services such as a business account or a loan.

Find out what types of accounts your bank offers. You might find that you can switch to a different type of account that pays interest or gives rewards for making payments through the account.

If you haven't yet activated your checking account through Mint.com, go to Chapter 2 for instructions. Then Mint.com can compare your existing account to others when making its recommendations for how you can save money on your checking account.

If you have cash in one bank and want to maintain a relationship with that bank, you can still open an account at a bank that pays a higher interest rate. That way, you have longevity at one bank and great savings potential at another.

If you're interested in opening a new checking account, use Mint.com to help you find an account. First click the Ways to Save tab at the top of the Mint.com page and then click the Checking button. In the big blue box at the top of the screen is the average bank balance and rate of interest (labeled Current APY) that you earn on your account. Below that information is a selection of banks that offer online banking. Mint.com compares the following factors so that you can see how your bank stacks up against the competition:

> ✔ **Minimum to open:** Many interest-bearing accounts require that you open your account with a minimum balance to qualify for interest earnings. Make sure you're willing to deposit the required minimum balance before choosing one of these accounts.

✔ **No fee balance:** Many bank accounts require that you maintain a monthly balance if you don't want to get hit with a monthly fee. You probably want an account with a no fee balance of zero. That way, if your balance drops below the required amount, you don't have to worry about having to pay a service charge.

✔ **Monthly fee:** If the account has a monthly service charge, that amount appears in the Monthly Fee column. The monthly fee is assessed when your balance drops below the no fee balance amount, so look at the Monthly Fee and No Fee Balance columns together.

✔ **APY:** APY, or *annual percentage yield*, is a fancy way of telling you how much interest your account earns annually. Suppose that you normally keep about $1,000 in your bank account and the APY is 1.5 percent. You would earn approximately $150 a year on the money you keep in this account, or $12.50 a month ($150 divided by 12).

You can scroll through the list of accounts that Mint.com suggests. Or you can save time by using the Filter Results option at the left side of the screen to get to exactly the type of account you want.

Following are the various ways in which you can filter your search:

✔ **Rates and Fees:** In the Rates and Fees section, move the sliders to lower or raise the amounts of each of the factors that determine the cost of and earnings on checking accounts. Figure 3-3 shows the results of a search of all banks that require less than $250 to open an account and with a no fee balance of less than $500, a monthly fee of less than $10, and an annual interest rate greater than .5 percent.

✔ **Check boxes:** Narrow your search by selecting the check box for features that interest you (such as free ATM withdrawals and free bill pay).

Search criteria            Click for more info

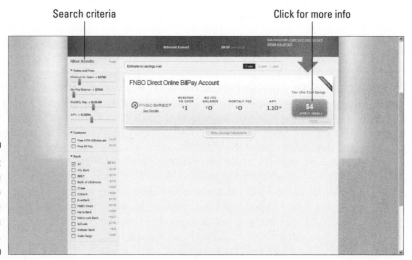

**Figure 3-3:**
Use the sliders to change the search criteria.

Mint.com displays its search results, explaining that, "We've found the best checking accounts for you, based on your activity on Mint." Scroll through the results of your search to see whether any of them interest you. To investigate an account further, click the blue Apply Now button to the right of the account description to display information about the bank and the account.

You don't have to close one account to open another. If you're happy with your existing bank account you might want to sign up for an additional account.

# Saving with Savings Accounts

Savings accounts are just like checking accounts in that they are places at the bank where you put your money. But unlike checking accounts, savings accounts always pay interest. Most savings accounts don't let you write checks against the balance, but the line between savings and checking accounts can be fuzzy, especially if your account is at a credit union or with an investment broker.

The criteria when choosing a savings account is similar to that used when you consider a checking account (see the preceding section):

✔ The minimum amount to open the account

✔ The no fee balance

✔ The APY, or interest rate you receive

In addition, savings accounts sometimes charge a *low-balance fee* if your balance falls below a certain amount. Furthermore, if your balance is so low that you're paying a monthly fee, the fee is probably higher than the interest you're earning, which defeats the purpose of having a savings account in the first place.

To select a displayed savings account, click the Savings button on the Ways to Save page. The Savings page, which is shown in Figure 3-4, works just like the Checking page. You can compare bank suggestions and filter results so that you see banks that meet certain criteria. You can also click 1 Year, 2 Years, or 3 Years to see what your potential savings will be for each time period.

Finding an account that gives you a good return on your deposit might be the impetus you need to keep more money in your savings account. If you're inspired to deposit more, Mint's projected three-year savings amount will be lower than your actual savings.

Change time frame

Search criteria

Click for more info

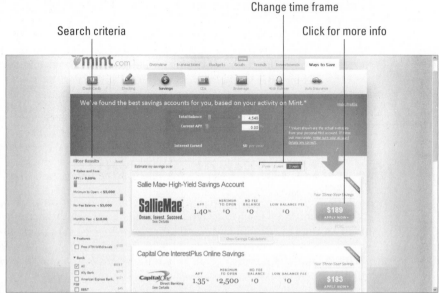

**Figure 3-4:**
Compare
savings
accounts to
see which
ones offer
you the best
deal.

# Saving with Bank CDs

You might think a CD is a round metal disk that plays music or downloads a program when you shove it in your computer's CD drive. But you can find another type of CD, called a *certificate of deposit*, at a bank. A bank CD is a lot like a savings account, except you agree to let the bank hang onto your money for a fixed amount of time (anywhere from three months to five years). In exchange, the bank agrees to pay you a higher rate of interest than it would on a regular savings account.

If you have a true emergency, you can withdraw your money even if the term on your CD has not run out, but you will have to pay an *early withdrawal penalty*. The bank is allowed to charge whatever it wants for an early withdrawal penalty, so familiarize yourself with the penalty procedures before you purchase the CD. Depending on how long you've owned the CD and its term, the penalty might be anywhere from 100 percent of the interest (for a short-term CD) to three to six months' interest.

To find the CD that best suits you, click the CD's button at the top of the Ways to Save screen. Mint.com asks you to answer two questions, as shown in Figure 3-5:

✔ **How long do you plan to invest?** Select a time period that corresponds to how long you're willing to let the bank have the use of your money. The longer the time period, the higher your interest rate. For example, when we chose a one-year investment term, the best interest Mint.com could find was 1.55 percent. When we changed that investment term to three years, the interest increased to 2.7 percent.

✔ **How will you fund this investment?** Mint.com displays the accounts where you have money that could be used to purchase the CD. Select one (or more) of these accounts so that Mint.com can properly calculate your potential savings. If you're taking money out of a savings account, for example, you earn interest on the CD but lose the interest from the savings account. Mint.com takes this into consideration when making its calculations.

As you enter your answers to these two questions, Mint.com sifts through its database of financial institutions that offer CDs and provides you with the best deals it can find.

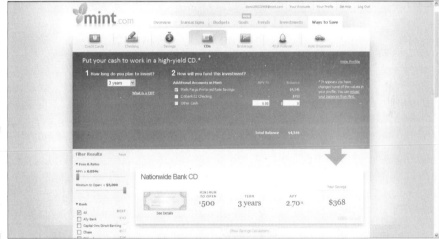

**Figure 3-5:**
Enter the answers to questions about your future CD.

# Saving while Investing

If you've experimented with online stock trading, you might already have an account with an online broker. But even if you do have an online broker, you might not be getting the best deal on your investments. Some online brokers charge more per trade than others or require an upfront deposit. Some offer better rates the more often you trade; others offer a certain number of free trades.

You should consider several options when choosing a broker. If you sign up with one online brokerage company, you can always change your mind and switch to a different company later.

To find a brokerage that meets your criteria, do the following:

1. **Click the Ways to Save tab and then click Brokerage button.**

   The screen shown in Figure 3-6 appears. If you've already recorded brokerage activity in Mint.com, your trading activity is reflected here. If you haven't entered a brokerage account, Mint.com uses averages from the Mint.com community to determine typical trading activity. You can override these numbers..

**Figure 3-6:**
How many
trades do
you make
per year?

2. **Describe your online trading activity.**

   Enter an estimate of how many trades you currently make per year in the categories of Stocks, Mutual Funds, and Options, and estimate how much each trade costs.

   When entering the number of mutual funds you trade per year, enter an amount here only if you pay a commission. Most people buy and sell mutual funds directly from the funds themselves, so no commission is applied to the trades. See Chapter 18 for more information on investing in mutual funds.

3. **Describe your current brokerage account.**

   If you use a brokerage account, enter the annual amount you spend for a maintenance fee, the amount you have in the cash account right now, and the amount of annual interest you earn on that cash account. It's possible that each of these numbers will be zero.

Mint.com has come up with a list of online brokers who are waiting to serve your trading needs. Several criteria weigh into the calculation of your estimated savings:

- ✔ **Trades:** You see separate costs for trades of stocks, mutual funds, and options. These costs apply to a single trade, be it a purchase or a sale. This is not a per-share price, but a price for the entire trade event, no matter how many or how few shares you trade.

- ✔ **Interest:** Mint.com displays the amount of interest you can expect to earn if you maintain a cash account with the broker. It's common for active traders to leave some cash in an account with a broker so that when they want to make a trade, cash will be ready to use without delay.

- ✔ **Fees:** Some brokerage accounts charge an annual fee for the privilege of using the account. This fee is in addition to the fees charged for each trade.

By default, Mint.com estimates a significant amount of trading activity among its users, so the estimated savings are much higher than the $1,000 Mint.com promised to save you in the first five minutes. If you trade at the level that Mint.com claims is merely average for its users — trading at least 60 stocks per year, 15 mutual funds per year on which you pay commissions, and 5 options per year — you're a power trader in our book.

Mint.com also estimates some hefty trading fees, at a minimum of $20 per trade. Most online brokers charge significantly less than $20 per trade, thus the thousands of dollars Mint.com claims it can save you if you switch to one of the recommended online brokers.

Filtering sliders on the left side of the screen, as shown in Figure 3-7, let you change the amount you are willing to put up for your initial deposit, the interest your cash earns, and what you are willing to pay for trades. A check box enables you to specify whether you're looking for an account with no maintenance fees.

**Figure 3-7:**
Slide the bars to set your requirements for the ideal online brokerage account.

As with the other options in the savings section of Mint.com, click the blue Get Started button to find out more about how these recommended brokers work and to display an application for signing up for the brokerage's services.

# Saving when Rolling Over a 401(k)

Do you have a 401(k) or a similar tax-deferred retirement plan, such as a 403(b) or a 457(b)? These retirement plans are set up through your employer. Typically, contributions to these plans are not taxed; the money in the account is taxed when you ultimately withdraw it.

Not surprisingly, the idea is to save the money in your retirement plan for retirement. But when you leave your job, you must decide what to do with the money in your tax-deferred plan. In Chapter 16, we talk about several alternatives to consider when dealing with your retirement investments. This chapter, however, describes how you can save money if you roll over your tax-deferred plan from a 401(k) or one of those other numbered plans to an Individual Retirement Account (IRA), which is another tax-deferred plan.

The main difference between the two types of plans is that you're limited to your employer's selection of funds with a 401(k) but can choose whatever you want as an investment with an IRA.

Rolling 401(k) money into an IRA account gives you not only more investment options but also a significant tax-saving benefit. If you still have money in your retirement account when you die, 401(k) money must be distributed to the beneficiaries at the time of death and is immediately subject to income tax. An IRA can be made part of the estate, and the tax on the IRA funds can be deferred over the life of the IRA beneficiary. In addition, you might be eligible to convert your IRA to a Roth IRA, which can provide additional tax savings. You can't convert a 401(k) plan directly to a Roth IRA; the 401(k) must be rolled over to a traditional IRA first.

Follow these steps to take a quick look at the amount of money you can save at retirement if you roll over your 401(k) to an IRA:

1. **Click the Ways to Save tab.**

2. **Click the 401k Rollover tab.**

   The screen shown in Figure 3-8 appears.

**Figure 3-8:**
Play with
the numbers
and figure
out how
much you
could save.

3. **In the 401(k) vs IRA Calculator box, enter your age and the amount in your 401(k) fund.**

   Mint.com displays the amount that you might be able to save at retirement, along with a list of six investment companies to review if you're looking to park your IRA money. Click the Learn More button next to any company to find out more about their brokerage terms.

Note that the amount Mint.com indicates as a savings does not take into account a couple of important factors:

✔ If your 401(k) plan is with your current employer, you don't have the right to convert the money to an IRA. The example referred to in Mint.com is for 401(k) plans from former employers.

✔ The amount calculated by Mint.com is based on the assumption that you'll have the same earnings but a lower administrative fee with an IRA than you do with your 401(k).

You're not limited to these six companies should you decide to roll over a 401(k) plan to an IRA. You can choose to invest your IRA money in many types of investments.

# Saving on Auto Insurance

You've probably seen the television commercials that tell you how you can save 15 percent with Geico, or set your own price with Progressive, or stay in good hands with Allstate. But instead of calling around for prices, you can comparison shop for auto insurance in Mint.com.

The auto insurance calculation is another way in which Mint.com hopes to help you save money. Simply follow these steps:

1. **Click the Ways to Save tab and then click the Auto Insurance tab.**

   The screen shown in Figure 3-9 appears.

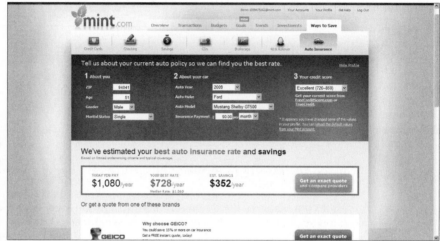

**Figure 3-9:**
Get an esti-
mate of your
insurance
savings.

2. **Enter some vital statistics about yourself.**

   Provide your zip code (auto insurance prices vary by geographic region), age, gender, and marital status. All these factors are taken into consideration when calculating auto insurance.

3. **Enter information about your car.**

   Provide the year, make, and model of your vehicle.

4. **Enter your current auto insurance payment amount.**

   Mint.com compares your current payment to the amount you'd pay to other insurers to calculate your potential savings.

5. **(Optional) Enter your actual or estimated credit score.**

   Your good credit is not a factor in the calculation of your auto insurance savings, so this step is optional.

6. **Click one of the grey Get an Exact Quote buttons or the blue Get an Exact Quote button.**

   If you click a grey Get an Exact Quote button next to the name of any of the major insurance companies, you see additional information about the company and the policies they offer. If you instead click the blue button, Mint.com provides quotes from a variety of insurers, not just the ones listed on the main insurance page.

# Chapter 4

# Getting Minty with Credit Cards

· · · · · · · · · · · · · · · · · · · · · · · · · · · · · · · · · · · · · · · · · · · · · · · ·

## In This Chapter

▶ Understanding how credit cards are your financial friend and foe

▶ Seeing how you use credit

▶ Deciding what kind of payment card is best for you

▶ Making the best use of your credit card

· · · · · · · · · · · · · · · · · · · · · · · · · · · · · · · · · · · · · · · · · · · · · · · ·

redit cards, which are essentially loans made to a consumer, can turn into a quicksand that ruins your financial future. One of Mint.com's biggest strengths is its capability to guide you through the process of using credit wisely. In this chapter, you find out how to turn credit into your servant, rather than the other way around.

## Living in a Plastic World

The financial crisis that kicked off in 2007 contained a crystal-clear lesson: We're addicted to debt. When scholars look back at the crisis, they will point to a *debt bubble*, or an overuse and abuse of borrowed money, as a cause.

Perhaps you've experienced a debt bubble in your own life. Thanks to credit cards, you can buy just about anything you want, when you want it, without handing over cash. Eyeing a new MP3 player? Rather than saving your money, you can simply swipe a credit card, start rocking out to tunes, and worry about paying the bill later. Mint.com is designed to help you spot such errors in financial judgment early — and adjust before it's too late.

Credit cards are loans. But unlike other loans, which require you to explain to a lender why you need the money and how you plan to repay it, credit cards automatically put a *credit line* in your back pocket. Borrowing with credit cards it easy — and abusing them is easy.

And abused they are. The median income of U.S. households was $50,303 in 2008, according to the latest data available at press time from the U.S. Census Bureau. Meanwhile, the median owed by U.S. households on their credit cards in 2008 was $7,008, says CardTrak.com, a firm that tracks industry trends. That means typical Americans owe nearly 15 percent of what they bring in each year to credit card companies.

Credit card debt is dangerous because it typically comes with a payload of very high interest rates. The *interest rate* is how much a *credit card issuer*, usually a bank, charges you to borrow its money. The higher the interest rate, the more expensive it is for you to borrow. Interest rates charged on credit cards typically range from 15 percent to 20 percent, which is up to four times higher than interest rates charged on other forms of debt, such as mortgages. These high interest rates make it much more difficult to pay down a credit card balance because much of your payment goes toward interest, not reducing the size of the loan, or *balance*. Mint.com is a helpful tool when managing credit card interest rates: It can not only monitor how much you're using credit but also detail how you used the credit and assist you in finding cards with lower interest rates.

Mint.com often refers to the interest rate charged by credit cards as the *APR* (*annual percentage rate*). The APR is the interest rate you're charged on credit card balances, expressed as a rate that you will pay for the entire year. This is confusing to some consumers because credit cards charge interest monthly, not yearly. However, the APR shows you how much the loan is costing you and allows you to compare interest rate offers from different credit card companies. For instance, if one credit card has an APR of 15 percent and another is 20 percent, you know that the one with the lower APR is the better deal, all other things being equal. In this chapter, though, I refer to the interest rate because it's more readily understandable than APR.

## Getting a grasp of payment card types

Credit cards are the largest and best-known *payment card,* but they're not the only one. Mint.com will help make sure you're using the payment card that's best for you by studying your spending habits.

Some of the most important payment cards follow:

- ✔ **Credit cards:** With credit cards, you borrow money from a credit card issuer and repay the money over time, with interest. Most credit card companies require that you make a *minimum payment* each month. This minimum payment is usually very small, and it could take a long time to repay the debt if you pay only this amount.

- ✔ **Charge cards:** Unlike credit cards, which allow you to pay back the balance over time, charge cards are usually due in full at the end of each month. Charge cards offer you the convenience of a credit card without the associated costs of borrowing.

✔ **Debit cards:** Debit cards work like electronic checks. When you pay for something with a debit card, the money is whisked out of your checking account. You don't get a bill. Instead, items you pay for are subtracted from your account and show up on your checking account statements.

✔ **Prepaid cards:** With a prepaid card, you give the bank money ahead of time, and charges are drawn against your balance. Prepaid cards appeal to consumers who may not qualify for a credit card and do not have a checking account but want the convenience of a payment card.

## *Putting credit cards to good use with Mint.com*

It's easy to demonize credit cards, but they do serve valid purposes when used wisely. Following are some reasons why credit cards, despite their dangers, deserve a place in your wallet:

✔ **Reaching goals:** The greatest use of credit cards is solving the classic dilemma faced by many people with great ideas. You might have an outstanding idea for a career or business, but you need money to get started. You could use your credit card to charge the equipment you need and then quickly pay back the loan using the money you collect from customers. For instance, you might need to buy a decent suit for an interview before you can land a job. Some entrepreneurs push the use of credit even further by launching a business with credit cards. Using credit cards to pay for a new business, though, is a dangerous and expensive use of credit and isn't recommended if you have other options.

✔ **Guarding against fraud:** When you buy items on credit, you're gaining some protections. For example, suppose you use a debit card to buy a $10 T-shirt, but the merchant accidentally enters the purchase as $100. That $100 hit immediately sucks money out of your checking account, which might make your account short for other bills. If you used a credit card instead, you can protest fraudulent charges and ask the bank to help you resolve the issue without tying up your cash.

✔ **Rewarding you with bonuses:** Most credit card companies offer perks to cardholders. Some perks, such as frequent flier miles, usually must be paid for in the form of *annual fees*. But many other perks are free, such as 1 percent cash back on purchases, free insurance on rental cars, and warranties on things you buy. The Mint.com blog discusses such perks at `www.mint.com/blog/saving/little-known-credit-card-perks/`.

✔ **Providing a cash-flow cushion:** A credit card can help manage several simultaneous expenses without drawing your cash balances too low. Mint.com can also warn you by e-mail if you're in danger of exhausting your checking account funds with its alerts feature, discussed in Chapter 6.

Just because you have a credit card doesn't mean you have to be in debt. Simply pay off your balance every month. By doing so, you beat the system by getting an interest-free loan, racking up rewards, and getting access to perks — without paying steep interest costs.

## Avoiding the pitfalls of credit

Although credit cards have big-time advantages, the downsides are even more important. Mint.com can warn you of the following credit card pitfalls:

- ✓ **Spending too much:** Mint.com helps you keep a constant eye on how much you're charging, so you can nip out-of-control spending early, before it becomes a big problem.

- ✓ **Getting hit with fees and other charges:** If you don't pay your entire balance at the end of the month, you will have a *revolving balance*, or a tab you must pay down. You not only have to pay interest on that balance but also risk late fees if you don't pay the minimum amount on time.

- ✓ **Carrying the wrong credit card:** Mint.com helps you make sure that the card in your wallet is the best one for you, based on your spending, income, and financial goals.

- ✓ **Having too many credit cards:** Department stores, gas stations, and other retailers are eager to muscle into the profitable credit card game. Consumers are often tempted into having too many credit cards, making it easy to overlook how debt is adding up. Mint.com shows you how much you owe in total across all your cards.

## Saving a fortune

It's easy to overlook how credit card fees and interest can snowball over time. And it's even easier to charge small amounts that build into a massive pile of debt. Suppose that you're carrying $7,008 in credit card debt (the median amount, as mentioned). And let's say that you have a 15 percent interest rate on that balance and pay only $100 to your credit card company each month. Ready for some depressing news? Paying off the balance would take about 14 years (169 months) and cost $9,796 in interest, more than the amount you borrowed.

Table 4-1 shows you why interest rates are so important. If you were able to find a card charging 7 percent using Mint.com's credit card tools, you could pay off the debt in less than 8 years (91 months) and pay $2,028 in interest.

| Table 4-1 | Repaying $7,008 in Debt | |
|---|---|---|
| *Interest Rate* | *Months to Pay Balance at $100 a Month* | *Total Interest Paid* |
| 0% | 71 | $0 |
| 5% | 84 | $1,297 |
| 7% | 91 | $2,029 |
| 15% | 169 | $9,796 |

Are you ready to have Mint.com help you manage your credit? You begin by entering your credit card account in Mint.com. If you don't have a credit card, you can skip this step.

To enter a credit card account in Mint.com, you need a user name and password with the credit card company. Different credit card companies use different procedures for setting up a user name and password, but most companies make the registration process painless. Citibank, for instance, provides a Register button at its Web site (www.citicards.com), as shown in Figure 4-1. You are prompted to enter your credit card number and account information, choose a password, and select security questions that may be used later if the site needs to verify your identity.

Chapter 2 describes in full detail how to add all your accounts to Mint.com, including your credit card.

**Figure 4-1:** Citibank, like most credit card companies, makes registering easy.

# Understanding How You Use Credit

Before you can find the best credit card, you need to know how you will use the card. Mint.com can do some amazing things when it comes to finding the best credit cards for you, but it needs the following basic information first:

- **Your typical monthly credit card spending:** If you're using your credit card to pay for just a cup of coffee a few times a month, you won't save much with Mint.com's suggestions for a better credit card. But if you charge most things, the potential savings with a different credit card are huge.

- **Categories you spend the most on:** Some credit card companies provide greater rewards for certain types of purchases, such as gas or groceries, than for other areas. Knowing where you're spending the most will help Mint.com find the best card. Mint.com can separate your expenses into *categories*, or groups, such as food and entertainment.

- **Whether you pay off your credit cards each month:** If you pay your credit card in full each month, the interest rate charged by a credit card is meaningless and your interest expense on your charges is zero. However, if you carry a balance, and that balance is getting bigger, the interest rate is the number-one factor to consider.

The best way to turn credit cards into a financial asset rather than a money pit is to pay your balance in full every month. Doing so gives you all the perks of credit cards at no cost.

- **Your credit score:** If you ever feel like you're just a number to credit card companies, you're right. Well, actually, you're two numbers: an *account number* and a *credit score*. Consumers are given numerical grades that measure how likely they are to repay the debt. Mint.com can help you get your credit score, as described later in this chapter.

- **Credit card perks or bonuses:** If you have a credit card already, you'll want to have an idea of the perks you're getting. Perks can be an important advantage of using credit cards. Mint.com may automatically show the perks on your current credit cards, but in many cases, you'll need to look up this information using the credit card company's Web site.

- **Credit card interest rate:** If you carry a balance on your card, the interest rate you're paying is critical.

So how do you go about finding all the pieces of information listed in the preceding list so you can find a better credit card? Mint.com can help you determine the information you need, if not generate the numbers itself. But the way Mint.com helps you gather your credit information differs based on your situation, which probably falls in one of three scenarios, as outlined in the following sections.

## Monitoring your credit rating

In the wake of the credit crisis that began in 2007, credit card companies have been more restrictive in who gets credit and how much. Whether or not you are given credit and the interest rate, you must pay come down to one number: your credit score.

Your credit score is a number calculated by three *credit bureaus:* Equifax, Experian, and TransUnion. The credit score number measures how good you've been at paying your bills, how responsible you've been in managing your debt, and how likely you are to repay your debt. Credit bureaus measure your credit score in several ways. Mint.com relies on a method that involves a three-digit credit score called FICO. Your FICO score determines how much credit a credit card company will let you borrow, which is called your *credit line.* Each credit bureau may calculate your FICO score slightly differently. You can read more about credit scores at www.myfico.com/CreditEducation/CreditScores.aspx.

Credit score ratings are in the following ranges:

✔ Excellent rating: 720 to 850

✔ Good rating: 690 to 719

✔ Average rating: 630 to 689

✔ Poor rating: 300 to 629

✔ Very poor rating: 0 to 200

To see your credit score, log in to Mint.com and click the Ways to Save tab. On the right, go to Step 3, "What Is Your Credit Score?" Below this step is an area labeled Get Your Current Score from FreeCreditScore.com or TrueCredit. Click either link and then follow the prompts to get your report. Both services provided through Mint.com have free offers.

You can also go to www.annualcredit report.com, a site run by Equifax, Experian, and TransUnion to comply with Federal regulations that require credit bureaus to provide consumers with a free credit report per year. The credit report is free, but you have to pay for the credit score. For a free credit score, go to www.quizzle.com.

## Analyzing debit card spending

Mint.com analyzes your debit card spending like a hard-nosed accountant. If you use a debit card and have added your checking account to the site. Mint.com classifies all your expenses, except ATM withdrawals, into a primary category and then a subcategory. (ATM withdrawals are discussed in the next section.) If you go to McDonald's and spend $10 on lunch, for instance, that expense goes in the Fast Food subcategory under Food & Dining. This information will help you find the best credit card. Mint.com's categories and subcategories are shown in Table 4-2.

| Table 4-2 | Categories and Subcategories in Mint.com |
|-----------|-------------------------------------------|
| *Category* | *Examples of Subcategories* |
| Auto & Transport | Auto Insurance; Gas & Fuel; Parking; Public Transportation |
| Bill & Utilities | Home Phone; Internet; Television |
| Business Services | Advertising; Legal; Office Supplies |
| Education | Books & Supplies; Tuition |
| Entertainment | Amusement; Arts; Music; Newspapers & Magazines |
| Fees & Charges | ATM Fee; Bank Fee; Late Fee |
| Financial | Financial Advisor; Life Insurance |
| Food & Dining | Alcohol & Bars; Coffee Shops; Fast Food; Groceries; Restaurants |
| Gifts & Donations | Charity; Gift |
| Health & Fitness | Dentist; Doctor; Eye Care; Gym; Sports |
| Home | Furnishings; Home Improvement; Lawn & Garden |
| Income | Bonus; Paycheck |
| Kids | Allowance; Baby Supplies; Babysitter & Daycare |
| Personal Care | Hair; Laundry; Spa & Massage |
| Pets | Pet Food & Supplies; Pet Grooming; Veterinary |
| Shopping | Books; Clothing; Electronics; Hobbies |
| Taxes | Federal Tax; Local Tax; State Tax; Property Tax |
| Transfer | Credit Card Payment |
| Travel | Air Travel; Hotel; Rental Car & Taxi |
| Uncategorized | Cash & ATM |

If you've added your checking accounts to Mint.com (see Chapter 2 for details), you can easily see where your money is going. Here's how:

1. **On the Overview page, click the Trends tab, as shown in Figure 4-2.**

2. **Select a time frame.**

   For this exercise, I recommend using the This Year time frame, which shows you how you're doing so far this year. Mint.com attempts to gather transactions going back as far as it can, but some banks let the program download only the last 90 days of activity.

**Figure 4-2:**
The Trends
tab helps
you see
where your
money is
going.

3. **Select the Spending option and then select the By Category option.**

4. **Adjust the spending for monthly values.**

   Divide the total amount of spending by 12 to see, roughly, how much you're spending each month. Also note in which categories you're spending the most.

## Analyzing cash spending

If you're an ATM addict, Mint.com's usefulness will be limited to showing you the total amount of cash you take out of the bank each month. Follow the steps in the preceding section for a summary of your spending.

But here's the catch. You may not know in what categories you spent that wad of $20 bills. You could estimate the amount. Or if you're willing to take the time, you could categorize your cash spending for a month or so before signing up for a credit card. To categorize cash amounts, first add your checking account to Mint.com and then follow these steps:

1. **On the Overview page, click the Transactions tab.**

2. **In the accounts list on the left, click the name of your checking account.**

3. **Highlight your cash withdrawal by clicking the transaction in the list.**

4. **Click the Edit Details tab under the transaction.**

5. **Click the Split button.**

   The Split button enables you to classify how you spent the cash you withdrew. However, the Split button is available only when you're editing an existing transaction, not when you're adding a new transaction.

6. **Divide your ATM withdrawal based on how you spent the money.**

   For instance, suppose you withdrew $100 and spent $60 on dinner and $40 on gasoline. You'd categorize the $60 as Food & Dining⇨Restaurants and the $40 as Auto & Transport⇨Gas & Fuel.

The more you categorize your spending, the more information Mint.com will have to determine where your money is going.

## Analyzing credit card spending

If you already have a credit card and are just wondering whether you should have a different card, Mint.com has you covered. More times than not, all the information you need to know to evaluate credit cards is already in Mint.com. Most or all of your spending is classified for you into categories and subcategories. Just skip to the next section to find the best card for you.

# Finding the Best Card

By now, you have most of the information you need to either find a better credit card or see which card would be ideal for your first credit card. All the hard work is finished.

To use Mint.com to find ideal credit cards for you to consider, follow these steps:

1. **On the Overview page, click the Ways to Save tab, shown in Figure 4-3.**

2. **Make sure the Credit Cards tab is selected.**

3. **Enter your monthly credit card spending.**

   This amount is the total you think you'll put on your card each month. You should have this information from following the preceding section. If your credit card is already entered in Mint.com, your expected spending will be filled in for you.

4. **If you know the categories for your spending, enter those.**

   If you've entered a credit card account, Mint.com fills in the categories automatically.

5. **Indicate if you pay off your credit cards each month.**

**Figure 4-3:**
Your head-
quarters for
finding a
better credit
card.

Respond Yes only if you actually do pay your cards off each month, not if you plan to. Your answer to this question is a big determining factor in the cards Mint.com recommends.

6. **Enter your credit score.**

   If you don't know your credit score, see the "Monitoring your credit rating" sidebar, earlier in the chapter, or estimate your score.

7. **Scroll through the credit card options.**

   Mint.com suggests cards that should save you money, along with an estimate of how much money you could save by switching.

8. **Narrow the list.**

   The number of cards Mint.com recommends can be overwhelming. Use the check boxes on the left side of the screen to focus on cards that appeal to you. For instance, you can view only cards that offer cash back rewards.

Most of the cards at the top of the list are *sponsored*, meaning the credit card companies pay Mint.com to pitch the card to you. Be sure to scroll through all the cards offered so that you don't miss a card that doesn't pay to be included on Mint.com but is the best card for you.

# Using Credit Prudently

Mint.com's founder, Aaron Patzer, said that the best way to control your spending is to monitor it. He's right. If you don't know where your money is going, how can you expect to control your spending?

# Tracking balances

Mint.com shows you how much you owe on each card, what you're buying on credit, and how those expenses fit into your overall financial picture, such as your budget.

Watching your spending like a hawk is especially important when you spend with a credit card because you don't take an immediate cash hit. A $20 charge here, a $45 charge there, and before you know it, you have a big bill at the end of the month.

### Monitoring spending with categories and the Transactions tab

Log into Mint.com, and you'll see seven primary tabs across the top of the screen. These tabs help you get an idea of where your money is going. For example, click the Transactions tab to see the individual transactions that have taken place in each of your accounts. You can then click the name of the account to examine how much you spent for each merchant. If you want to examine transactions from a single account, click the credit card account, which is listed on the left side of the page.

The Transactions tab is especially valuable when studying credit card spending because it's easy to examine what you're charging and filter other spending you do using cash and debit cards.

For a credit card account, the Transactions tab is the Mint.com equivalent of a paper credit card statement, showing everything you've bought and any credits to your account. All your transactions are divided into the following four elements:

- ✔ **Date:** This is the date the credit card company recorded the transaction.

- ✔ **Description:** This field is a brief text description of the transaction. You'll see the name of the merchant, such as Target or Starbucks. Sometimes, you might see something cryptic such as *No* or a transaction number, although Mint.com attempts to remove such confusing descriptions.

- ✔ **Category:** Mint.com takes a stab at what category the transaction belongs in. Some transactions are easy to categorize, such as McDonald's (Food & Dining category, Fast Food subcategory).Mint.com needs help with other transactions, such as those at a store that sells different types of items. If the category Mint.com chooses is incorrect, just click the down arrow in the row and select the correct category and subcategory.

- ✔ **Amount:** The amount is the dollar value of the transaction. The two main types of transactions are charges and credits. Most transactions in your credit account will be *charges,* which are the values of things you've bought. Charges are displayed in the transaction list as negative numbers. A *credit* is when you return an item, are issued a refund, or pay your credit card bill. Credits are displayed as positive numbers.

Note that purchases often don't fit into just one category. For instance, you might have a $30 charge from Target, consisting of $20 for a basketball and $10 for shampoo and conditioner. The entire $30 doesn't fit in a single category, and Mint.com needs your help in figuring out in what categories the money should go. Here's how:

1. **Click the transaction in question.**

2. **Click the Edit Details tab under the transaction line and then click the Split button.**

   A new window appears.

3. **Enter the price for the basketball.**

   Click the down arrow next to the category and choose Health & Fitness⇨ Sports. Enter **20** for the amount.

4. **Click the Split button and repeat the process for the shampoo and conditioner.**

   Choose Personal Care⇨Hair. Enter the amount.

5. **Click the Save button.**

   Now Mint.com knows how you spent the $30.

Mint.com's Transactions tab can do more than just display your purchases and payments. Click a transaction you're interested in studying, such as the dinner at that fancy restaurant you went to last week. On the right side of the screen is a snapshot of how much you've spent in the category that corresponds to the transaction you clicked and how your spending in that category compares with the average amount spent by other Mint.com users. You also see how your spending in the category has been rising or falling over the past three months, as shown in Figure 4-4.

### Monitoring spending with tags and the Transactions tab

Another way to monitor credit card spending is through *tags,* which you use to group expenses in different but related categories. For instance, suppose that you want to see how much you're spending on an upcoming camping trip. You can't use categories alone because the pack of hot dogs would go in the Food & Dining category but the tent would go in the Shopping category.

With tags, you can pull together all expenses across several categories in one group, such as Vacation. You can also create a unique tag for the trip, such as Camping Trip 2010. Here's how to use tags to group your credit card spending:

1. **Click the Transactions tab.**

2. **Click the credit card account on the left side of the page.**

3. **Click the transaction in the list that you want to tag.**

4. **Click the Edit Details tab under the transaction.**

5. **Assign a tag in one of two ways:**

   • **Click the box next to a tag that describes the tab, such as Vacation Tag.**

   • **Create a tag by clicking the Manage Your Tags link, clicking the Add a New Tag button, entering the name of the tag, and clicking Okay.**

6. **If you have additional transactions to tag, go back to Step 3.**

7. **When you're finished, click the I'm Done button.**

**Figure 4-4:**
Spot categories that are eating up your paycheck.

After you've set up your tags, it's easy to see how much you're spending in particular categories. From the Transactions tab, select your credit card account and then click the appropriate tag from the list on the left, such as Vacation. Mint.com displays all transactions that pertain to that tag.

## Monitoring spending with the Trends tab

The Transactions tab is great when you want to isolate how much you're spending in a particular category on a specific credit card or other account. When you want a bird's-eye view of spending across all your accounts, however, check out the Trends tab. Because the Trends tab adds how much you've spent using all payment methods, including cash, debit cards and credit cards, you can quickly see whether a certain type of spending is messing up your budget.

Click the Trends tab. Select one or more months from the selection bar at the top of the page. Click and drag to the left or right to select multiple months. Some trends you'll expect, such as more charges on gifts in November. Look for expenses that are creeping up in categories you don't expect.

If the Trends tab shows that you're spending too much in a category, it's time for a budget. Read Part II for all the details on creating a budget.

## Watching fees and interest rates

Guess what? Credit card companies aren't giving you loans because they like you. They're in the business of making money. Credit card companies make most of their money on interest charges, but that's not their only source of revenue. Mint.com enables you to see all the fees that various credit card companies, perhaps including yours, are charging.

Click the Ways to Save tab, and then click the Credit Cards tab. Scroll down to see a list of hundreds of credit cards. Below the picture of each credit card is a See Details link. Click this link and you'll see a laundry list of fees, including the interest rate and any annual fee.

For a more detailed look at how credit card fees pertain to your situation, click the Show Savings Calculations tab below the image of the credit card. Mint.com displays how fees affect your total cost of using that card. An example is shown in Figure 4-5.

The calculation to measure the total costs of a card is a bit confusing at first. For the Fees & Bonuses amount, Mint.com subtracts all the perks you get (such as sign-up bonuses) from the fees you pay (such as annual fees). Mint.com also estimates your rewards from using the card, such as calculating a 1 percent cash back bonus on future spending.

Some credit cards that offer perks such as frequent flier miles charge an annual fee. Don't assume that these fees are a good deal. If you don't charge enough, you'll end up paying more in annual fees than you would to just buy the airfare. You might be better off buying an airplane ticket with a card that has no annual fee and no frequent flier miles but pays 1 percent cash back. Some cards offset annual fees by offering you a sign-up bonus. Mint.com helps you evaluate this confusing array of bonuses, perks, and fees in the See Details link.

## Paying on time and in full

A cardinal rule for using credit cards wisely is to pay the entire balance each month. Getting tired of hearing this yet? Paying off your credit cards in full turns credit cards into a powerful financial tool that gives you benefits with no cost. Paying your bill on time is also important.

Most credit card companies charge about $30 as a fee for a missed payment. That's just wasted money.

Mint.com is like your guardian angel when it comes to making sure you pay on time. You can set up an alert that triggers Mint.com to remind you when your credit card payment is due. You can get the alert when you sign into Mint.com, or have the alert e-mailed to you or sent to your mobile phone. See Chapter 6 for details on setting up alerts.

**Figure 4-5:**
Fees that credit card companies sock you with.

## *Whittling credit card debt*

Being debt-free is a goal for many consumers. Mint.com can help you dig yourself out of the hole. For example, Mint.com shows you all the fees and interest you're paying with a credit card. If you use several credit cards, Mint.com can find the card that's costing you the most money with interest rates or other fees, so you can pay off that one first.

In the "Watching fees and interest rates" section, previously in this section, you found the fees charged by your cards by using the Ways to Save tab. A more direct way to see these fees is to use the account setup page. Here's how:

1. **On the Overview screen, select the Edit option at the top-left corner of the page under the Mint.com logo.**

2. **Find your credit card account and hover your mouse pointer over the name.**

   The words *Edit Details* appear.

### 3. Click the Edit Details link.

In some cases, you'll see the card's interest rate or APR, the annual fee, if it charges one, and information on the card's rewards, as shown in Figure 4-6.

**Figure 4-6:** The account setup page provides a quick look at many of your credit card's fees.

If Mint.com isn't able to download that information from your credit card, click the Edit Details link and enter the information yourself, based on what you find on the credit card's Web site

One of the smartest ways to wiggle out of debt is with a *balance transfer,* where you move your debt from one credit card to another. Credit card companies often give you a temporary lower interest rate if you transfer a balance to them. Mint.com will help you find credit cards with attractive balance transfer rates. You can keep transferring your balance until you pay down the debt.

Be careful because this strategy has potential downsides. If you transfer your balance to a credit card with a low balance transfer rate but a high interest rate for purchases, you could get stuck if you're not able to find another credit card company to transfer the balance to later. Also, a low transfer interest rate might revert to a high rate, leaving you in a bad position if you can't transfer your balance again.

## Setting a goal to cut your debt

The Goals tab helps you create a plan to tackle some of life's biggest financial problems. Paying down debt, including credit card balances, certainly qualifies.

Click the Goals tab and select the Get Out of Debt option. A series of pages appear to help you think through digging out of the debt hole. Mint.com asks how much extra you think you can afford to pay toward your credit card debt and then estimates how quickly you'll reduce your debt with those extra payments, as shown in Figure 4-7.

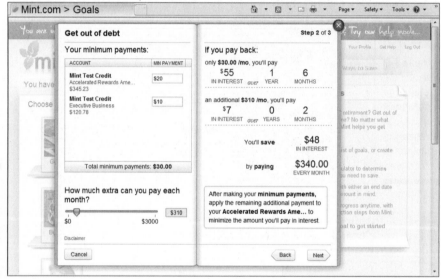

**Figure 4-7:**
Create a game plan for reducing debt ahead of schedule.

As you can see, Mint.com is a valuable tool in digging into how you use credit, how much it costs, and whether you can save money. Credit can be a useful tool if you manage it correctly. We hope this chapter and Mint.com can help you do just that.

# Chapter 5

# Tracking Your Cash

*In This Chapter*

▶ Paying for items with cash

▶ Tracking your cash expenditures

▶ Keeping tabs on income received in cash

*F*rom our earliest days, we are spenders of cash, from asking for change for the gumball machine to buying peanuts and beer at ball games, and from shelling out for taxi fares to paying the babysitter. You need to record those cash activities if you want Mint.com to provide a full picture of your personal finances. In this chapter, you see how easy it is to make your Mint. com financial records, budgets, and spending reports more robust by keeping track of the cash you spend and receive.

## Spending Cash

You know the drill. You stop by the bank, pop your card in the ATM, and walk away with a wad of cash. Or maybe you swipe a debit card to buy groceries and take the option to get extra cash. Or perhaps people pay you in cash for your labors.

If you want some control over and understanding of your finances, you need to track the cash you spend and combine that information with records of your other financial activity. However, keeping track of cash spending can be difficult. You start the day with 50 bucks, but all you have left by nighttime is a few singles and some change. We aren't going to tell you to carry around a pocket-sized notebook and write every cent you spend. Instead, we suggest that you don't sweat the small stuff. Concentrate on big expenses, the ones that are easier to remember. For example, as you sift through the small amount of cash left in your pocket at night, you can probably recall that you went out to lunch and the meal cost about $10. You can also remember that your neighbor stopped by in the afternoon and hit you up for a $20 contribution to a school fundraiser.

You don't have to remember every nickel and dime you spend. If you take a few minutes each day recording where the bulk of your cash went, you can get stated tracking your cash expenses in Mint.com.

The budget you create in Part II will be more robust and meaningful if your record keeping includes your cash activity.

The flip side of withdrawing a wad of cash and paying for everything in real dollars and coins is swiping a credit or debit card for every expenditure. One major benefit to being a full-time swiper is that every financial transaction in your busy day is tracked in your bank account (debit card) or your credit card account and therefore automatically recorded in Mint.com.

You might think that keeping track of every cash expenditure is more nit-picky than you want to be. But if you want a sense of where *all* your money goes, adding your cash spending to your financial record keeping gives you an additional level of information.

The best time to enter a cash transaction in Mint.com is right after you perform the transaction, when you are more likely to remember it. You can get an app for that! Chapter 23 includes a section on using your cell phone to record transactions in Mint.com.

# Recording Cash Expenditures

When using Mint.com to track the amounts of cash you spend, the hard part is remembering when and where you spent your money. Getting the information into Mint.com is the easy part.

To enter a cash payment into Mint.com, simply follow these steps:

1. **On the Overview page, click the Transactions tab.**

   You see a list of your recent cash and credit transactions, as shown in Figure 5-1.

2. **Click the Add a Transaction button.**

3. **Select the (approximate) date of your cash transaction.**

   Click in the Date field to display the date menu shown in Figure 5-2. Select one of the displayed dates or click the up or down arrow to see more dates. It's probably not essential to remember the exact date of the transaction unless the purchase was tax-related (see Chapter 21 for information about using information in Mint.com to prepare your tax return).

4. **Describe your cash transaction.**

   What did you buy with that cash? Enter a brief description, such as *lunch* or *ball game*.

**Figure 5-1:**
Your recent
cash trans-
actions.

**Figure 5-2:**
Select the
transaction
date.

The amount you spend in cash needs to be fully described if this is a tax-related expense. For example, a business lunch expense requires that you enter the names of the people who joined you and the reason for the lunch.

**5. Select a category.**

Organize your cash transaction by category by clicking the drop-down arrow in the Category field and selecting a category and a subcategory. If you don't find what you need in the subcategory list, select Add/Edit Categories, which is at the bottom of each subcategory list, and create your own category.

Mint.com uses categories to produce your budget, the trends report that analyzes your spending, and many other reports. The more precise you are when selecting categories for your transactions, the more useful your Mint.com reports. Choose categories that specifically describe the transaction. For example, don't just choose Food & Dining as your category when you can select a Food & Dining subcategory of Alcohol

& Bars, Coffee Shops, Fast Food, Groceries, or Restaurants. Adding this type of detail to your category selection provides you with much clearer information about where your money is going.

6. **Enter the amount.**

   Suppose you're recording the amount you spent at the movies last Saturday. If you know that you spent about $25, enter that amount. You don't have to remember that you spend exactly $28.75 for tickets and popcorn and soft drinks.

   *Note:* For amounts you spend, use a minus sign.

7. **Leave the Type field set to Cash.**

   In the Type field, you choices are Cash, Check, or Pending. Because this section is all about recording cash transactions, go ahead and leave this field set to Cash.

8. **(Optional) Select the appropriate tags.**

   If you use tags to organize your finances (see the "Playing tag" sidebar), select the check box for any tag that applies to your cash expense.

9. **Enter appropriate notes.**

   The Notes area is your place to enter the information that helps you remember more about this transaction than just the name of the payee, the amount, the category and, if applicable, the tag. The Notes feature comes in handy when you plan to take a tax deduction for the amount of the transaction.

10. **Click the I'm Done button.**

    The cash transaction becomes part of your transaction list and is used in the calculations of budgets and trend reports.

# Recording Cash Revenue

In addition to spending cash, sometimes you get cash revenue. We're not talking about the change you get from making a $5 purchase with a $20 bill or the cash you get from the 24-hour teller. You've already received that money once; you're just handling it again. In other words, you already own the money in your bank account and the receipt of that money has already been noted in the form of a paycheck, or a loan, or however else you received the money. Examples of cash revenue for purposes of this chapter are money from a friend or relative who gives you a loan or pays back a loan, money you receive from a cash-paying job such as babysitting, an allowance, or money you get from your dinner companions to pay for their share of a meal that you charged.

# Playing tag

Tags are Mint.com's cool tool for keeping track of a particular type of financial item, regardless of the category you use to classify the transaction. For example, suppose you want to track how much you spend on your children. Start by creating a tag named Children:

1.  **On the Transactions tab, click the Edit hyperlink that appears next to Tags on the left side of the screen.**

2.  **In the window that appears, click Add a new tag.**

3.  **Enter** Children **in the field provided.**

4.  **Click Save It and then click Okay.**

    Note that the tag you added is available for all transactions, not just new transactions.

Now, each time you spend money on your children, select that transaction in the transaction list, click the Edit Details tab, select the Children tag, and then click I'm Done. ***Note:*** You can assign a single tag to financial transactions in different categories. For example, you might have kid-related expenses in your food, clothing, furniture, entertainment, and education categories.

Now the next time the kids ask for an allowance increase, you can show them how much you're already spending and tell them to go outside and play.

If you're going to deposit the cash in your bank account, you don't need to record the cash revenue now because Mint.com will pick up the transaction when the deposit appears. But if you're going to hang onto the cash and spend it, you need to record the cash revenue transaction.

To enter a cash revenue transaction, follow the steps in the preceding section, except enter the amount of cash you received as a positive number in Step 6.

# Chapter 6

# Staying On Track with Alerts

. . . . . . . . . . . . . . . . . . . . . . . . . . . . . . . . . . . . . . . . . . . . . .

. . . . . . . . . . . . . . . . . . . . . . . . . . . . . . . . . . . . . . . . . . . . . .

*W*ouldn't it be great if someone tapped you on the shoulder before you were about to do something foolish with your money. Before joining a heated eBay bidding war for a $1,000 Darth Vader action figure, imagine a little voice saying, "Do you really need that?" (Well, it might be a little creepy.)

The urge to spend and consume can jeopardize long-term financial needs, such as education, home ownership, and retirement. Mint.com's alerts monitor your spending and caution you against making bad financial moves. In this chapter, you see how Mint.com's alerts keep you focused on long-term goals and prevent you from getting sidetracked by consumer impulses.

## Understanding How Alerts Can Help

Professional stock traders know the value of avoiding mistakes. Just one poor investment decision can sour an entire portfolio, which is one reason why a popular adage on Wall Street is "Cut your losers short, but let your winners run." Traders know that it's human to make a mistake but plain silly to ignore the mistake and let it ruin you.

Mint.com's alerts function brings this same error-avoiding discipline to your personal finance life. In short, alerts are designed to stop you from continuing to make mistakes that can set back your financial goals.

## Monitoring your financial progress

If you're like many people, you don't think about money until a problem occurs. Maybe your financial problem threatens the roof over your head when you find that you're suddenly unable to afford your rent or mortgage. Other times, the problem is more subtle. Perhaps you want to achieve a financial goal, but as the time for the goal approaches, you realize you don't have enough money to make it happen.

Alerts wave a red flag as soon as a financial problem starts. By following Mint.com's alerts, you can keep on top of your money and be in control every day, rather than respond to crises that are difficult to manage or even to spot. This constant monitoring can help you do the following:

- ✔ **Correct a small financial problem rather than deal with a big one:** Catching bad financial habits early is a key to staying on track. For example, financial planners love to demonize getting a cup of joe on your way to work. Clearly, buying a premade cup of coffee for $2.00 is a luxury when you can make it at home for 25¢. But one cup of coffee is financially insignificant. The extra money you spend getting take-out coffee once in awhile isn't going to spoil your long-term goal of retiring at 65. If you put that $1.75 you saved in the bank for 30 years at 2 percent interest, it would be worth only $3.17. That's hardly enough to worry about over a 30-year period.

  What does make a difference, though, is the snowballing effect of a bad financial habit that goes unchecked for years. Suppose that you spend an extra $1.75 to buy coffee versus making it yourself not from time to time but every workday. That spending adds up to $35 a month, or $420 a year. And had you saved the $420 at 2 percent interest each year for 30 years, you would have more than $17,000. Now that's something worth worrying about. Mint.com is a useful tool for finding financial habits that might be subtracting from your financial future.

- ✔ **Capitalize on the fact that success breeds success:** Don't underestimate the power of positive feedback. Being financially sound requires diligence, and encouragement from time to time can help. After all, saving money doesn't give you the same kind of instant gratification as spending money can. Mint.com can be your financial coach by pointing out areas where you're doing well financially as well as areas where you need to improve. If you stay on track with Mint.com alerts, you'll be encouraged and keep moving ahead because you'll feel more in control of your finances.

- ✔ **Detect unnoticed financial problems:** Homeowners will tell you that the worst problems are the ones you can't see, such as a hidden water leak. The same is true for your finances. You may not even know what financial problems to watch for, such as when your bank suddenly cuts the interest rate being paid on your savings. Or perhaps you know what to look for but don't have time to pay as much attention as you should. Mint.com alerts get your attention with e-mail or phone messages to make sure that you don't overlook these problems.

✔ **Stop a financial mistake before you make it:** In the short story "The Minority Report," police used a Precrime system that knew which people would break a law in the future, sometimes even before the people knew. The police used this intelligence to arrest future criminals before they did anything illegal. Don't worry. Mint.com isn't going to toss you in jail. But Mint.com's alerts are a financial Precrime unit that tries to stop you from committing a financial crime against yourself.

## Staying focused on the long term

Mint.com monitors your spending and saving, on the lookout for ways you can do better. If you're steering off-course in the short term, alerts notify you so that you can adjust at once. The true beauty of alerts is that they watch over short-term issues so that you can focus your efforts on long-term financial goals. In Table 6-1, we outline the items that alerts can help you manage.

| Table 6-1 | Financial Items That Alerts Monitor |
|---|---|
| *Alert* | *Examples of Financial Aspects Monitored* |
| Banking | Low account balances, changes in interest rates, bank fees, large deposits becoming available for withdrawal |
| Credit | Bills coming due, amount of credit available |
| Planning | Over budget in different categories, unusual spending, credit available, large purchases |
| Investing | Trade commissions |

Letting Mint.com handle the short-term stuff listed in Table 6-1 enables you to focus your time and energy thinking about the following:

✔ **Retirement:** If you should be worried about only one long-term goal, it's your retirement. If you're like most people, you'll need to save enough money to support yourself, without a job, for 20 or more years. More on retirement planning in Chapter 16.

✔ **Rainy-day fund:** You should have enough cash on hand to cover your expenses for six months or even longer.

✔ **College savings:** A degree from a four-year college is becoming increasingly important in our information-based economy. College isn't cheap. In 2010, tuition and fees for four years cost $32,600, on average, at a public college and $121,800 at a private college, according to Savingforcollege.com, citing data from The College Board. You need to start saving now or face huge loans.

✔ **Wedding:** Listen up, future Bridezillas and Groomzillas. If you expect to have a five-star wedding at a fancy hotel on the beach, you might need to start saving now. And if you're the father or mother of the betrothed, you might be tapped to save too.

✔ **Travel:** If you're the typical young user of Mint.com, travel is probably important to you and a big part of your budget. You need to plan to make travel possible without sending you on a trip to the poorhouse.

Part III details how to use Mint.com to track your progress toward specific long-term goals.

# Discovering the Types of Alerts

If you pull a fire alarm, there's no question what kind of alert you're going to get. Expect loud sirens, flashing lights, and the arrival of the fire department. Mint.com's alerts are far less dramatic and include a weekly summary e-mail and alerts that tip you off to developments in specific accounts, such as your brokerage or credit card accounts.

## Trusting Mint.com: Alerts everyone gets

In this section, we describe the alerts and other types of notifications you get when you first sign on to the Mint.com service. These premade alerts may be all you need.

### Weekly summary e-mail

Each Friday, Mint.com e-mails you an electronic document that resembles a customized paper bank statement for all your accounts. The top of the weekly summary e-mail typically contains a financial tip, such as how rolling over a 401(k) from an old job to an IRA can be beneficial (more on that in Chapter 16). Scroll down and you get a rundown of key aspects of your financial life, such as the amount of money in your checking and savings accounts, the amount you owe on your credit cards, and the worth of your investment portfolio.

Scroll down a bit further in the summary e-mail and you'll see a list of the biggest purchases you made during the month. At the bottom of the e-mail is a rundown of your budget and how much you've spent in different categories, such as Fast Food, Coffee Shops, and Gas & Fuel.

Most people will find Mint.com's weekly summary e-mail helpful and want to keep receiving it. However, if you want to turn off your weekly summary e-mails, click the Change Your Alerts link, at the top of Overview page, as shown in Figure 6-1. Note the default alerts in the Alerts section. In the Send Summary Emails drop-down list, select Never.

Click to change the alerts you receive

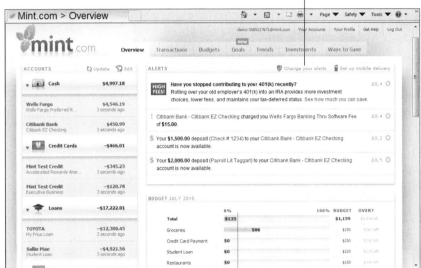

**Figure 6-1:**
Your gate-
way to
customizing
alerts.

## Alerts on the Overview tab

When you log in to Mint.com, all your alerts are prominently displayed. On
the right side of the page (refer to Figure 6-1), you see the alerts that Mint.com
thinks you should know about. These alerts might include news that your bank
charged you a fee, that a large deposit is available for withdrawal, or that a
credit card bill is due. More on these types of alerts from Mint.com in a minute.

## Mint.com trends on the Overview tab

Mint.com tries to use everything it knows about you and your wallet to alert
you of relevant financial events. The Trends section of the Overview tab is a
great example of how Mint.com flags important information. The Trends section isn't called an alert, but it provides some of the same types of financial
information as Mint.com's alerts.

To find the Trends section, start at the Overview tab. Scroll down until you
see the Trends section on the left, as shown in Figure 6-2. This section displays how much you're spending in cash versus what you're charging, how
your income is shaping up this year, and more.

# Banking on alerts

Banks advertise that they're your friends. Well, we're here to tell you that
they're not. Banks survive on fees they charge. Sometimes fees are connected
with banking services you've selected, such as online bill payments. Other
bank fees are connected to your financial screw-ups, such as spending more
than you have, or *overdrafting* your account.

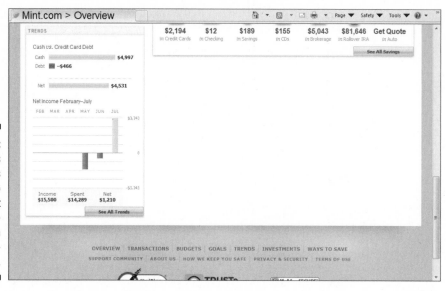

**Figure 6-2:**
The Trends
area alerts
you to
important
develop-
ments in
your finan-
cial life.

Mint.com's banking-related alerts can help you avoid such costly mistakes. Of all the alerts offered by Mint.com, the banking alerts are the most numerous and detailed. All but two of the alerts, over budget and interest-rate changes, have default monetary values that you can change. Following are Mint.com's banking alerts:

- **Low balance:** Mint.com tells you if the balance of any of your checking or savings accounts falls below $500. This alert can save you a bundle if it stops you from writing a check that's bigger than your balance. These so-called rubber checks *bounce*, or are rejected by the bank, and can result in high overdraft fees. Sometimes the bank covers the check but charges interest on that amount.

- **Unusual spending:** If your spending in any category jumps $200 more than average, you are notified. You can see what categories Mint.com tracks in Chapter 4.

- **Over budget:** If you spend more than you've allotted in any category, Mint.com will bring it to your attention so that you can get back on track.

- **Interest-rate changes:** Banks lure you in with a high interest rate on a savings account but later lower the rate to next to nothing. Mint.com can tell you when your bank changes your interest rate.

- **Bank fees:** Banks love to charge fees but don't like to draw attention to them. Mint.com is designed to let you know about any bank fee, but you can change the setting so that it tells you only about large fees.

✔ **Large purchases:** Sometimes you splurge. Mint.com's alerts remind you of your indulgences by notifying you of purchases of $1,000 or more.

✔ **Large deposit:** Just because you deposit a big check doesn't mean you can spend that money right away. A deposit can take several days to clear the banking system and be available in your checking or savings account. Mint.com lets you know when you can start using the money you've deposited. The default setting is to send an alert when deposits of $1,000 or more are available.

## Tracking your credit

Many of Mint.com's banking alerts notify you of charges or fees you've already incurred. Mint.com's credit alerts, however, can help you avoid making a financial mistake, such as paying a credit card late or wrecking your credit score. Mint.com's credit alerts follow:

✔ **Bill reminders:** If you pay your bills late, you can incur late fees and other nasty charges. Avoid these setbacks with Mint.com alerts, which default to reminding you seven days before a bill is due.

✔ **Credit available:** If you don't have a high credit card limit, you may need to conserve your credit for certain upcoming large purchases. Mint. com's credit available alert lets you know if you draw your available credit below a default level of $1,000.

✔ **Reckless credit card usage:** Mint.com sends an alert if you go on a plastic-spending rampage that might threaten your credit score.

Instead of paying for costly credit monitoring services from your credit card company, set up alerts to flag large or unusual purchases. That way, if someone does steal your credit card or your credit card number, you'll catch it early.

## Putting your portfolio on high alert

Mint.com has only one alert pertaining to investments: Letting you know if your brokerage charges you a trading commission.

Most investors will question the value of being informed when they've paid a commission. Investors typically expect to pay a commission and know what the commission will be when they make a trade. Also, trading commissions have shrunk, with some online brokerages letting you trade for free and others charging less than $9 for trades.

If you're serious about investing and like the idea of alerts, you'll need to look beyond Mint.com. Many online brokerage firms and financial Web sites will e-mail you or otherwise alert you when, for example, the price of a stock you own falls a certain percentage or trading in a particular stock gets heavy. Yahoo! Finance (`www.finance.yahoo.com`), for instance, will alert you by e-mail if a stock price rises or falls by a preset amount. To find out how to use the Internet to boost your investment success, check out *Investing Online for Dummies* by Matt Krantz (Wiley).

If you're an investor, read Chapters 18 and 19, which deal with how to use Mint.com to track mutual funds and stocks, respectively.

# Customizing Alerts

Have you ever spent time in a building that gets frequent false fire alarms? The first time the fire alarm goes off, almost everyone in the building gets the heck out. But if the alarm goes off again and again and there's no fire, everyone ignores the alarm before long. The same is true for financial alarms.

If you get constant warnings about your finances, including trivial financial events, you'll soon start ignoring them. Mint.com enables you to tailor alerts as follows:

- **Delivery method of the alert:** You can always access your alerts by going to Mint.com. In addition, you can have alerts sent to you by e-mail or even as a text message to your cell phone or smartphone.

- **Types of alerts:** Not all types of alerts are valuable to everyone. Mint.com lets you decide which alerts you want to receive on your cell phone or as e-mails.

- **Triggers that cause an alert:** You can set thresholds that are serious enough to warrant Mint.com sending an alert to your cell phone or e-mail.

## Determining the types of alerts you receive

One of the best ways to make sure the alerts you're getting from Mint.com are helpful is to tailor them to your situation. You can tell Mint.com which types of alerts you receive on your cell phone or in your e-mail box.

To change the types of alerts you receive, do the following:

1. **Click the Overview tab.**

   If you just logged into Mint.com, the Overview tab is selected automatically.

2. **Click the Change Your Alerts link, which is in the Alerts section.**

   The window shown in Figure 6-3 appears.

**Figure 6-3:**
Your dash-
board to
controlling
your alerts.

3. **Choose the alerts you want to receive.**

   Scroll down the list of all the alerts and select the boxes to the left of the
   alerts you want to receive. If you want to receive the alert as a text message on your cell phone, select SMS option. You can read more about
   getting alerts on your cell phone later in this chapter. If you want the
   alert as an e-mail, select the Email option.

   You can't permanently turn off alerts. This information is presented to you
   each time you log in to Mint.com.

   After you have set the alerts that are relevant to you, you must next decide at
   what point alerts are triggered, which is discussed next.

## Setting an alert threshold

The point when a financial event becomes significant enough to warrant an
alert is subjective. For instance, what's a large purchase? If you're living on a
shoestring budget, a purchase of $500 is probably massive. However, if you're
a tycoon, you might not think twice about spending $500 a night for a hotel
room. Because Mint.com users are in different places financially, the capability
to tell Mint.com when financial events are worthy of an alert is important.

Follow these steps to set the thresholds for alerts sent to your cell phone or
by e-mail:

1. **Click the Change Your Alerts link on the Overview tab.**

2. **Find the alerts for which you want to set thresholds.**

   It's easy to spot the alerts that allow you to set thresholds because they have a default value entered in a pull-down menu bar.

3. **Click the down arrow near the alert and select the threshold that will trigger the alert.**

You can't set a threshold for the alerts you get at Mint.com because those alerts are generated automatically. However, you can tell the program to stop displaying an alert at Mint.com, as described in the next section.

## Deciding how to receive alerts

Location. Location. Location. These are the three most important things about investing in real estate. The same is true with Mint.com alerts. Your location when you get a Mint.com alert can make all the difference in the value of the alert.

You can tell Mint.com not only the types of alerts you want to get but also where you want to receive them. You can get alerts in the following four ways:

- ✔ **At Mint.com:** You can't hide from your alerts when you log in to Mint. com. The upper-right side of the screen lists all your alerts. All Mint.com users receive these alerts and they can't be customized with thresholds.

- ✔ **By e-mail:** You can tell Mint.com to e-mail you a particular type of alert. You can also designate a secondary e-mail address for the alert if, for example, you have a separate e-mail address for your smartphone.

- ✔ **To your cell phone:** Mint.com can send a text message to your cell phone if an alert is triggered.

- ✔ **From your smartphone:** Most smartphones can receive text messages. In addition, a version of Mint.com is available for the Apple iPhone and smartphones running Google's Android operating system. The mobile version of the Mint.com application, or *app,* lets you get on your smartphone some of the same information you get at Mint.com. The apps don't yet provide Mint.com's alerts, but they can serve a similar role. For instance, using the Mint.com app, you can view the balances of all your financial accounts as well as see how much you've spent so far this month on specific categories, such as restaurants. If you're about to make a big purchase and aren't sure you can afford it, fire up the Mint.com app.

You can't customize the alerts displayed automatically at Mint.com's Overview tab. If you don't want to see the alert again, however, you can tell Mint.com to stop displaying it. View the Mint.com alerts on the right side of the Overview page. Click the X in a circle to the right of the alert you no longer want to see.

Finally, to receive an alert by e-mail or to your cell phone or smartphone, follow these steps:

**1. Click the Change Your Alerts link on the Overview tab.**

You see the screen shown in Figure 6-4.

**Figure 6-4:** Receive an alert by e-mail or as a message to your cell phone.

**2. Scroll to the Alert Configuration section.**

**3. For an alert you want to receive on your cell phone, select the check box in the SMS column for the alert.**

Mint.com sends alerts to smartphones and standard cell phones using the messaging technology known as SMS, or *Short Message Service*.

**4. For an alert you want to receive by e-mail, select the check box in the Email column for the alert.**

**5. Click the Close button.**

# *Reacting to an Alert*

Uh oh. You just received a text message from Mint.com telling you that your ongoing wild weekend in Las Vegas financed by your credit card isn't such a good move. If you've just busted your budget, Mint.com will alert you right away. But remember that alerts are only warnings. Mint.com can't stop you from spending money because you're the ultimate Mint.com override system.

But before you exercise your override authority, you might want to consider the following:

- **Is the alert informed?** Suppose that Mint.com tells you that you've exceeded your monthly budget for clothing. But perhaps you've been forgoing clothing purchases for the past six months. Or maybe you've been eating ramen noodles every night so you could buy that sweater of your dreams with the food money you've saved. Although Mint.com may correctly alert you that you've spent more on clothing than you've budgeted, that doesn't mean you're necessarily in danger of running out of money this month.

- **Is the alert meaningful?** You might get an alert that the balance in your checking account has fallen below $500. Sounds scary, right? But what is the actual amount? A balance falling to $499 is different than one falling to $10.

- **Is the alert relevant?** Mint.com sets many alerts automatically, so you might get alerts that aren't right for you. You can't change the alerts you see on the Overview tab, but you can change the ones you receive by e-mail and on your cell phone. (See the preceding section for details.) Also, if you haven't been using Mint.com long, the program might not yet have a handle on your typical spending.

You risk ignoring all alerts if you don't stop the ones that you don't care about. And if you start ignoring alerts, you're short-circuiting a big reason to use Mint.com in the first place. If you are deleting e-mails from Mint.com without opening them, you probably need to tailor your alerts.

Don't be afraid to tinker with Mint.com's alerts. You can tweak them to become more meaningful and relevant to your situation. To make your alerts useful, do the following:

- **Weed out alerts you're not going to act on.** You might think that you want to be notified when your brokerage charges you a trading commission. But if you're not going to alter your investment strategy or change brokers, the information could become a distraction.

- **Drop alerts you're getting elsewhere.** If you already get an alert from your credit card company when a bill is due or an alert from your bank when a check clears, turn off the similar alert in Mint.com. Otherwise, you might feel like you're being nagged.

- **Add alerts that are painful.** Sometimes the best alerts are the ones you hate getting. If you're a shopaholic, a Mint.com e-mail alert when you blow the lid off the budget in the shopping category will be especially unwelcome but exactly the kind of alert you need — and need to heed.

# Chapter 7

# Feeling Safe and Secure Using Mint.com

*T*o use Mint.com most effectively, you must violate several guidelines of online security, such as giving all your account numbers and passwords to a third party you've never met. If that doesn't make you nervous, it should. To be fair, though, the security of financial information has been a serious concern as long as there's been money. Before widespread use of the Internet, financial information was stolen the old-fashioned way — by rummaging through dumpsters for credit card receipts and bank statements.

In this chapter, we outline the risks — and the rewards — of entrusting so much personal financial information to Mint.com. We also discuss what Mint. com says about its security.

## Giving Info to Mint.com

The beauty of Mint.com is that it can pull all your vital financial information into one easy-to-access site. But from a security standpoint, such a consolidation of financial information can be a bit risky because one Web site has access to all your most sensitive information.

Just about any Internet site you use erodes at least some of your privacy and security. Many Web sites, for instance, track you so that they can put targeted advertising on your screen. If you understand the risks of giving your financial information to Mint.com, you can minimize those risks.

Security is important for all Mint.com users to consider. But you might be especially interested about security if you

✔ **Have concentrated financial relationships:** If you have just one checking account and one savings account and a crook breaks into your accounts, your entire cash horde is at risk. But if you have your money spread around in different banks and brokerages, you get some built-in security just from the fact that the crook would have to crack several institutions.

✔ **Lack the technological savvy to spot early-warning signs:** If you're unfamiliar with technology, you may not know how to spot evidence that your financial security has been violated. However, if you're regularly using Mint.com and logging in to your bank, brokerage, and credit card accounts, you'll quickly see if anything is amiss.

---

# Financial data breaches do happen

If you think security breaches can't happen to you, keep reading. Following are a few recent hair-raising examples of stolen online financial information:

✔ **The Heartland Payment Systems Visa and MasterCard breach:** What is believed to be the largest identify theft in U.S. history was revealed in January 2009. *Identity theft* is a type of fraud in which criminals steal your personal information to, for example, use your credit cards. A group of criminals broke into Heartland Payment Systems, a large processor of credit card transactions, and had access for several weeks to the payment system. They allegedly stole millions of MasterCard and Visa credit card and debit card numbers.

✔ **Electronic money transfer hacking:** Criminals have targeted financial transactions that move money between institutions. Between 2008 and 2009, the Federal Bureau of Investigation pursued more than 200 cases in which online crooks pulled off fraudulent transfers of money, stealing $40 million as a result, as reported in *USA TODAY.*

✔ **The RBS WorldPay hack:** In 2009, eight people were indicted on charges of stealing debit card information from payments processor RBS WorldPay. These criminals used the financial information to steal millions from ATMs in just a few hours.

Trojans, rogue computer programs that allow criminals to take control of your computer, are one of the biggest threats to anyone using the Internet to perform banking functions. More than 200,000 Trojans were used in 2009, up from 194,000 in 2008, says *USA TODAY,* citing data from PandaLabs.

Risks from online security breaches have exploded to such a degree that in early 2010, the American Bankers Association (ABA) backtracked from its longtime insistence that online banking is 100 percent safe. The association advised small and midsized businesses to use a locked-down and dedicated computer for online banking. Also in 2010, the ABA started to ask individuals to "partner" with banks to keep their accounts safe.

# Information you give to Mint.com

To register with Mint.com, you must provide information about important aspects of your financial life. (Flip to Chapter 2 to find out how to sign up for Mint.com and enter your account information.) Following is the data you enter in Mint.com:

- ✔ **Your e-mail address:** Your e-mail address is the primary way Mint.com identifies you. Mint.com uses your e-mail address, not your actual name, as your *user name*, or the identifier that tells Mint.com who you are when you sign in.

  One of Mint.com's biggest security claims is that it doesn't require you to enter your first or last name. (This claim is discussed later in this chapter in the "Safeguards" section.) However, many people have an e-mail address that at least partially resembles their name. If you have two e-mail addresses, and one does not include your name, consider using that one when signing up for Mint.com.

- ✔ **Zip code:** Mint.com doesn't ask you for your exact address, but does ask for your five-digit postal zip code.

- ✔ **Password:** To use Mint.com, you must select a password that consists of 6 to 16 characters.

  Choosing a *strong password*, or one that's difficult for other people to guess, is a critical first step in protecting your Mint.com account. When you sign up for Mint.com and choose a password, Mint.com tells you if the password you selected is strong or just okay. See the "Smart security practices" section for help in choosing a password that's hard for criminals to crack.

- ✔ **Agreement to Mint.com's Terms of Use:** Most Web sites and software require you to agree to the rules of the product. Mint.com is no different. To use the site, you must click the Yes, I Agree to the Mint.com Terms of Use option. When you do, you are agreeing that you will not hold Mint.com or its parent company Intuit liable if you suffer any loss as a result of using Mint.com.

- ✔ **Your financial institutions' names:** To pull in your financial information, Mint.com needs to know where to look. That means you must enter the names of the banks, brokerages, and credit card companies with which you have accounts.

- ✔ **Online ID:** When you sign up to use a bank, brokerage, or credit card company's Web site, you either choose or are assigned an online ID. This is the name you use to tell the company's Web site who you are when you log in. You must enter the online ID for all the accounts you choose to add to Mint.com.

- ✔ **Passcode:** Yes, you must give Mint.com the password for your accounts. And yes, Mint.com will have both your online ID and passcode for your accounts, which could enable someone to access your account information online.

✔ **Challenge questions (for some bank and brokerage accounts):** For extra security, many banks and brokerage firms require you to choose several questions when you sign up for access to their Web site, such as the name of your first pet or mother's maiden name. The theory behind financial institutions' usage of these challenge questions is that even if someone were to get your online ID and passcode, they wouldn't have the answers to your challenge questions. Mint.com requires that you answer these when you add some bank and brokerage accounts. Mint.com says that 90 percent of the time, you are not required to enter your challenge questions. But that means you have a one-in-ten chance that you'll need to provide this sensitive information when adding an account. Whether you need to enter the challenge question is determined by your financial institution.

✔ **Trading passwords (for some brokerage accounts):** Most online brokerages take security seriously. And that's a good thing because people keep a vast majority of their wealth in this type of account. Most brokerages have multiple layers of security. Even if you have the online ID and passcode, most brokerages require you to have a third piece of data, called a *trading password*, to buy and sell stocks. The trading password is your most guarded secret when it comes to brokerage security. Mint.com states that on rare occasions, you may be asked to enter your trading password.

## What Mint.com gives you in exchange

All the information that you enter in Mint.com, including your passwords, is transferred to powerful computers, called servers, that Mint.com controls. Putting all that information *in the cloud*, or on a server controlled by someone else, might make you pause.

Giving up personal financial information is the price of entry to use Mint.com. But by providing that information, you get the following:

✔ **A comprehensive picture of your money:** The more information you give to Mint.com, including data about accounts, the more complete a picture Mint.com can give about your accounts. You might want to play it safe and give Mint.com information about only your savings account. But then Mint.com's Trend tab, which shows useful changes in your balances and spending, won't have access to your credit card account, where you might do most of your spending.

✔ **Extra security:** Wait a second. Didn't we say you're giving up security when you provide all your information to Mint.com? That's right. But giving Mint.com your personal financial information can also protect your financial information. Suppose you enter the online ID and password for your credit card and allow Mint.com to access your account.

From now on, Mint.com will watch that account. If someone were to tap into your credit card account and make charges, Mint.com's alerts feature would notify you immediately of unusual or large spending. Meanwhile, if you check your Mint.com account regularly, you might be more likely to spot something fishy going on in your accounts. This safeguard would be on top of those you already have in place, such as when your credit card company calls to alert you of suspicious charges. So in a way, by giving your personal information to Mint.com, you get an extra safeguard against fraud. You can read more about Mint.com's alerts feature in Chapter 6.

Here's another potential security boost from using Mint.com. If you start getting your account statements online from Mint.com, you can tell your banks, brokerages, and credit card companies to stop mailing paper statements to your house. Paper documents have their own security risks because they can be stolen from your trash can.

✔ **Insights about your finances:** If you're not tracking your money at all, your online ID and password may be secure, but your finances might be a wreck. In exchange for your financial information, Mint.com gives you a way to keep closer tabs on your money.

# Safeguards

Mint.com goes to great lengths to describe the security measures in place to safeguard your financial information. Mint.com's founder, Aaron Patzer, appears in a video on the site that steps through the reasons why you can trust him and Mint.com to keep your financial information safe. To view the video, go to `www.mint.com/privacy/` and click the Patzer box, which is in the upper-right corner.

## Mint.com's security claims

Rather than just saying "Trust us," Mint.com spells out the following ways it makes sure the information you enter doesn't fall into the wrong hands:

✔ **Mint.com does not ask you to enter your name.** Mint.com claims that none of your financial information, including passwords or account numbers, are linked to personally identifiable information.

Again, it bears mentioning that although Mint.com doesn't ask for your name, it does ask for your e-mail address. If you have several e-mail addresses, including one that's not easily associated with your name, consider using that one with Mint.com. If you want to be extra careful, create another e-mail address not associated with your name and use it with Mint.com.

✔ **Mint.com uses bank-level security.** Mint.com says it uses many security techniques practiced by top banks and brokerage firms. The site makes the following claims. One, all data you transmit to the site is digitally scrambled, or encrypted using 128-bit Secure Socket Layer (SSL) technology. Two, all Mint.com employees must pass background checks before they're hired. Three, the facility is in unmarked from the outside and locked down with Mission Impossible–like security that includes a hand scanner, two guards, and a long corridor called a "man trap" that prevents a second person from following an authorized user into the facility. Four, no one Mint.com employee can defeat the technology used to scramble the data.

✔ **Mint.com won't let you move money.** You can view information from your accounts online, but you can't see account numbers or passwords. In addition, the site doesn't let you transfer money between accounts or buy and sell stocks. If someone were to get into your Mint.com account, that person could see how much money you have but couldn't move the money into another account from Mint.com. The crook would need to crack your bank's Web site to transfer the money and, according to Mint.com, wouldn't get much help in that endeavor from information on the Mint.com site.

✔ **Mint.com provides immediate notifications of any changes to your account.** If you use the Mint.com Web site regularly, you'll know right away if any money is missing from any of your accounts because Mint.com displays the balances and transactions from all your accounts in one place. You can also check balances from your cell phone and sign up for alerts to warn you of any big changes to your accounts.

✔ **Mint.com is owned by Intuit, the financial software giant.** Mint.com doesn't directly list the fact that it's owned by giant financial software firm Intuit as a security advantage, but it is. Intuit is behind some of the most trusted financial software available: TurboTax tax preparation software, Quicken personal finance software, and QuickBooks small-business software. Intuit stakes its reputation on making sure your financial data is safe in Mint.com. The data in Mint.com is saved on servers controlled by Intuit, which has decades of experience safeguarding financial data.

## Wiping out your information in Mint.com

Online privacy experts have long expressed concern that online personal information seems to stick around forever, not unlike nuclear waste. *Web crawlers*, or computers trained to automatically explore the Internet and create maps to all available information online, are constantly looking for anything new online and saving a copy. Top search engines, such as Google and Bing, store copies of Web sites and make them available as *cached pages*, even if the pages have been deleted. Conversely, Mint.com makes it easy to zero out your financial information.

### Erasing a bank, brokerage, or credit card account

Just because you add a bank, brokerage, or credit card account to Mint. com doesn't mean it's permanently burned into Mint.com's servers. You can remove any financial account from Mint.com at any time. You might decide you no longer want to divulge a particular account to Mint.com, or you might want to delete an account if you've stopped using it.

Deleting an account in Mint.com does not close your account with the bank, credit card company, or brokerage. When you delete an account in Mint.com, you're simply telling the site to delete the information that has already been pulled in and to stop downloading new information.

Deleting an account in Mint.com is simple:

1. **Log into Mint.com and click the Your Accounts link at the top of the page.**

   The link is labeled in Figure 7-1.

2. **Scroll down the list of banking and brokerage accounts in Mint.com until you find the one you want to remove.**

3. **Click the Delete button for the account you want to remove (see Figure 7-2.**

4. **Type the word** DELETE **in the blank.**

   Use all uppercase letters.

Click here to access your accounts

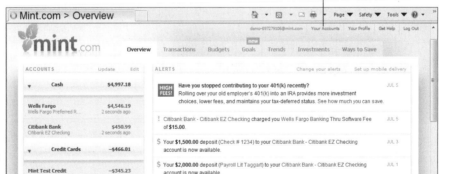

**Figure 7-1:** Click the Your Accounts link to delete an account.

**Figure 7-2:**
Delete bank,
brokerage,
and credit
card info
you've
entered.

**5. Click the Okay button.**

Just make sure you mean it. You can't get the account back after you delete it.

### Erasing your entire Mint.com account

Even if you delete individual banking or brokerage accounts that you've connected to Mint.com, you haven't deleted your Mint.com account. You can still add banking, brokerage, and credit card accounts to your Mint.com account and track the accounts you haven't deleted.

But if you decide that you want to stop using Mint.com, you can delete everything. Follow these steps and it will be as though your account never existed in Mint.com:

**1. Log into Mint.com and click the Your Profile link, at the top of the page.**

**2. Scroll down and click the red Delete Your Mint.com Account link.**

Mint.com asks if you really want to delete the information.

Be sure that you want to delete your Mint.com account when you click this link. After clicking it, your account is removed immediately. If you decide you want to use Mint.com later, you have to set up everything again.

**3. Click Yes, Delete My Mint.com Account link.**

**4. Enter your password.**

Mint.com asks you to enter your password as a safeguard to make sure you're an authorized user.

**5. Click the Finish button.**

If you change your mind and decide to not delete your Mint.com account, click the Close button instead.

Mint.com eliminates all traces of your financial data from its computers within 48 hours of the deletion of your account.

Deleting your Mint.com account does not close any of your bank, brokerage, or credit card accounts and doesn't change how you log into the Web sites operated by those accounts.

## Smart security practices

Mint.com runs in the cloud. In other words, the information is stored on computers connected to the Internet and controlled by Mint.com, not on your computer's hard drive. Because Mint.com is running mainly on their equipment, most data security issues are out of your hands, which is why you need to trust Mint.com and its security practices if you're going to use the site.

However, you can take steps to protect your information. Locking a building with the best locks made doesn't matter if you leave a window open. Likewise, you can follow some smart security practices to help ensure that your financial information remains safe when using Mint.com:

✔ **Keep your computer's operating system browser up to date.** Regardless of the type of computer you use, criminals will eventually find a weak spot. Such vulnerabilities often show up in your computer's operating system, which is the software that tells the machine how to function. The main computer operating systems used by consumers are Microsoft's Windows and Apple's Mac OS. Download the latest updates, or *patches*, required to close security holes discovered by researchers.

For instance, most recent versions of Windows include a program called Windows Update, which automatically checks for, downloads, and installs patches that make Windows more secure. You can also start Windows Update yourself. In Windows 7, click the Windows Orb in the lower-left corner and type **Windows Update**. Click the program name that appears and follow the instructions for Windows Update, as shown in Figure 7-3.

✔ **Keep your Internet browser up to date.** Just as operating system makers release security updates, so do makers of Internet browsers. Your *browser* is a program that accesses the Internet, including the Mint.com Web site. The top browsers used by consumers are Microsoft's Internet Explorer, Mozilla's Firefox, Google's Chrome, and Apple's Safari; all can check for updates.

If you're using Internet Explorer, Windows Update will keep not only your operating system but also your browser up to date.

✔ **Make sure browser add-ons are up to date.** A handful of small programs often attach to your browser for legitimate purposes. These browser add-ons are a big reason why Web browsers can do more than just display text and photos, but their power comes with potential security breaches. One browser add-on that is especially important to keep up to date is Flash, which enables Web pages to display videos and users to interact with Web pages. Normally, you don't have to do anything to update Flash. (If necessary, you can get the latest version at `get.adobe.com/flashplayer`.)

✔ **Choose a strong password.** Because the password you choose when you sign up for Mint.com is your first line of defense, you want it to be a decent deterrent. Mint.com will tell you if the password you chose is strong or just okay when you enter it. Some ways to make the password stronger include using a combination of letters, numbers, and symbols. Also consider making the password closer to the maximum limit of 16 characters. It's also a good idea to change your Mint.com account password periodically, such as every three months. And try to avoid words that a snoop could figure out, such as the name of your street.

✔ **Use antivirus software.** Antivirus tools helps prevent malicious software, called *viruses*, from tampering with your computer. Keeping viruses off the computer used to access Mint.com is especially important.

For most personal users, Microsoft's free Security Essentials is all you need. You can download Security Essentials from `www.microsoft.com/securityessentials`.

✔ **Use a firewall.** A *firewall* acts as an electronic gate that separates your computer from the Internet, controlling the information sources or programs that may communicate with your computer. A firewall is critical in ensuring that your computer is not being taken over by criminals. Most versions of Windows come with a built-in firewall, but you should make sure it's turned on. You can read more about firewalls at `windows.microsoft.com/en-us/windows7/What-is-a-firewall`.

✔ **Share private information only with secure Web sites.** When you use a Web site that asks for personal information, especially Mint.com, make sure the site is encrypted. In Internet Explorer, simply look for a gold padlock icon to the right of the Web site's address in the address bar. Also make sure the site you're connecting to is the one you think you're connecting to. Internet Explorer can help. When you go to a financial Web site, such as Mint.com, the address should turn green, indicating that the site is indeed what it claims to be. You can also click the company name just to the right of the gold padlock icon. Doing so will show you the site's security certificate and confirm that it's correct. Currently, the green address bar feature is unique to Internet Explorer, so tread carefully if you're using Firefox, Chrome, or another browser.

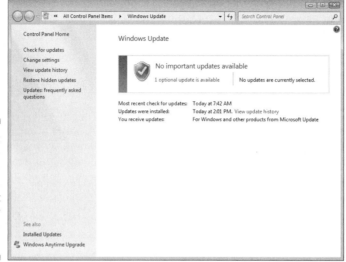

**Figure 7-3:**
Make sure
your operat-
ing system
and Internet
Explorer
browser are
current.

Don't be fooled into thinking that you're safe if you use an Apple Macintosh computer. Fewer viruses have been written for the Macintosh, perhaps because Macs are less popular than computers running Windows. But several high-profile cases show that Mac users have to be as concerned as Windows users with security.

During a contest in 2009, Charlie Miller needed only a few seconds to take control of a MacBook computer that was fully up to date with all patches. He told technology Web site ZDNet, "Hacking into Macs is so much easier. You don't have to jump through hoops and deal with all the anti-exploit mitigations you'd find in Windows."

In addition, in 2009, security research firm Intego found Trojans on some gaming Web sites that could infect Macs. And in 2010, Intego found another Trojan that infects Mac users after they download and install seemingly legitimate screensavers and other free software. No matter what computer you use, if you connect to the Internet, you need to think about security.

# Protecting Your Mint.com Data from Loss

After you start using Mint.com, you may get hooked on how the site pulls together various aspects of your financial life. Mint.com can become your financial control center, showing you how much money you have, what you owe, and how much you should save to meet future goals. However, you should remember that none of the information you see on the site is stored on your computer's hard drive. All the data is stored remotely on computers controlled by Mint.com.

The fact that Mint.com stores all your data on Mint.com's servers, not your computer's hard drive, is a key distinction between Mint.com and personal finance software such as Intuit's Quicken.

## Downloading your personal information

Storing your financial information on Mint.com's computers is convenient because you can access the information from any Internet connection. There's no need to copy your data onto a portable memory card if you need to move the data to another computer. In addition, Mint.com handles the data backup. If your laptop goes kaput, you can use another computer to access all your financial information, as though nothing ever happened.

Even so, you might want to save to your hard drive a copy of the data stored on Mint.com. To download your financial information stored at Mint.com, do the following:

1. **Select the account for which you want to download transactions.**

    The list of accounts appears on the left side of the Mint.com home page.

2. **Click the Export All *x* Transactions link (where *x* is the number of transactions in that account), as shown in Figure 7-4.**

    You need to scroll to the bottom of the list of transactions to see the link. Your computer's operating system displays a message asking where you want to save the file.

3. **Select a location on your computer's hard drive to save the information.**

    Save the file to a place on your hard drive you'll remember. The file will be a comma-separated values (or CSV) file. Most spreadsheet programs, including Microsoft Excel, can read and open CSV files.

4. **Repeat Steps 1–3 for your other accounts.**

5. **Open the CSV file in a spreadsheet.**

    Just to make sure the download worked properly, open the CSV files you saved on your computer's hard drive using a spreadsheet program.

Even if Mint.com were to lose your financial transactions, all your original information would still be available from the Web sites of your bank, brokerage, and credit card companies. Note, however, that the number of years that financial institutions keep transactions varies widely.

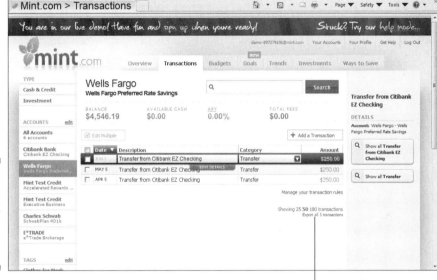

**Figure 7-4:**
Use the
Export link
to download
your info to
a file.

Export link

---

# The cloud's downside

Because Mint.com and other online personal finance Web sites store your personal information on their computers or in the cloud, you can access your financial information from any computer and even on a cell phone. But there's a downside. Because your data isn't on your computer, your financial information can sometimes be unavailable or vanish. We're not suggesting that Mint.com will disappear. The fact that Mint.com was bought by Intuit shows that deep pockets are behind the service. But when you don't control your data, you need to be prepared for the possibility that you might sometimes have trouble accessing it. Every few weeks, for instance, Mint.com takes down its Web site late at night to perform maintenance. During these times, you are unable to log into your Mint.com account and view your financial information.

Even more startling, though, a Mint.com-like service was essentially unplugged. Cake Financial, an online personal finance system that was one of the top rivals of Mint.com, was launched in 2007. Cake, like Mint.com, allowed consumers to store all their financial information in one place. When the site was abruptly taken offline in January 2010, people could no longer access their information on the site. Then in July, another popular online personal finance site, Wesabe, was discontinued without warning. Fortunately, Wesabe provided tools to help abandoned users download their financial information and delete their accounts from the site. Still, the abrupt closures of Cake and Wesabe are reminders of the chance you're taking when you trust a third party to keep track of your financial information.

## Accessing Mint.com away from home

One of the great features of Mint.com is that you can access your financial information anywhere. If you're in a coffeehouse with a *hotspot* (a site that provides wireless Internet access), you can log into your Mint.com account and see how your budget is shaping up for the month. But now that you're outside your home, your security radar should kick into high alert.

Beginning in July 2010, Starbucks began providing free Internet access to its customers. Previously, customers were required to use a Starbucks card and make a certain number of purchases to qualify for several free hours a day of Internet use in their stores. To find other establishments offering free public Wi-Fi, go to www.wififreespot.com.

When you connect to Mint.com or other Web sites from a hotspot, you're exposing yourself to a new set of security issues. With just a little experience, other people sitting in the hotspot may be able to try to intercept your Internet traffic and steal any passwords you type into your computer.

When connecting to the Internet through a hotspot, be sure to read the "Smart security practices" section, earlier in the chapter. Make sure you see the gold padlock icon in the address bar of any Web site you access from a public Wi-Fi hotspot. Also have a firewall running when accessing sensitive data online from a public Wi-Fi hotspot.

It's generally a bad idea to access any Web site, especially one that contains sensitive information, from a public computer. It's one thing to use your own computer while connected to a hotspot, but avoid logging into your Mint.com account from a shared public computer, such as one in a hotel lobby. Such public computers can steal your password with software designed to record your keystrokes.

A feature in Windows 7 handles most of the security regarding hotspots. The first time you connect to a hotspot, Windows asks if you're using a home network, work network, or public network. If you choose public network, Windows 7 makes sure your firewall is running and tweaks other system settings to make you safer.

If you'd like to be extra careful when accessing your Mint.com account from a hotspot, you might consider using a *virtual private network,* or *VPN,* which is like a private tunnel for your Internet traffic that blocks outsiders. You're most likely to use a VPN by

✔ **Linking with your company's VPN:** If you get a laptop for work, it most likely comes with VPN software that lets you connect securely to your work network. Some companies also provide software you install on a personal computer to connect to a VPN. Be sure to check with your company's information technology department to make sure the software is okay for personal use.

✔ **Connecting to an existing VPN:** Here you instruct your laptop to connect with a VPN that's provided for public use. This solution raises its own problems, such as insisting that you download software that might contain distracting ads and requiring that you trust the security of the existing VPN. One example of a public VPN is PublicVPN.com (`http://publicvpn.com`).

✔ **Creating your own VPN:** Some software programs let you create a VPN network using a computer at home. You can then securely connect to that network using your laptop and a hotspot. Windows 7 has a built-in VPN system. You can also use VPN software from third parties such as LogMeIn Hamachi[2] (`www.logmein.com/products`).

# Part II
# Budgeting

The 5th Wave          By Rich Tennant

"My portfolio is gonna take a hit for this."

## In this part . . .

Creating a budget and sticking with it are probably on the top of the list of things you know you should do, but don't. The idea of sitting down, analyzing your spending, and then deciding how much you can afford isn't at the top of most lists for weekend fun.

But Mint.com can do almost all the heavy lifting when it comes to creating a budget. The site can scour through your spending patterns and help you find out how much you're allocating in major categories such as housing, food, and entertainment. You can then create reasonable spending limits using Mint.com's budget features. And if you do blow your budget in one area, Mint.com will help you do damage control and cut spending in other areas so you stay on track. After reading Part II, you'll have your budget set up and working for you in no time.

# Chapter 8

# Budgeting Income and Expenses

· · · · · · · · · · · · · · · · · · · · · · · · · · · · · · · · · · · · · · · · · · · · · · ·

· · · · · · · · · · · · · · · · · · · · · · · · · · · · · · · · · · · · · · · · · · · · · · ·

*1*n its simplest form, a budget is a plan, one that shows how much money you expect to earn and how you expect to spend that money. For some people, budgets are a way of life: Nothing is spent unless it fits in the budget. For others, a budget is a necessary evil. Maybe you have a budget but ignore it. Or maybe you struggle to pay your bills every month, so even short-term planning goes out the window.

Having a budget is the key to getting the things you want out of life. And using a budget provides you with the peace of mind of knowing how you are going to distribute your money to pay your bills.

Mint.com makes it easy to examine your budget, futz with the numbers, and keep track of how close you are to reaching your monthly spending limits. The examples in this chapter illustrate budgeting techniques to control your spending and plan for your income.

# Budgets, Simplified

You can look at a budget in two ways. One, you can think of a budget as an estimate of your expected income and expenses, a roadmap to help you see what you can expect in the months and years ahead. This kind of budget is your financial friend, reminding you when you're on track and helping you when you're off track. Two, you can think of a budget as a stern guardian that helps you manage your money by monitoring your spending and by slapping your hand when you don't stay within the limits you've set.

Friendly guide or taskmaster, a budget, in its simplest form, is a list showing how much you expect to earn and spend for a period of time in the future.

# Budgeting Your Income

You know how much money you earn at your job, and if the amount you earn from month to month doesn't change, budgeting for this income is effort-less. Assuming you deposit your paychecks in your bank account, Mint.com already has a handle on how much money you make each month.

But is there more to your income than your paycheck? Income comes in many shapes and sizes, and some income sources might not seem obvious. Here are some examples that might apply to you:

- ✔ Interest that you earn on bank savings accounts and other interest-bear-ing investments

- ✔ Dividends on stocks that you own and earnings on mutual fund investments

- ✔ Rent from rental property that you own, boarders, people who pay to use your summer home, adult children who are still at home

- ✔ Retirement income, including pension income, Social Security, and amounts you're withdrawing from an individual retirement account or another tax-deferred account

For a complete income picture, we include the earnings in our retirement account and employer matching amounts as income. We can't get our hands on that money until we retire and start drawing down the account, but the money is still income, just like the amounts we earn in a savings account that we don't use except for emergencies. Chapter 16 provides more information about retirement earnings.

Mint.com makes budgets based on the information it accumulates from all your accounts. These budgets are adjusted automatically over time, based on your financial activity. If you have income from other sources that Mint.com hasn't detected, you can add those items to the budget as follows:

1. **On the Overview page, click See All Budgets.**

   The standard budget that appears by default is a spending budget, which doesn't display your income. The See All Budgets feature displays a more robust budget page that includes your income.

2. **View your budgeted income.**

   Budgeted income for the current month appears at the top of the screen. In Figure 8-1, paycheck income for the month is budgeted at $4,000, and $4,000 has been received.

3. **Click Create a Budget to add a new income item to your monthly budget.**

   The Set a Budget window appears.

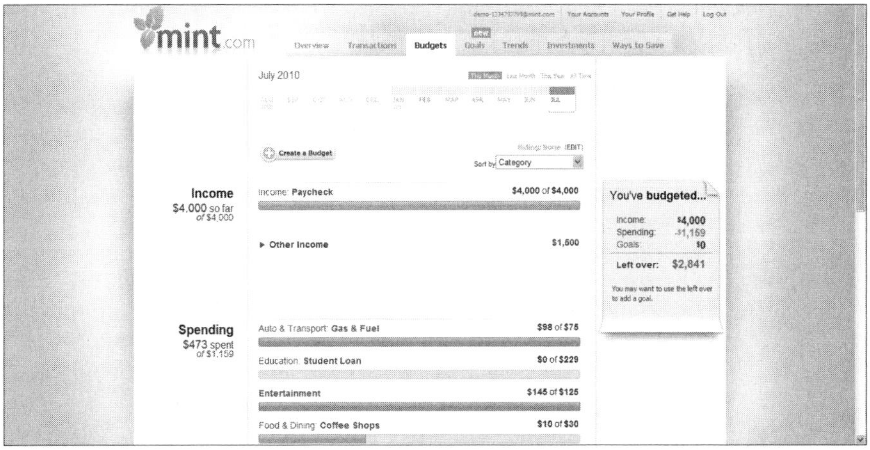

**Figure 8-1:** I received my total budgeted amount of pay this month.

**Figure 8-2:** Projected interest income is $10 per month.

4. **Select a category.**

   Click the drop-down arrow in the Choose a Category field, mouse over the Income item in the list, and then click the type of income you're adding from the side menu. In Figure 8-2, we selected Interest Income.

5. **Enter the budgeted amount.**

   Enter how much income you expect to receive each month from the income type you selected.

6. **Click Save to add the new income item to your budget.**

# Budgeting Your Expenses

In stories and in the movies, imaginary characters do good deeds when no one is looking. Fairy godmothers wave magic wands and dreary days become filled with sunlight and rainbows, ragged clothes turn into finery, and lowly mice become grand horses. The budgeting process at Mint.com is a lot like those magical scenes.

The imaginary elves at Mint.com sift through your bank and credit card accounts and figure out what types of expenses you incur on a regular basis. Presto! Each time you open your Mint.com account, the home page presents your budgeted expenses, as shown in Figure 8-3. This display is updated each time you open Mint.com, reflecting any new spending.

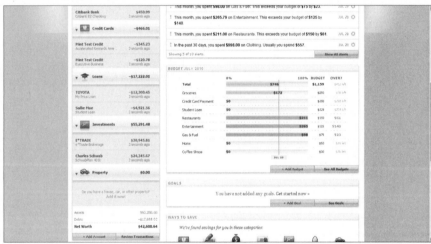

**Figure 8-3:** The vertical bar represents today's date, so you can see how much of the month remains.

The home page budget includes a list of your major recurring expenses, the anticipated monthly amount of each expense, a colorful chart showing how much of your budgeted amount has already been spent, and a vertical line showing you how far into the month you've progressed as of today.

Click the name of any budget item to see the details of the spending in that category so far this month. If a transaction is misclassified, click the item, click the Category field, and select a new category in the drop-down list.

To get a list of all your monthly spending, click the Budgets tab or click the See All Budgets button that appears at the bottom of the budget list on the Overview page.

By default, Mint.com presents your budget on a monthly basis. If you look at the top of the Budgets tab, you'll see options to change the budget to Last Month, This Year, and All Time. You can also click a specific month from the calendar at the top of the screen. Click This Month at any time to go back to the current month's budget.

As mentioned, Mint.com determines your monthly spending mostly by reviewing your bank and credit card accounts, but some items might not be recorded properly. For example, you might have a monthly payment to Sterling Sports that Mint.com classifies as Entertainment or Gym expenses, when actually your brother owns Sterling Sports and the store loaned you $1,000 that you're paying back over time.

Also, you might have periodic payments that aren't occurring every month, so Mint.com hasn't determined the frequency of those payments. For example, you might want to budget a certain amount for medical expenses even if you haven't spent anything on medical care this year.

Following is a list of common payments to include in a budget:

- Rent or mortgage payments.
- Utilities and related services: Electricity, gas, water, sewer, trash service.
- Transportation: Gas and oil, public transportation, auto payments, auto repair and maintenance, auto insurance.
- Medical care: Health insurance, doctor and dentist visits, ongoing medications, contact lenses.
- Children: Education, day care, diapers, school lunches.
- Clothing.
- Job-related costs: Tools, books, dry cleaning, uniforms, union dues, lunches, parking, professional dues, professional liability insurance.
- Debt service: Loan payments, interest on credit card bills. The amounts you charge on your credit card should go in the proper categories, such as food, clothes, and entertainment. When you make a credit card payment, you can split the payment, including the finance charge, into appropriate categories.
- Insurance: Life insurance, property insurance, insurance not included elsewhere.
- Pets: Food, boarding, veterinarian, equipment.
- Charity: Religious organizations, other not-for-profit organizations.
- Gifts: Birthdays, other holidays, graduations, anniversaries, showers, weddings.

✔ Entertainment: Cable television, movies, restaurants, sporting events, concerts, music, night clubs, vacations, books, magazines, newspapers, Internet, satellite, home movie service, videos.

✔ Personal: Haircare, makeup and other toiletries, fitness.

✔ Savings: Short-term and long-term savings investments, including contributions to retirement funds (unless your retirement fund payments are withheld from your paycheck).

If you make any of these payments and they're not being accounted for properly in the budget as determined by Mint.com, follow these steps to add the appropriate expense to your budget:

1. **Click the Add Budget button, which appears at the bottom of the budget on the Overview page.**

   Or click the Create a Budget button that appears at the top of the budget on the Budgets page. In either case, the Set a Budget screen appears.

2. **Select a category to add to your budget.**

   Click the drop-down arrow in the Choose a Category area. Mouse over the main category list to select a category from one of the side menus.

   Don't see what you need? Click Add/Edit Categories on any side menu to display the Manage Your Categories window. Select a category from the left side of the window, click Add a New Category, and then enter your new category, as shown in Figure 8-4. Click Save It and then click Okay. Your new category is added to the drop-down list.

**Figure 8-4:** The new Long Term Care Ins category will appear in the Category list.

3. **Indicate the frequency of this budgeted item.**

   Your choices are Every Month, Every Few Months, or Once. Select Every Few Months for an amount that will be budgeted periodically but not every month; select Once for a one-time budgeted item. For monthly or one-time-only payments, you are asked to enter the amount of the payment. If you select Every Few Months, you also need to enter the frequency (anywhere from every two months to once a year) and the month in which the next payment occurs (or when the last payment was made — your choice).

4. **Click Save.**

   Mint.com adds the expense item to your budget.

If you're not sure how much to enter as a budgeted item, be safe and err on the side of overstating your expenses and understating your income. Having extra money at the end of the month is better than coming up short.

# Chapter 9

# Working with Your Budget

## In This Chapter

▶ Understanding the components of the budget displays

▶ Looking at ways to increase income and decrease spending

▶ Sending your budget report to another program

▶ Putting your budget to work

*L*earning to work with a budget is like learning to play the piano. You start with the simplest of concepts, studying a few expenses at a time, widening your reach, until eventually you're stretching across the financial keyboard, combining all aspects and layers of your various sources of income and expenses. Just like anything that takes practice, your ability to understand and benefit from using a budget will improve with time. Before you know it, you'll be a budget virtuoso!

People who create budgets on paper can put their paper budget in a drawer and never look at it again. Those who use a personal finance software program such as Quicken or Microsoft Money can open the program but not open the budget screen. If you use Mint.com, however, you see your budget the minute you log in. You can't fold up your budget and stick it in a drawer, and you can't open Mint.com without seeing the numbers. Mint.com makes sure you get a full dose of your budget whenever you use the program.

Onscreen isn't the only place where you get budget immersion. When you slip up and go over-budget on an expense, Mint.com sends an alert to your e-mail inbox, reminding you to shape up and get back on track. (You can also ask Mint.com to send alerts to your phone — Chapter 6 explains how to turn on phone alerts).

You can't avoid your budget in Mint.com, so why not take advantage of it and make this tool work for you?

In this chapter, you discover how Mint.com calculates budget numbers and how to customize the budget to fit your needs. You also get plenty of tips on how to make your own financial lifestyle fit within your budget. You also find put how to send your Mint.com budget to a spreadsheet, where you can make your own budget reports, just the way you like them.

# *Touring the Budget Displays*

The first step in using your budget is finding out what the information in the budget means. In this section, you take a tour of your budget on both the Overview tab and the Budgets tab.

## *Categories*

The Overview tab, shown in Figure 9-1, displays a summary of the balances in all your accounts, alert messages about your recent financial activity, tips for saving money, some of your more frequently used budget items, a few charts showing trends in your spending and income, and some quick links to click to find out how to save money. In the Budget section, you see a list of expense categories that represent a standard selection of common budget items.

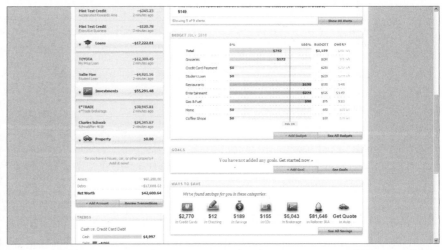

**Figure 9-1:**
The budget
categories
on the
Overview
page are
standard in
Mint.com.

The Overview screen displays expense categories used most often by the average Mint.com user, not necessarily the expense categories you use most often.

## *Horizontal bars*

You've probably figured out that the horizontal bars on your budget graph represent your spending. But why so many colors? And why are the colors on the Overview tab different from those on the Budgets tab? And why do you have to buy a 96-count box of Crayola crayons to get Razzmatazz?

## Creating a budget yourself

The more history you have in Mint.com, the closer your budget comes to your actual spending. However, the budget is at best a close representation of past performance and only an approximation of future performance.

For serious budgeting, we recommend that you use Mint.com as a starting point to help with your estimates and as a daily reminder of your current spending. Then create your own budget on a spreadsheet or in a personal finance program such as Quicken. Instead of relying on averages of past performance like Mint.com does, you can use your knowledge of your expected future earnings and expenses and make a budget that incorporates anticipated changes.

To create a budget that is easy and meaningful, start with your current income and expenses. You can use the numbers from Mint.com as a starting point for a monthly budget for the current year. Then set near- and long-term financial goals, such as increasing your income or paying for a college education. (Read more about goal setting in relation to budgets in Chapters 15 and 16.)

If you need to make changes to your budget, see the "Balancing Your Budget" section for ideas for increasing your earnings and decreasing your spending.

I can answer at least some of these questions. The bars on the budget portion of the Overview screen come in orange and chartreuse. The chartreuse color represents spending within your budget, and the brighter orange color is spending that is over-budget.

The color system changes when you flip to the Budgets tab, as shown in Figure 9-2. Instead of keeping with the chartreuse and orange scheme, the color police at Mint.com have switched to a red, yellow, green system. Red means "Stop! You're spending too much!" You have gone over-budget for the selected time period. Yellow means you're moving along nicely but getting close to your limit. And green means all is well — you can carry on.

We're only speculating, but maybe the folks at Mint.com have soothing, happy budget colors on the home page to lure you into your budget, and then use colors that mean business on the Budgets tab.

## *Vertical bar*

The vertical line drawn through your budget on the Overview page of Mint.com represents where you are in the current month. This Overview budget displays the current month's spending in major categories.

If the line is positioned in the middle of the budget graph, you can bet the date is approximately the 15th of the month. If the line is close to the right side of the graph, the month is coming to a close. Note that this vertical line appears only on the budget presentation on the Overview tab, not on the Budgets tab.

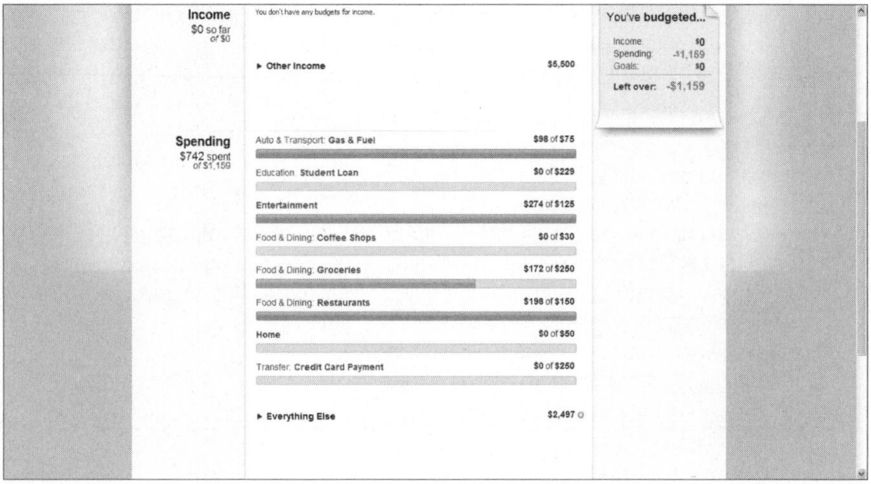

**Figure 9-2:**
Bolder colors mean business.

# Budget column

Mint.com uses your average spending in different categories to establish a baseline amount for your budget categories. You can alter these amounts if they are not accurate estimates of your anticipated spending.

To make a change in a budgeted amount, go to the Budgets tab. Move your cursor over any budget category, and an Edit Details tab appears. Click the Edit Details tab and you can change the amount of the budgeted item.

# Are you over-budget?

Have you spent more than your Mint.com budget recommends? If so, the orange amount in the Over? column on the Overview page displays how much you have exceeded your budget for the current month. A dim blue number shows you how much you have left before you get into budget trouble.

On the Budgets tab, each line of the budget displays how much of your total budgeted amount you have used so far this month. A box to the right of the budget screen shows how your actual income and actual expenses for the month compare to your budgeted amounts.

## Different views

Are you tired of seeing the same budget information over and over again? By default, Mint.com displays your budget for the current month only. If you're on the Overview page, the current month is your only choice for your budget presentation.

On the Budgets tab, however, you can change your view of the budget. At the top-right corner of the screen, shown in Figure 9-3, you see options for displaying your budget in various forms:

**Figure 9-3:** You can change your budget to display a year or particular months.

✔ By the current month (the default)

✔ By last month

✔ By year

✔ For all time

You can also click a month on the calendar bar to display a different month than the current one. To select contiguous months, click a calendar bar month, hold down the Shift key, and click a different month.

# Balancing Your Budget

When you examine your budget, some categories might be over-budget. Perhaps you've already spent your month's allotment on clothes, so you have to make do without more t-shirts of your favorite music group or reduce the grocery budget.

You should regularly analyze your budget and try to determine not just how you can make ends meet today but also how you can make sure that you have enough left over for future expenses such as retirement, travel, or a college education for your child. Part III discusses how to plan for future events. For now, you need to get a handle on how to take control of your budget and how to use your budget to help make ends meet.

You can increase the bottom line in two ways:

✔ Increase your income.

✔ Decrease your expenses.

This section provides tips for accomplishing both tasks.

## *Increasing your income*

You can increase your income in obvious and not-so-obvious ways. Many methods for increasing income entail working harder. Other methods require that you be more clever with the way you use your money, which can be risky. And still other methods involve situations over which you have no control.

Following is a list of suggestions for ways in which income can be increased. See if some of these tips can work for you:

✔ **Get a raise.** If your employer gives out raises each year, position yourself to get the highest possible raise. Go to work early, get involved in extra projects, make your superior's job easier, mentor people in your company, and just do the best job you can.

✔ **Think ahead.** Are you hoping to get promoted someday? Do you want to move into a new position or a better job? Start making yourself ready for that next job by acquiring new skills or practicing new techniques on your own time. Develop a plan for learning what you need to know to get that next job.

✔ **Ask about other earning opportunities.** Your job might have overtime opportunities, extra shifts, or special projects that pay extra.

✔ **Add another job.** Look for additional work, something you can do part-time when you're not at your regular job. Tell friends, family, and acquaintances that you're interested in extra work. If they don't know of something available today, they might later. Use the Internet and check the ads in your local paper.

✔ **Dust off your piggy bank.** It's time to get back to saving. As a child, you loved the sound of coins dropping in the piggy bank and thinking about how much money you had and what you were going to do with it. Start saving again. Send some of the money from your checking account over to savings each month. Consider investing some money in mutual funds, a money market account, or an investment club.

✔ **Change your withholdings.** Are you accustomed to getting a large tax refund each spring? Why wait until April? Ask your employer for a W-4 form and adjust your withholding to claim more exemptions now, thus increasing your take-home pay for the rest of the year. You can always change back to a lower number of exemptions later or next year.

Before adjusting your income tax withholding, consult with your tax accountant to make sure you don't come up short in the spring. Ideally, you want to have enough tax withheld so that you don't owe money on your tax return. Underpayment of taxes can result in your owing penalties and interest to the Internal Revenue Service.

## Decreasing your expenses

You've worked on various ways to make more money, so now it's time to reduce your spending by finding ways to save on expenses.

Following are several tips for cutting expenses. All these ideas probably won't work for you, but chances are good you can find some money-saving ideas in this list:

✔ **Cut back on utilities**. This section is too big to cover in a single bullet point, so see the "Reducing utility costs" sidebar.

✔ **Pay bills online**. Forget about postage and envelopes. Use your bank's online service, or go directly to the Web site for the company from which you received a bill, and pay your bills from your computer. The payment is delivered quickly and securely. If your bank charges for bill paying, Mint.com can help find you a bank that won't (see Chapter 3).

✔ **Make your home safe.** By installing a smoke detector in your home, you can reduce the cost of your homeowner's or renter's insurance. If you add a security system, you can lower your insurance rates, too.

✔ **Get rid of your junk.** Do you have items taking up space — things you don't want any more? If so, get busy selling these items and turn the things you don't want into cash. Then save that cash.

✔ **Move.** Moving might seem like a drastic measure, but it's possible you can slice your monthly living expenses if you move to less expensive housing. If you own a house and want to make a quick getaway, consider finding a tenant for your house to cover your mortgage expenses and then rent something cheaper for yourself.

✔ **Take in a boarder.** If you'd rather not move but your living expenses are exceeding your budget, maybe it's time to bring in someone to share the cost of your home. Place an ad online or in the local newspaper if you're willing to have a stranger move in. Alternatively, check whether a friend or family member is looking for a place to live.

If you plan on taking in a boarder, talk to a lawyer and have a formal lease drawn up. Even if your new roommate is a family member or close friend, you'll be happier in the long run if the legal issues are agreed upon up front.

✔ **Buy in bulk.** Team up with a friend, neighbor, or coworker and buy items in large quantities. The price breaks can be significant when you shop this way.

✔ **Save money on auto insurance.** Check with your agent to make sure you're getting all the price cuts to which you're entitled. Auto insurance companies often provide lower prices when you go for three years or more without a ticket, use the same company for other types of insurance such as homeowner's or renter's insurance, or insure other family members at the same company. Teenage drivers receive better insurance rates if their grades are high or they do well in driver's education class. If you live in a large city but don't drive to work, you might get a lower rate.

✔ **Reduce gas usage by combining errands**. Do multiple errands at the same time or take turns doing driving trips with a friend.

✔ **Make timely payments.** Avoid interest and late charges by making all your bill payments on time.

✔ **Switch shifts to avoid daycare.** You or your spouse can look into working a different shift so that one of you is always home with the children.

✔ **Eat at home.** When you get a yearning to eat out, think about what you would order if you were at a restaurant and then figure out how to make that same dish at home.

✔ **Bring your lunch to work.** Cook large quantities over the weekend so you can carry food to work and avoid having to get take-out or go to restaurants.

✔ **Take a staycation.** Instead of traveling when you have time off, turn your home into a vacation getaway. Camp out in the yard or on the living room floor; make ethnic food; sleep late; don't answer the phone. Be a tourist in your own town by visiting local museums and attractions. Consider having friends or family visit you instead of traveling to see them.

✔ **Cancel magazine subscriptions.** Read magazines online or at the library.

# Exporting Your Budget

It's helpful to have a copy of your budget so you can monitor your progress and make notes in the margins. Onscreen reports in Mint.com list your income and expenses, and colorful onscreen charts provide graphic illustrations of your financial activity.

# Reducing utility costs

You can save money by reducing utility costs in many ways. Following are some examples:

✔ Familiarize yourself with state and federal tax breaks for energy-saving insulation and devices.

✔ Turn down the temperature on your water heater, particularly if you're leaving the house for more than a few days.

✔ Reduce your use of air conditioning in the summer and heating in the winter. Adjust the thermostat if you're leaving the house for more than a few hours.

✔ Check and replace furnace filters frequently. Not only does a clean filter make your furnace run more efficiently but some furnace maintenance contracts are not enforceable if you don't change the filter on schedule.

✔ If you have an old furnace or air conditioner, look into upgrading. Newer models pay for themselves quickly with the money they save on lower utility costs.

✔ Close vents and doors in rooms you don't use.

✔ Use the time feature on your thermostat (or look into upgrading an older thermostat to add this feature) to lower your heat or air conditioning usage when you're sleeping.

✔ Install ceiling fans to improve the efficiency of the furnace or air conditioning system.

✔ Reduce the time you spend in the shower. Turn off the water when shampooing or shaving.

✔ Switch to cold water in your washing machine.

✔ Run the washing machine and dishwasher only when you have a full load.

✔ Turn off music and the television when you leave the house.

✔ Put timers or motion sensors on outside lights.

To view the charts that display your income and spending trends, do the following:

1. **Click the Trends tab.**

2. **Select a timeframe option at the top of the screen.**

   Your choices are This Month, Last Month, This Year, and All Time. You can also click a month from the list that appears at the top of the screen. To select a contiguous range of months, hold down the Shift key, click Home Month, and then click another month.

3. **Select the type of graph.**

   In the left column, select Spending, Income, Net Income, Assets, Debts, or Net Worth. The Spending and Income graphs provide the most detail and are the most applicable for budget-related graphs.

4. **In the Choose a Graph area, select By Category.**

   You see all spending categories (or income categories, depending on your choice in Step 3) displayed in a pie chart, as shown in Figure 9-4.

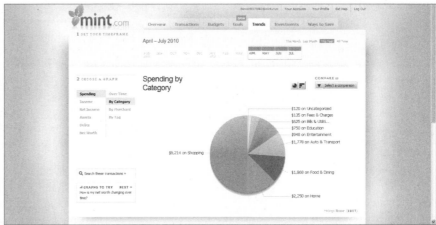

**Figure 9-4:**
The Spending graph is a good choice when graphing your budget.

### 5. View details of any category.

If you want to see the detail behind a spending category amount, click the category in the chart itself or click the description next to the chart. A new chart appears, illustrating the detail behind the category you chose.

### 6. After viewing details, click Overview above the chart to return to the main chart.

### 7. View the report.

Scroll to the bottom of the screen to see the information in a standard report format, as shown in Figure 9-5. Click the Show All option at the bottom of the category list to view all your budget categories. When you do this, the option changes to Show Fewer, as shown in Figure 9-6, which returns you to the original condensed report.

**Figure 9-5:**
Click Show All to see all your budget categories.

8. **Send the report to another program.**

   If you want to export the report to a spreadsheet program or another
   program where you can manipulate the numbers, or save the report in its
   current form to a file on your computer, click the Export to CSV option at
   the bottom of the report. Then choose Open and the report opens in an
   Excel spreadsheet, as shown in Figure 9-7. In Excel, you can use the numbers to create any type of report you want and then save your Excel file
   on your computer by choosing File➪Save. If you prefer to open the Mint.
   com report in a different program, click Save instead of Open. In the Save
   As window that appears, save the file to a location you choose on your
   computer, and then open the file with the program of your choice.

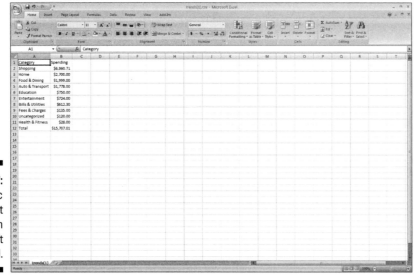

# Using Your Budget Report

Now that you have a budget report, what should you do with it? Use your report as the foundation for family discussions about your financial strategy. In the short run, the report can be a daily reminder of where you are in your monthly income and spending cycle. In the long run, use the report as a planning tool by viewing how you spend your money each month and by discussing how to control particular areas.

You might find it useful to take your budget report to a financial planner if you want to seriously consider long-term plans for your financial security.

Remain mindful of the fact that you, not the budget report, are in charge of financial activity in your household. The budget is a guide to where you want to go. If your budget isn't pointing you in the right direction, review the "Balancing Your Budget" section to see how to increase your income and decrease your expenses.

However, there are limits to what a budget can do for you. Following are five tips for how *not* to use your budget. These techniques should help you use your budget information wisely:

- ✔ **Don't rely on the budget alone to do the job.** A budget is a tool for helping you monitor your income and spending. Earning the income and keeping the spending in line are your responsibilities.

- ✔ **Don't try to pass off your budget as a financial statement.** If you're applying for a loan, the financial institution will ask you to provide financial statements. Although you can include a budget in the package you give to your potential lender, the lender is looking for your actual income and spending, not a monthly estimate of your desired income and spending.

- ✔ **Don't think that your budget is inflexible.** You can do your best to predict your financial circumstances, but you can't control life. Understand that your budget must be flexible and you might need to make budgetary changes during the year.

- ✔ **Don't change the budget to meet every whim.** A fixed budget that you create outside Mint.com won't be useful if you change it every time your income or expenses don't agree with the budgeted amounts. (A Mint.com budget incorporates changes as they occur.) Analyze the differences between your actual earnings and spending and your budgeted amounts, make sure you understand what caused those differences, and try to get back on track. Remember that you can make adjustments in future months to make up for problems in months gone by to keep your actual income and spending for the entire year where you want it to be.

- ✔ **Don't think that your budget prevents you from spending money on items you want or need.** Your budget should have the opposite effect. Keep tabs on your budgeted categories and see when money is available for spending. By following your budget, you know whether it's okay to spend.

# Chapter 10

# Budgeting Irregular Income and Infrequent Expenses

. . . . . . . . . . . . . . . . . . . . . . . . . . . . . . . . . . . . . . . . . . . . . . .

. . . . . . . . . . . . . . . . . . . . . . . . . . . . . . . . . . . . . . . . . . . . . . .

*I*n a perfect world, we would receive all the income we need on a regular, predictable basis, and that income would be enough to pay all our bills with enough left over for us to take trips, buy all the material goods that would make us happy, and sock away a comfortable nest egg for retirement. Good luck with that. Instead, we live in a world of unpredictability, and many people have a hard time making ends meet, let alone setting aside enough for a comfortable retirement.

Some folks earn money sporadically because they change jobs, are out of work sometimes, or earn their income in fits and spurts. Financial planning is frustrating when your income isn't received according to a strict schedule but your expenses keep coming in, month after month. If your receive income at irregular intervals, you must save enough in the lucrative months to cover fixed expenses in the unprofitable months. In this chapter, we explore ways to address in your budget this up-and-down process of earning a living.

# Understanding Inflexible versus Flexible Budget Items

You can receive two types of income — we like to call these income types flexible and inflexible. Much of your *inflexible income* is in the form of paychecks received on a regular schedule: weekly, biweekly, semimonthly, or monthly. *Flexible income,* on the other hand, is sporadic and difficult to budget.

Even if you receive your income sporadically during the year, it can be easier to make a budget from the perspective of earning income evenly. At the beginning of the year, estimate your earnings and expenses for the entire year, and then adjust those numbers so that the income figure remains higher than the expenses figure. These adjustments will involve *flexible expenses,* which are items that you can control, at least to a certain extent. *Inflexible expenses* are fixed expenses over which you have little if any control.

Mint.com reports your income and expenses just as they come into your bank and credit card accounts and doesn't have a way of determining in advance how frequently or infrequently you might incur these financial transactions. This section provides examples of how you can budget for flexible and inflexible income and expenses.

# Budgeting Inflexible Income

You receive inflexible income items month in and month out. Following are the most common examples:

- **Paychecks:** As long as you're at one job, you can count on a steady paycheck.
- **Interest income:** Bank savings accounts and other interest-bearing accounts typically make monthly payments.
- **Dividend income:** Stocks and mutual fund shares provide predictable dividends. Stocks usually pay quarterly dividends; mutual funds generally pay monthly dividends, although some funds pay quarterly or year dividends.
- **Rent:** If you own rental property, you receive a monthly rent payment.

To enter in your budget an item that is the same each month (inflexible item), follow these steps:

1. **On the Mint.com home page, click the Budgets tab.**

   The Budgets screen appears.

2. **Click the Set a Budget option at the top left.**

   The Set a Budget screen appears.

3. **In the Choose a Category list, select an inflexible income category.**

   Refer to the preceding section for a list of inflexible income items. We selected Income and then Interest Income as our category.

4. **In the When Will This Happen? area, select an option, if necessary.**

   Because we chose Interest Income in Step 3, and Mint.com knows that interest is received on a monthly basis, the timing options (When Will This Happen?) change so that Every Month is the only choice, as shown in Figure 10-1.

**Figure 10-1:**
Interest
is auto-
matically
designated
as monthly
income.

5. **In the Amount field, enter an amount.**

   Estimate how much interest you expect to earn each month. You can always go back and change this amount.

6. **Click Save.**

   Your interest income is now part of your monthly budget. To record any other inflexible income items, repeat Steps 2–5.

## Budgeting during unemployment

Are you out of work, looking for a new job, drawing unemployment compensation, working part-time jobs, doing odd jobs, or worried about losing your job? These unpredictable job situations make budgeting more difficult — and more necessary. When you have a secure job and a regular paycheck, making ends meet can be difficult. But when you don't know whether revenue will be coming in next month, it can seem impossible to make all your expense payments. The better you plan for the future, the easier it will be to get through the difficult times. Using a budget helps you see into the future and plan for inevitable expenses.

# Budgeting Flexible Income

Flexible income often arrives on an irregular schedule. Following are some common examples:

- **Paychecks:** Paychecks can appear in both the flexible and inflexible categories. If you change jobs or are between jobs, your paychecks might not be coming regularly.

- **Payment for contract work:** Some people, such as actors, sculptors, writers, and musicians, are paid for projects instead of pulling in a regular paycheck, so their pay is sporadic.

- **Seasonal income:** Some workers are busy at some times of the year and not so busy other times. For example, in cold climates, some construction workers and other outside laborers are busier in warm months. Tax preparers are really busy in the spring. Many businesses add employees during the holiday season.

You have two choices when entering flexible income items into your budget. First, you can determine your expected income for the entire year and divide each type of income by 12. You enter these amounts into your budget the same way you enter an inflexible income item, as described in the preceding section.

When you budget sporadic income as though it were regular, fixed income, you will be under-budget in certain months and over-budget in others. If you look at a particular month, your budget might look skewed, and you might think that your expenses aren't being met or you're making way more than you're spending. Everything will work out (we hope!) at the end of the year, when you receive and record all your income.

The second way to include flexible income items in your budget is to enter your actual anticipated income each month. With this method, your budget is more finely tuned and your income is more precisely matched against your expenses.

For example, suppose that you get a freelance job in March, and expect to earn $1,000 a month for three months. Here's how you would enter that flexible income in your budget:

1. **On the Mint.com home page, click the Budgets tab.**

2. **Click the Set a Budget option at the top left.**

   The Set a Budget screen appears. Mint.com doesn't have a Freelance Income category, so we have to create one.

3. **Set up a new income category as follows:**

   a. **In the Choose a Category field, click the down arrow, mouse over the Income category, and choose Add/Edit Categories.**

      The Manage Your Categories window appears.

   b. **Click Add a new category.**

   c. **Start typing** Freelance, **and a drop-down list appears.**

   d. **Choose Freelance Income in the list, as shown in Figure 10-2.**

   e. **Click Save It and then click Okay.**

      Freelance Income is now one of your income categories.

**Figure 10-2:**
Adding a new budget category.

4. **Click the down arrow in the Choose a Category field, mouse over Income, and then choose Freelance Income from the side menu.**

5. **Enter** 1000 **in the Amount field.**

   By default, Mint.com has designated your freelance income as monthly income. Because this freelance gig lasts only three months, you have to come back after three months and change the amount of your monthly freelance income to 0.

6. **Click Save.**

You can use this new Freelance Income category for several types of income, or you can set up separate categories for different jobs. Maybe you do outside house painting in the summer and inside carpentry in the winter. You can put all the income together in one category, or you can repeat Step 3 to set up a category for each type of income.

# Budgeting Inflexible Expenses

Just as income can be divided into flexible and inflexible, so too can expenses. An *inflexible expense* is a fixed payment that occurs monthly, quarterly, yearly, or on another basis. Whatever the timetable, an inflexible expense is the result of a contract or an agreement you have entered into, and you have a legal commitment to make those payments.

Following are examples of inflexible expenses:

- **Rent or mortgage payment**: You might be able to refinance your mortgage to reduce your monthly payment amount.

- **Insurance (homeowner's, renter's, health, auto)**: If you pay your insurance annually instead of monthly, you may qualify for a lower rate. You can also increase the deductible on your home or auto insurance policy and thus reduce the premium payment.

- **Alimony and child support payments**: Child support may fluctuate depending on the season. As your children get older, you might be able to renegotiate child support amounts.

- **Utilities**: Heating and electricity expenses will probably change from month to month. You can cut down on your utility usage (see Chapter 9 for examples on cutting utility expenses).

- **Auto and other loan payments**: Shop around to make sure you get the lowest rate possible.

- **School loan payments**: If you're unemployed, you're entitled to up to a three-year deferment on your school loan. Many states offer loan deferment or even loan cancellation if you agree to teach in an inner-city school or in certain areas. Also, look into consolidating school loans with one lender for a lower payment. Setting up an automatic payment plan can result in a lower interest rate.

Suppose that you owe $500 in auto insurance each year and make quarterly payments. Here's how to set up this inflexible expense item as a budget item in Mint.com:

1. **On the Mint.com home page, click the Budgets tab.**

   The Budgets screen appears, and you can see the income and spending you've already budgeted or that has been budgeted for you courtesy of Mint.com. Time to add something new.

2. **Click the Create a Budget button, as shown in Figure 10-3.**

   The Set a Budget window appears. This is where you enter the specifics about your auto insurance.

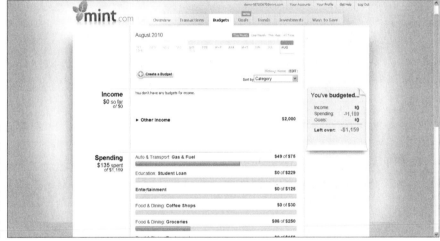

**Figure 10-3:**
Set up a budget for an inflexible, recurring expense.

3. **Enter the payment type and frequency:**

   a. **Choose Auto & Transport⇨Auto Insurance as the category.**

   b. **In the When Will This Happen field, select Every Few Months.**

   Additional fields appear for entering the payment details.

4. **Enter the payment amount and frequency.**

   We entered 125 and 3 months, as shown in Figure 10-4. My next payment is due in January 2011, so I selected Next Is and entered the date, January 2011.

5. **Click Save.**

   Your budget item is now part of the master list, so you'll receive friendly alerts reminding you to make your payments.

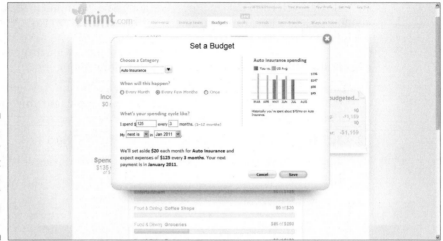

**Figure 10-4:**
Enter
budget
details
for your
recurring
payment.

# Budgeting Flexible Expenses

You can't necessarily do without flexible expense items, but you can control some of the amounts you spend. And in some situations, you have control over when you make the payments.

Here are some typical budget items that afford a certain amount of flexibility, along with some suggestions for taking control of these items:

- ✔ **Food:** Stop eating out. Learn to cook new and interesting dishes that either make a lot or don't cost much (or both). Have pitch-in meals with friends, in which you make one part of the meal. Clip coupons and shop at stores that offer double the value of the coupon. Buy in bulk (consider shopping with friends and splitting the cost).

- ✔ **Medical care**: Look for discounts if you buy a new prescription at a particular pharmacy. Consider using generic drugs. If your doctor writes a prescription, ask for a free sample. Schedule nonessential medical treatments for the entire family in the same year so that you can take advantage of a tax deduction for medical expenses.

- ✔ **Contributions to savings:** If your cash flow is too tight to put money in savings for a particular month, try to double up next month. You're not making a monthly contribution to your savings accounts? Get busy saving or you'll never be able to afford the things you want.

- ✔ **Home repairs and maintenance:** Learn how to repair and maintain the house. Books and Web sites are filled with instructions for household repairs, and big do-it-yourself stores are ready to help you with workshops and tips. If you can't afford to fix the leaky faucet this month, make sure you get it on the list for next month.

✔ **Life insurance:** Reassess your life insurance policy each year. Some people continue having a term policy when their kids are older and supporting themselves. Decide how much insurance you need and shop around for the best policy. A good agent will help you find the best purchase for your lifestyle. As of this writing, Mint.com doesn't provide recommendations for life insurance options.

✔ **Transportation:** Save on commuting by carpooling or using public transportation. Look for the lowest fuel costs in your area by going to www. gasbuddy.com. If it's time for a replacement vehicle, look for something that gets great gas mileage. Make sure your air filter is changed regularly, and make a conscious effort to reduce your driving speed.

✔ **Child care:** Share child care with other parents or ask relatives to help, even if it's only once a month. Consider sharing the cost of an at-home care provider with another family. Adjust work schedules so that both spouses aren't working at the same times and one spouse can stay with the children.

✔ **Clothing:** Look for quality second-hand clothing shops. Schedule a clothes swap with friends who have children of a similar age. Push clothing purchases off to months when you're likely to have extra cash; for example, if you are paid weekly or biweekly, you get an extra paycheck at least two months a year.

✔ **Home supplies:** Buy cleaning supplies in bulk and try generic supplies. Search the Internet for instructions on making your own cleaning supplies from items you already have in the house. Use reusable cloths, sponges, and mops. Share the rental of a carpet steam cleaner with friends.

✔ **Gifts:** Shop flea markets and sidewalk sales for gift items and save your purchases for future gifts. Purchase Christmas gifts year-round when you find bargains so you don't have to do all your spending in December. Make homemade gifts and regift items you received but don't want.

✔ **Entertainment:** You have ultimate control over entertainment. Treat yourself to movies and shows and sporting events when you have the money and can enjoy them guilt-free. When money is tight, rely on free entertainment such as television, movies from the library, Little League games, and evenings with friends.

Mint.com is one step ahead of you when it comes to budgeting for expenses that you normally pay on a monthly basis. Suppose that you spend an average of $70 per month on entertainment, but you want to cut back to $50 a month for movies and DVD rentals. Easy. Just follow these steps:

1. **On the Mint.com home page, click the Budgets tab.**

   Your budgeted items appear.

2. **Click Entertainment: Movies & DVDs in your list of budgeted expenses.**

   The list of your transactions in this budget category appears.

3. **In the Date field, click the x (after 8/1/10 and 8/31/10 in Figure 10-5).**

   By removing the date restriction, you can see all the amounts that have been categorized into this group and used for determining your average spending.

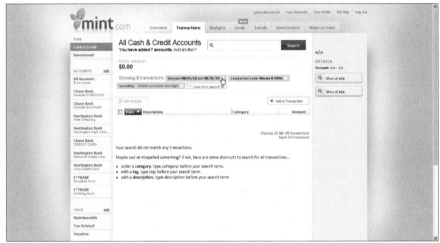

**Figure 10-5:**
Click to
close the
date filter
and all
expenses
in this cat-
egory are
displayed.

4. **Click the Budgets tab again to go back to the main Budgets screen, where you can work on customizing this budget item.**

5. **Highlight the budget item you want to change.**

   No clicking involved. Simply mouse over the item, and a box appears around the item. You also see an Edit Details button and two arrows, one on either side of the budgeted amount, as shown in Figure 10-6.

6. **Change the budgeted amount by clicking the left arrow twice to change the amount from $70 to $50.**

7. **Click the Edit Details button for that Entertainment budget item, and the Set a Budget window appears, as shown in Figure 10-7.**

   Here you can type a new amount (an alternative to using the arrows in the preceding step) and change the frequency of this budget item from monthly to something else. You can also set this item to rollover (see the "Using the Rollover Budgeting Feature" section).

8. **Click Save to save your new budget restrictions.**

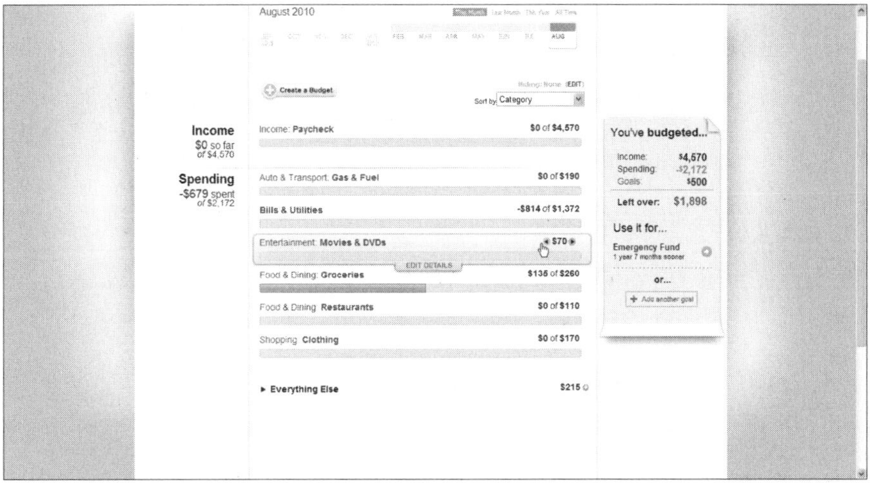

**Figure 10-6:**
Click an arrow to raise or lower the budgeted amount.

**Figure 10-7:**
Spending too much on videos and movies?

# Using the Rollover Budgeting Feature

Mint.com provides a rollover feature that takes budgeting to a higher level. In the standard process in Mint.com, the budget begins over again at the end of each month. If your budget allows you $150 per month for utilities, and in April you spend only $135, your budget for May utilities starts over at $150.

By using the rollover feature, however, you can adjust your next month's budget with the amount you are over (or under) at the end of the current month. Using the preceding example, if you spend only $135 on April utilities and have turned on the rollover feature for your utilities budget, your budget for May utilities is $165. The extra $15 that you didn't spend in April is carried forward and applied to May, giving you some extra room for utilities expenses.

To set your utilities expense to roll over to the next month, follow these steps:

1. **On the Mint.com home page, click the Budgets tab.**

2. **Select Utilities in the budget list.**

    If Utilities appears in the top half of your budget list (with a red, yellow, or green bar below it), mouse over the Utilities budget item and choose Edit Details. If Utilities is not in the top list, click Everything Else at the bottom of the screen to open your complete budget list, find Utilities, and click the plus button to the right of the utilities amount. Whichever method you use, the Set a Budget window appears, showing you the details of your utilities budget.

3. **Select the Make This Budget Roll Over option, as shown in Figure 10-8.**

    The rollover feature is activated.

4. **Click the Save button.**

    You've activated the rollover feature for your budget item. This rollover goes into effect at the end of the current month. Repeat these steps with any other budget items to which you want to apply the rollover feature.

**Figure 10-8:** We told Mint.com to make the Utilities budget roll over.

You can't make changes in your Mint.com budget for previous months. You can make changes only for the current month and going forward.

The rollover feature treats your budget amounts as an annual expense instead of a monthly expense and allows you to annualize payments that aren't made every month. Types of expenses that lend themselves to the rollover feature include quarterly, semiannual, or annual insurance payments; quarterly tax payments; and school tuition payments paid each semester. Some budget items are automatically set to roll over when they are created. For other budget items that don't necessarily require monthly payments from you but that you want to budget for on a monthly basis, you can turn on the rollover feature manually, as shown in the following example.

For example, if you pay $420 in automobile insurance twice a year, that works out to an average of $70 per month. You can set up your budget to reflect a $70 per month auto insurance payment and instruct Mint.com to make this a rollover budget item. Then $70 will be applied to your auto insurance budget each month and rolled over until you actually make your payment. When it's time for the six-month payment, you have $420 properly budgeted.

For example, follow these steps to set up a semiannual auto insurance payment with an automatic rollover:

1. **In Mint.com, click the Budgets tab.**

   The Budgets screen appears, displaying the current month's budget.

2. **Click Create a Budget.**

   The Set a Budget window appears.

3. **In the Choose a Category field, choose Auto Insurance.**

   Click the down-arrow in the Choose a Category field, mouse over Auto & Transport, and click Auto Insurance.

4. **Select the frequency of your payments.**

   In the When Will This Happen? field, click the Every Few Months option, which enables you to specify how often you make this particular payment.

5. **Fill in the fields in the What's Your Spending Cycle Like? area:**

   a. **In the I Spend field, enter the total amount to budget for the time period.**

   b. **In the Every x Months field, enter the time period in months.**

   c. **Select Next Is and then select a date.**

   In Figure 10-9, we entered $420 as the amount to budget for auto insurance and then entered 6 to indicate that the actual payment is made every 6 months. We also entered a next payment date of December, 2010. Mint.com calculates that we need to set aside $70 each month to be ready for the December auto insurance payment.

6. **Click the Save button.**

   Mint.com saves your new budget item.

**Figure 10-9:**
Auto
insurance
accu-
mulates
monthly
until you're
ready to
make a
payment.

Note that no related spending is associated with this budget item in the current month. Because the unused portion of this budget amount is automatically rolling over to the next month, that month's budget will show $140
budgeted for auto insurance. The auto insurance amount will continue to
increase until you make the payment in December, at which time all the accumulated amounts will be applied to the December payment and your budget
item will appear to be in balance.

# Chapter 11

# Handling Emergencies

. . . . . . . . . . . . . . . . . . . . . . . . . . . . . . . . . . . . . . . . . . . . . . . . . . . . . . . . . . . .

. . . . . . . . . . . . . . . . . . . . . . . . . . . . . . . . . . . . . . . . . . . . . . . . . . . . . . . . . . . .

*W*hen an emergency occurs and you need cash in a hurry, you don't want to have to count on the spare change in pockets and drawers. It's far better to have already set aside cash. In this chapter, we describe the all-important task of creating an emergency fund.

## Identifying Emergency Fund Expenses

Emergencies are by definition unexpected events. Some events, such as car wrecks and storm damage and medical crises are covered by insurance. Other emergencies, such as the need for a new car or major home repairs or costs associated with a death in the family, might not be covered by insurance. Perhaps the most ominous emergency that many people face, particularly in today's tenuous economy, is the potential loss of a job. With no income to cover even daily expenses, you can quickly deplete the money in your bank accounts.

You can buy yourself some valuable time by having an emergency fund that is available to cover big items such as a new car, repairs, or funeral costs, or several months of basic expenses that will keep you afloat financially if you find yourself out of work.

Experts suggest that you should be able to cover at least six months' worth of basic living costs from your emergency fund. Basic living costs don't include everything you spend when you're feeling flush. If you lose your job, you're probably going to cut back on some of your spending. The basic costs you should be able to cover for at least six months include the following:

✔ Rent or mortgage payments

✔ Groceries

- ✔ Utilities (electricity, gas, water, sewer, telephone, cable, Internet, trash)
- ✔ Medical expenses
- ✔ Education costs, including current tuition, school loans, books, and supplies
- ✔ Loan payments, including car loans
- ✔ Clothing (necessities only)
- ✔ Transportation expenses, including public transportation and automobile expenses
- ✔ Insurance, including home or rental insurance, auto insurance, health insurance, and life insurance

Some of these expenses won't apply to you. Young people, for example, might be able to survive a job drought by moving back home with their parents, without having to pay for most living expenses

---

## Borrowing against your retirement fund

Warning! We don't recommend borrowing against your retirement plans. That said, if you are truly in a bind and can't get money any other way, consider borrowing money from an Individual Retirement Arrangement (IRA) or a tax-deferred employer-sponsored retirement plan such as a 401(k). This is risk borrowing and potentially expensive borrowing, so be sure to exhaust all other options before turning to this type of borrowing.

**Borrowing from an IRA:** If you are not yet of retirement age (that is, 59 1/2), the law permits you to take money out of your IRA account for up to 60 days at no cost. If you don't get the money back within 60 calendar days, you have to pay tax on the money at your regular income tax rate (both Federal and state income tax) and you have to pay a penalty of 10 percent of the amount you borrowed. Suppose you are in the 25 percent income tax bracket; live in Indiana, where the income tax rate is 3.4 percent; and take $5,000 out of your IRA. You pay 25 percent Federal income tax, 3.4 percent state income tax, and a 10 percent penalty, for a whopping 38.4 percent fee ($1,920). You can find a loan shark with better rates than that.

**Borrowing from a 401(k):** If your 401(k) plan is structured in such a way that you can take a loan from the plan, you get a pretty decent interest rate on the money you borrow, and you can have up to five years to repay the money. Not a bad deal on the surface. However, when you look at the interest rate on your 401(k) borrowing, you should add to that rate the amount of earnings you're not getting on the amount your borrowed, and increase your interest rate accordingly. So, if you borrow from your 401(k) at 8 percent, and the plan was paying a return of 10 percent a year, you're really borrowing at 18 percent. Furthermore, you lose the future value of the money that you took out of the 401(k) plan. And finally, if you decide to keep the money and not pay it back to your 401(k), you run into the income tax and penalty situation just described.

Remember that the old, retired you is not going to be happy with the young you if you start messing with retirement money before you reach retirement age.

An emergency itself is often associated with expenses. For example, you might not be fully covered for an emergency medical situation. Or if you lose your job, you not only need emergency money to cover your daily expenses, but also have the expense of searching for a job, including the cost of preparing and producing a resume or the cost of training to learn new skills. In addition, if you lose your job, you might have to start paying for certain benefits that you were receiving from your employer, such as health insurance.

# Saving for Emergencies

When you're trying to make ends meet, it's difficult to think about putting aside money for emergencies. But when an emergency strikes, you'll be thankful that you saved.

Following are some tips to get you started saving:

- **Put aside a little each week.** You might find it hard to save each week, particularly if you have trouble meeting your current expenses. Try redirecting $20 per week to savings for your emergency fund. That amount adds up to $1,040 for the year, not including interest. If you can increase the amount above $20, even better.

- **Save your raise.** If your employer gives you a raise or a bonus, put that money aside in your emergency fund.

- **Stash your tax refund.** When you fill out your tax return in the spring and it turns out you have a refund, put the refund into your emergency fund.

- **Save your change.** At the end of each day, stash all your coins in your piggy bank or some other container. Once a month, take the coins to the bank and deposit them in your account. Coin money adds up quickly and painlessly.

# Creating an Emergency Fund

The best way to set aside money for an emergency is to create a separate savings or investment account. By using a separate account, your money can grow, undisturbed, and you are less tempted to draw on those funds for everyday spending.

Following are some tips for choosing an account where you can stash your emergency savings.

- **Don't use your checking account for saving emergency money.** Money sitting in your checking account is money waiting to be spent. Long-term savings should go where they won't be accidentally spent at the grocery store.

✔ **Don't speculate with your emergency money.** The last thing you need is to put your emergency savings in a "sure thing" investment, only to see the oil rig blow up and your money go south. Emergency money has to be available when you need the cash, so use a bank account or a money market fund for this type of saving. Don't use emergency money to invest in stocks. Speculate only with money you can afford to lose.

✔ **Choose an interest-bearing account.** As long as you're saving money, you might as well earn a bit of interest. Interest rates are low as of this writing, but every little bit helps. Select a savings account or a money market account that provides you with positive cash flow. Stay away from mutual fund accounts, which can lose money.

✔ **Look for a free account.** You defeat the purpose of earning interest on your account if you have to turn around and pay the bank a fee. Plenty of options are available for free saving. Shop around and compare account options.

✔ **Make sure you can get to the cash fast.** Arrange for online access to your money so you can transfer the funds at any time, or set up an account that has check-writing privileges. Stay away from accounts that require you to request a withdrawal by phone or in writing because those requests can take a week or more and waste precious time.

Use the Mint.com emergency saving feature to determine how much you should save in your emergency fund and then set up your emergency fund account. Simply follow these steps:

1. **Click the Goals tab on the Overview page and then click the Save for an Emergency goal.**

   The window shown in Figure 11-1 appears.

**Figure 11-1:**
Saving for basic expenses each month.

2. **Enter your average monthly spending.**

   Mint.com automatically enters an average monthly spending amount that is based on your own spending activity for the past three months. This average spending amount doesn't necessarily take into account frugality measures that you might follow if you're drawing on emergency funds. Using the emergency fund list presented in the "Identifying Emergency Fund Expenses" section, determine your required monthly spending and enter that amount.

3. **Indicate the number of emergency months and then click Next.**

   As mentioned, experts suggest that you save enough so that you can live on your emergency fund for 6 months. Mint.com lets you plan for anywhere from 1 to 12 months of emergency saving. Drag the slider to choose the savings goal that best fits your plan; the amount on the right side of the screen changes to show you how much you need to save for the amount of months you select.

   Look closely at the savings goal you are creating. If the number seems too high to reach or too low to cover your actual expenses, rethink the average monthly amount.

4. **Give your fund a name.**

   Emergency Fund is the default title for this savings goal. Call it whatever you want — Life Preserver, Piggy Bank, or I Hate My Boss and Want to Quit My Job Fund.

5. **(Optional) In the Set a Goal Amount field, change the amount.**

   The goal amount was calculated in Step 3. You can increase the amount if you need to save more, or decrease the amount if you don't need to save that much or think the goal is unreachable.

6. **Choose a realistic timetable.**

   By default, Mint.com has chosen a one-year timetable for setting aside this emergency money. Are you going to need this money sooner than a year from now? Do you already have some money set aside so that you don't need to hurry with this savings plan? Determine the date when you want to have this money in place and enter that date in the spaces provided.

7. **Enter the monthly contribution and then click Next.**

   Mint.com tells you how much you need to save to meet your goal according to the timetable you established. If you think you can set aside more per month than the calculated amount, enter a higher amount. If the number is too high and you can't save that much each month, enter a lower amount and Mint.com recalculates the date when you will achieve your goal, as shown in Figure 11-2.

### 8. Select your savings option.

Choose how you plan on carrying out this savings plan. You can open a new account based on Mint.com's suggestions by clicking the Apply Now option next to the suggested account. Use an existing account by selecting the second option. Mint.com displays a list of your current accounts, as shown in Figure 11-3, and you can select the account you want to use. If you want to select an account at a later time, your savings goal is put on hold until you come back and make an account selection.

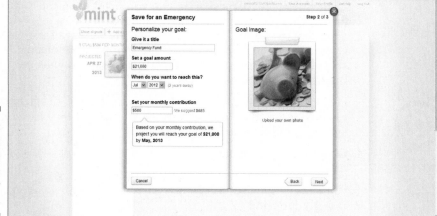

**Figure 11-2:** Seriously? I can't afford to put aside $500 per month.

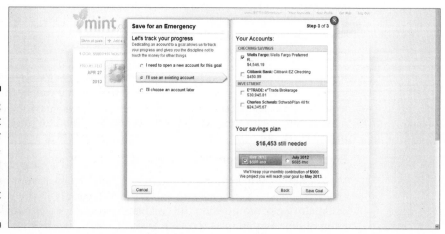

**Figure 11-3:** The amount you save for your emergency fund is tracked in the account you select.

Select an account that hasn't been used for another goal in Mint.com. Only one goal is allowed per account.

9. **Click the Save Goal button, and you're ready to start saving.**

Now when you click the Goals tab on the Mint.com home page, the Emergency Fund appears as one of your goals, and Mint.com tracks how much you've saved toward that goal, as shown in Figure 11-4. Need to make a change? Click View Details (below the thermometer) and then click Edit at the top of the Goal Details box.

**Figure 11-4:**
You see the progress of your emergency savings program.

# Keeping Tabs on Your Emergency Fund

Each time you log into Mint.com, your emergency fund status is listed in the Goals section on the Overview page, right below your budget items. Click the name of the fund if you want to see the details. Note that Mint.com tells you whether you're on track or behind with your emergency savings.

By setting up this emergency fund savings plan, you are enabling Mint.com to track your saving program and remind you of your plan. The actual process of saving is still up to you!

To get that money into your emergency savings account each month with no effort on your part, set up an automatic transfer of funds from your regular banking account to the emergency account. Or have a portion of your paycheck automatically deposited in your savings account. Most employers that offer direct deposit programs give you the option to route some of your money to a second account.

Reassess your emergency needs from time to time — once a year is probably sufficient. Check your monthly living expenses because some items may have changed in the last year. Perhaps you paid off a car loan or are sending a child to college. Make any necessary adjustments to your emergency fund savings plan so that you're still on track to have enough saved to get you through hard times. Also, make sure your emergency fund investment is still where you want it to be. Perhaps another account can earn a higher rate of interest.

Sometimes staying up to date can be difficult. If you miss a month of saving or have to draw down the emergency account for, well, an emergency, make sure you get back on track as soon as possible and replenish your account.

# Part III
# Planning and Saving

The 5th Wave                    By Rich Tennant

"We took a gamble and invested all our money in a race horse. Then it ran away."

# In this part . . .

When you're first starting your financial life, it's all about getting established. You want to make sure you're doing all the basics right, such as not running out of money before payday. Before long, however, your financial needs become more complicated. Soon you start thinking about planning for big financial goals, such as saving for retirement, or tracking how much you're worth.

Part III is your guide to using Mint.com to help you go beyond just paying the bills to mapping your financial future. You find out how to track your financial value, or net worth, to make sure that you're on the right path. You also discover how to save and plan for large expenses, such as college and retirement.

# Chapter 12

# Managing Your Net Worth

· · · · · · · · · · · · · · · · · · · · · · · · · · · · · · · · · · · · · · · · · · · · · · · · · · ·

## In This Chapter

▶ Understanding net worth and how it's calculated

▶ Tracking your assets and bills

▶ Improving your net worth position

· · · · · · · · · · · · · · · · · · · · · · · · · · · · · · · · · · · · · · · · · · · · · · · · · · ·

There's long been an infatuation with wealth. The TV show *Lifestyles of the Rich and Famous* and several reality shows are popular largely because people like to peer into the world of the well-off. And couch potatoes aren't the only ones fascinated with wealth. Business magazines often publish lists of the wealthiest people in the world. Even successful CEOs and entrepreneurs can't help but look at such lists and dream of one day being listed themselves.

But you might find it even more interesting to watch your own wealth, more formally known as net worth. Your *net worth,* or the value of everything you own minus the value of everything you owe, provides a single number that tells you how you're progressing toward your financial goals and how well-positioned you are to withstand a financial blow.

Mint.com understands the importance of net worth and has several features that not only calculate your net worth but also help you monitor its ups and downs. In this chapter, you find out why net worth is so important, even if you're not on the list of the richest Americans. You also discover how to tabulate your net worth and to use that number to stay on track to reaching your financial goals.

# Understanding the Value of Net Worth

It might seem like overkill to monitor your net worth if you don't have a garage full of Rolls-Royces to count or far-flung homes to track. Even the term *net worth* conjures up images of Scrooge McDuck sitting in his vault, counting his gold coins. But people of all means should track their net worth because it shows them, at a glance, how much they have and what they owe.

## Formulating net worth

The term *net worth* is an instant turnoff for many people who are starting to get serious about tracking their money. Those words may conjure up images of complex financial statements and, gasp, accounting. For many people, the sight of a long list of numbers is about as inviting as a snake pit.

But net worth is really a simple formula with a fancy name. Specifically, your net worth is a total of all your assets, or things you own, minus your bills, or things you owe. Expressed as a formula, net worth looks like this:

net worth = assets − bills

That's it. Net worth is nothing more than a subtraction problem, and a basic one at that. If there's a tricky part to measuring your net worth, it's coming up with totals of your assets and bills. But Mint.com can help you with those tasks, as you discover later in this chapter.

Accountants often refer to the money you owe as *liabilities*. But Mint.com uses the word *bills* instead. To be consistent with Mint.com, we refer to liabilities as *bills*.

Calculating your net worth is worth your time and energy because the number tells you the following:

- ✔ **Your degree of financial security:** Your net worth is a good way to understand how prepared you are to withstand life's little financial surprises because it indicates how much savings you have beyond what you owe to pay for things that might go wrong. If your net worth is less than $1,000, for instance, getting in a car accident could be devastating if it means you couldn't afford to both fix your car and pay rent. In this case, you might choose to have an auto insurance *deductible*, or the amount you're responsible to pay after an accident, of much less than $1,000.

- ✔ **Your amount of debt:** Borrowing too much is one of the biggest mistakes people make with their money. Even big Wall Street banks couldn't resist borrowing too much, causing several to fail between 2007–2009. Many consumers who borrowed too much during the housing boom in the 2000s also risked losing everything. If you monitor your net worth, you'll have a good idea if you're living off too much borrowed money.

- ✔ **The amount of wealth you're accumulating:** The goal of working and saving is to make sure you're building your nest egg over time. Your net worth is like a report card for how well you're doing.

Making sure you're on track with your money doesn't have to be complicated. Just think of your net worth as your progress meter. If your net worth is rising, you know you're saving money and advancing toward financial self-sufficiency.

## *Your assets*

Want to know what an asset is? Quick. Open your wallet. That wrinkled-up $20 bill inside is an asset. *Assets* are things that you possess that have financial value. Your assets are your prized financial belongings that are worth something.

Understanding what assets are is critical to getting a grasp of net worth. Assets can be just about anything with value, including things you might not think of as an asset, such as your impressive Pez dispenser collection. Typically, though, the primary assets you might have that Mint.com tracks are as follows:

- ✔ **Checking and savings accounts:** Now that you've outgrown your piggy bank, some of your cold hard cash is probably stored in checking and savings accounts. This is the cash that's most readily available to you, or *liquid*, meaning you can use it instantly to pay bills.

  Checking and savings accounts are considered some of the safest places you can put your cash. If your financial institution is a member of the Federal Deposit Insurance Corporation, or FDIC, your deposits up to $250,000 are insured by the U.S. government. If something happens to your bank, the FDIC will make you whole. You can read more about the FDIC and understand the insurance limits and requirements at http://fdic.gov.

  The Dodd-Frank Wall Street Reform and Consumer Protection Act, signed on July 21, 2010, permanently extended the $250,000 insurance level, which formerly was $100,000. Initially, the increased coverage was temporary.

  Actual paper cash, or *currency*, in your possession, is one of the ultimate forms of an asset. Cash in your pocket is available now and accepted everywhere, and no one disputes what a dollar is worth. Mint.com can't download the value of cash stuffed in your jeans pocket or under your mattress, but can track your paper cash if you enter it manually, as you discover later in this chapter.

- ✔ **Money market accounts:** Some money market accounts attempt to fix one of the biggest problems with checking and savings accounts. While checking and savings accounts make your cash readily available and safe, with FDIC insurance, they tend to pay next to no interest.

Money markets sacrifice some convenience and safety in exchange for a higher interest rate. Money markets invest mostly in debt from the Federal government that's expected to be very safe and likely to be repaid. Some money market accounts also let you write some checks, usually greater than $500. However, money market accounts are not guaranteed by the FDIC.

✔ **Investment accounts:** As you save more money, you can afford to take more risk. Sooner or later, you will save money that you don't immediately need. Putting such excess money in a checking or savings account may not be a great idea because those accounts pay extremely low interest rates. When you have surplus savings, it's time to think about investing your money in stocks and mutual funds, which generally reward you with higher returns because you're risking losing money. Your holdings of stocks and mutual funds form your *investment portfolio,* which is a key part of your assets.

✔ **Collectibles and other property:** Baubles and other collectibles may have value, too. You might also have electronics, furniture, and other assets with monetary value. The problem with such physical assets, though, is that they're often not quickly converted to cash, and it can be unclear what they're worth. Your elaborate stamp and Matchbox car collections certainly have value, and you could sell them on eBay. But how long it would take to sell them and how much money you'd get are unclear. Mint.com allows you to enter the value of such assets, but establishing that value is largely left up to you. If you hold gold or ownership in other precious metals through an investment account, Mint. com might be able to help you track the value.

If you want to own gold and track its value in Mint.com, you can invest in a gold exchange-traded fund (ETF). This type of fund, which you can buy through any brokerage, is an investment vehicle that trades like a stock. Mint.com can easily pull the value of the gold ETF into your account. You can read more about exchange-traded funds in Chapters 19 and 20.

✔ **Special investment accounts:** Investors go to great lengths to avoid taxes. The government, too, encourages investors to save by dangling tax breaks in front of those who set up accounts designed for certain types of spending. 401(k) accounts and various individual retirement accounts, for instance, give you tax breaks toward saving for retirement. Other accounts, such as 529 accounts, give you tax breaks for saving for college. Because retirement accounts and 529 accounts are assets, Mint. com includes them as such in your net worth calculation. You can read more about tracking your retirement accounts in Mint.com in Chapter 16 and your education savings plans in Chapter 15.

✔ **Vehicles:** Your wheels aren't just for style. Your car is a financial asset, too. But vehicles are different from the other assets described so far. Unlike savings accounts, your car isn't a liquid asset that you can tap to pay bills with. It's an asset you use. Additionally, unlike investment accounts that are expected to increase in value over time, your car loses value, or *depreciates*, over time. Mint.com will help you keep track of what your car is worth and how much value it's losing, as you discover in the upcoming section, "Interpreting Your Net Worth."

✔ **Real estate:** For most people, the biggest financial asset they have is the roof over their heads. Mint.com adds the value of this asset to your account and helps you track its value.

# Your bills

Being free and clear financially is a goal held by many. But in the course of buying things you need, you often take on bills, including debt. Mint.com factors the size of your bills to give you an accurate picture of your net worth.

For instance, you might buy a new $20,000 sedan. That $20,000 is included as an asset in your net worth. But your net worth doesn't get a $20,000 boost if you borrowed $17,000 to buy the car. Your net worth is unchanged. The $17,000 loan you took on to buy the car is subtracted from your net worth. Meanwhile, remember that the $3,000 in cash you spent on the car is also subtracted from your net worth. As your car ages and loses value, its original $20,000 value erodes. Mint.com doesn't automatically track the erosion of value in your car (yet), but the program allows you to enter the value of your car and see how the purchase of large assets affects your net worth.

Mint.com helps you tally everything you owe, which includes bills such as the following:

✔ **Credit card balances:** Running up your credit card may give you instant gratification as you buy stuff. But your net worth takes a big hit as a result. The balance on your credit card is subtracted from your assets and reduces your net worth. You can read more about how Mint.com helps you track credit cards in Chapter 4.

✔ **Student loans:** The average college student racks up thousands of dollars of debt going to school. These loans will be a big liability many students will have to pay down as they get jobs and work. Mint.com helps you track student loans and see the bill shrink over time, which in turn gives your net worth a boost.

✔ **Car loans:** If you borrowed to buy your car, the balance of the loan is a hit against your net worth.

✔ **Mortgage loans:** Just as most people's biggest assets are their homes, their biggest bills in many cases are their home loans, or *mortgages*. Mint.com tracks your mortgage balance and monitors your progress in paying it down.

# *Interpreting Your Net Worth*

If all this accounting talk is making your eyes glaze over, you're in luck. Although understanding net worth, assets, and bills is helpful, Mint.com handles the gnarly number-crunching for you. You just help Mint.com figure out what assets and bills you have, and the Web site does the rest for you.

## *Adding your assets and bills*

Before you can start exploring your net worth, you need to tell Mint.com what you have and what you owe. Adding assets and bills is simple and similar to the steps you follow to add any account.

Follow these steps to add your assets and bills to Mint.com:

1. **Log in to Mint.com and click the Overview tab.**

2. **Click the Your Accounts link, which is on the top right.**

3. **Add your financial accounts.**

   Click the blue plus sign to add your accounts. Make sure you add your checking and savings accounts, which are your cash assets. Also add associated loans, including car loans, mortgages, and student loans.

4. **Add your real estate assets as follows:**

   a. **Click the Real Estate tab at the top of the window.**

   b. **Enter the address and zip code of your home, as shown in Figure 12-1, and click the Search button.**

   Mint.com searches a database of homes to see if it can determine the value of your home.

   c. **If your home is not in Mint.com's database, enter the value manually at the prompt.**

   Take a guess at your home's value, based on what you paid for it or the cost of similar houses.

5. **Add cash or loans not held at a financial institution.**

   You enter most of your cash and loans in Step 3. But if you have cash or loans not through a bank, enter them manually as follows:

   a. **Click the Other tab.**

   b. **Select the Money (or Debt) option and then click the blue Next button.**

   c. **Give the cash or loan a name.**

**d. Enter the value in the How Much Is It Worth? field.**

      If you're entering cash, type the amount as a positive number. If you're entering a loan, type the amount as a negative number.

      **e. Click the Add It button.**

  **6. Add your vehicles as follows:**

      **a. Click the Vehicle Selection button and select the type of vehicle you own.**

      Mint.com lets you add a variety of vehicles, including automobiles, boats, or even snowmobiles.

      **b. Enter the value of the vehicle.**

      At press time, Mint.com was finalizing an agreement with Kelley Blue Book to help you enter the value of your car and reflect its declining value. If Mint.com doesn't provide the value of your car, you can look it up at www.kbb.com.

  **7. Add other property.**

      Click the Other Property selection button. Here, you can add the value of your collectibles or other assets, including artwork, computers, furniture, and toys.

      When adding other property to your list of assets, don't overvalue items that might have sentimental value but aren't worth much to anyone else. If you add property at inflated values, Mint.com will tell you your net worth is higher than it really is. Check what items have sold for on eBay to get a realistic estimate of their value.

**Figure 12-1:**
Figure out
the value of
your home.

# Calculating your net worth

Now that you've entered all your assets and bills, Mint.com has everything it needs to guide you to net-worth-tracking goodness. Mint.com provides your net worth data in a summary account list on the Overview tab and also on the Trends tab. We describe both locations in this section.

## Net worth on the Overview tab

When you log in to Mint.com or click the Overview tab at the top of the page, you see a list of all your accounts on the left. Scroll down and you'll see that Mint.com has tallied the value of all your assets, subtracted the value of all your debts, and presented your net worth. You can see the summary account list's net worth display in Figure 12-2.

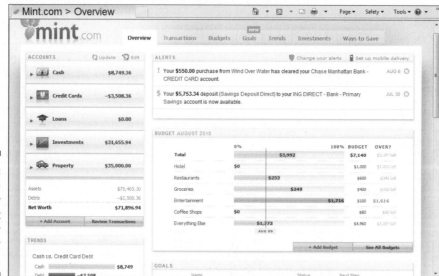

**Figure 12-2:**
Use the summary account list to quickly see your net worth.

## Net worth on the Trends tab

You use the Trends tab to dig deeper into your net worth and spot changes in the values of your assets and bills that are causing your net worth to rise or fall. The Trends tab makes it easy to investigate the components of your net worth so you can pinpoint financial moves that are paying off by boosting your assets and those holding you back by racking up bills.

To use the Trends tab to track your net worth, do the following:

1. **Click the Trends tab.**

   This tab displays your financial information in a series of colorful graphs.

2. **Click the Net Worth option.**

   Mint.com displays your net worth in the current month.

3. **Modify the time period for your net income.**

   By default, Mint.com shows your net income in the current month, but the Trends feature is even more helpful when you use it to see your net worth in different time periods. Click the three-letter month symbol at the top of the page to get your net worth for a month in the past. You can also click This Month, Last Month, This Year, and All Time. Or customize the display by clicking the first month you want to see, holding down the mouse button, and swiping over the remaining months. The months you've selected sport a green-colored indicator (see Figure 12-3).

**Figure 12-3:**
See your net
worth over
different
time
periods.

When using the Trends tab to track net worth, don't overlook the net worth line plotted on the chart (refer to Figure 12-3). This line subtracts your bills from your assets and plots the difference. The net worth line is like a stock chart showing how your value is rising and falling.

## Digging deeper into your assets

Your net worth is like a letter grade you get in a class. Yes, it's helpful to know if you received A, B, C, D, or F. But the grade doesn't really tell you where you're excelling or failing in the class.

The same downside is true when using your net worth as a single gauge of your financial success. Although Mint.com might show that you're successfully increasing your net worth, you still need to dig into the numbers to understand what is driving your success and what could threaten your finances.

The easiest way to dive into your assets, which are the starting point of your net worth, is through the Trends feature. From the Trends tab, click the Assets option in the leftmost column, in the Choose a Graph area. Three secondary options in the rightmost column in the table are as follows:

- ✔ **Over Time:** Click the Over Time option to see how your assets are rising or falling over different periods of time. Scroll down to see the dollar value of your assets in the months in the chart. You can also see what your peak, or highest, level of assets were during the time period as well as the biggest month-over-month change, as shown in Figure 12-4.

**Figure 12-4:**
See if your assets are rising or falling.

If your assets are in freefall, you should investigate further to find the cause. And that's where the By Type option, described in the next bullet, comes in.

✔ **By Type:** If you spot a trend in your assets in the Over Time option, click the By Type option. Mint.com provides a pie chart displaying your largest assets.

To use the Assets by Account Type chart to find the causes for your eroding or skyrocketing net worth, click the down arrow under the Compare To option on the right and select the previous year. You see a graph comparing your asset levels by account type this year and the preceding year, which is 2009 in the example shown in Figure 12-5. You see changes in the value of account types, including those for vehicles, investments, and bank accounts.

If your stock portfolio took a big hit during a bear market, you'll see a fall in your investment assets. To remove the comparison, click the Compare To option and select Remove Comparison.

**Figure 12-5:** The Compare To feature makes it easy to see where your items of value are shriveling.

✔ **By Account:** The Assets⇨By Account option shows you which accounts house most of your assets. Mint.com can display this useful information as a pie chart. If you click the small pie chart icon on the right side of the screen, you can see which accounts are the biggest slices of your assets. You can also use the Compare To option to see whether certain accounts have grown dramatically over the year.

## *Examining your bills more closely*

If you're like most people, many of your most valuable assets aren't really yours. You've probably borrowed money to pay for your car and house, and maybe home appliances, too. Bills, primarily debt of various forms, can take a huge bite out of your net worth. You want to pay close attention to your bills and make sure they're manageable and don't pull you into a financial abyss. The Trends tab makes it easy to see your biggest bills, just as it does with your assets. From the Trends tab, click the Debts option on the left side of the Choose a Graph area. Next, you can explore your debt loads further with the following options:

- **Over Time:** You can tell Mint.com to show your debts as they stand now or use the selection bar to select particular months. Don't miss the Compare To option, which shows how your debt levels each month compare to where they were a year ago.

- **By Type:** When you're in debt, half the battle is understanding what kind of debt is holding you underwater. Select the Debts⇨By Type option to break your debt into major classifications, such as credit card debt and mortgage debt.

   All forms of debt have downsides, but some types of debt are worse than others. If you have debt with relatively low interest rates and used the money to buy an asset that should increase in value, such as a mortgage on a house, that can be a tolerable type of debt. However, if you have debt with high interest rates and used the money to buy items that are consumed or lose value, such as credit card debt, that's the worse kind of debt. Use the Debts⇨By Type chart on the Trends tab to see how your good debt compares with your bad debt.

- **By Account:** If you want to see which banks own you, check out the By Account option. If you have several credit cards, for instance, the By Account option displays how much you owe each.

   If you're trying to dig yourself out of credit card debt, use the Debts⇨By Account list to see where most of your balance lies. Then, examine the terms of each credit card to see which one is costing you the most and pay that one off first. Refer to Chapter 4 for tips on paying down your credit card balances quickly.

# *Improving Your Net Worth*

There's no question that knowing your net worth is useful. But the true value of tracking your net worth is using the information to spot changes in your assets or bills that need to be addressed. Just as Mint.com can help you closely monitor your spending, it can also help you see how well you're moving along toward reducing bills and accumulating assets. If you're not moving in the right direction, Mint.com's net worth tools will help you get back on track.

## Spotting trends that boost or erode net worth

You may suspect that several bills are starting to sink your net worth, but you're not sure which ones are responsible. Similarly, it might seem as if you've been adding quite a bit to your net worth, and you want to track your progress. The Trends tab can take the mystery out of what's affecting your net worth. Click the Net Worth option in the Choose a Graph area. Keep changing the time frame until you can see a discernible trend up or down. You can then click the green part of the bars, and you'll see your assets by account. You can also click the red part of the bars to see your debts by account.

This exercise can quickly show you where your financial problems or victories might lie. If debt is the problem, you can start thinking about a game plan to wipe it out. Mint.com can help you tackle reducing debts, as you discover later in this chapter. If your assets seem to be eroding, that might be a sign that you need a new investment strategy or should think about turning some assets that are losing value into cash.

## Giving your assets a turbo boost

No one wants sagging assets. You can't go to a plastic surgeon to get your net worth nipped and tucked, but the Trends tab is the next best thing. Mint.com shows you where your assets, including savings, checking, and investment accounts, are losing ground. It's up to you to not only spot changes in your level of assets but also understand the reasons behind the change and decide what to do.

Following are some scenarios that can cause asset values to change by pleasant or alarming amounts:

✔ **Surging savings or checking balances:** The Net Worth option on the Trends tab can give you important insights into your assets. For instance, click the asset bar in the Net Worth chart and pay close attention to how large your checking and savings accounts are relative to your other assets.

If your balances in checking and savings accounts are soaring beyond what you need for your emergency fund and other short-term needs, congrats. You're saving money. But don't just pat yourself on the back. Surging balances in checking and savings accounts might mean it's time to start thinking about opening an investment account. By holding too much money in a savings account, you might be losing ground because the interest rate your savings account is paying is likely less than the rate at which prices go up, or *inflation*. You're losing purchasing power because your dollars won't be as valuable in the future as they are today due to inflation. Chapters 18 and 19 will show you how Mint.com can help you get started with investing so you can get better returns and beat inflation.

✔ **A big, unexpected financial hit:** Sudden financial problems can wreak havoc on your assets. Coughing up money to pay for the share of an auto accident that isn't covered by insurance can derail even well-intentioned savings plans. Mint.com's net worth calculation will show you if it's time to rebuild your emergency fund. For details on saving for an emergency, see Chapter 11.

✔ **Eroding value of other property:** Some assets are investments, and others are consumables. Investments, including stocks and bonds, generally rise in value over time. Consumable assets, such as cars and furniture, usually lose value as you use them. Mint.com can show you if you have too much of your net worth tied up in consumables.

## Shedding your bills

Bills can be a big liability. Most people don't have the level of net worth they want to have because of piles of bills that are a direct result from being too far in debt.

If you have too much debt, the variety of tools on the Trends tab, as explained previously, will make the fact abundantly clear. But are you going to keep suffering under a mound of debt or are you going to do something to reduce the debt? If you want to erase your debt, the Goals tab can help:

1. **From the Goals tab, click the Add a Goal button.**

2. **Click the Get Out of Debt goal.**

   You see a list of all your debts, their balances, and how much you're paying the lender in interest, expressed as an *annual percentage rate*, or *APR*. The higher the APR, the more expensive the debt.

When looking to reduce your debt load to reduce your liabilities, pay off the debt with the highest APR first.

3. **Select which debts you aim to wipe out first, and then click the Next button.**

Mint.com creates a debt-busting game plan by telling you how much you need to pay toward the debts to reduce them by a set time in the future. You can see a sample goal for limiting debts in Figure 12-6.

**Figure 12-6:** Reduce your bills by whittling outstanding debt balances.

# Chapter 13

# Avoiding Money Troubles

. . . . . . . . . . . . . . . . . . . . . . . . . . . . . . . . . . . . . . . . . .

## In This Chapter

▶ Banking online

▶ Paying your bills online

▶ Getting out of debt

▶ Avoiding overdraft fees

▶ Understanding bank fees

. . . . . . . . . . . . . . . . . . . . . . . . . . . . . . . . . . . . . . . . . .

*E*xtremely wealthy people have money managers who keep a close eye on their wealth and make sure it doesn't go away. These money managers keep all the accounts in balance, constantly look for the best financing deals, make sure the bills are paid on time, and move money around so as to collect the highest interest rates and avoid unnecessary bank fees.

You have to be that money manager for yourself. Instead of letting money events happen to you, you need to strive for a well-managed cash flow system. Sometimes life's events turn you in unexpected directions and you forget to keep a watchful eye on the financial part of your life. That's when trouble starts. You forget to make a payment, overdraw your account, pay unwanted fees, and on and on. One problem leads to another, and trouble is all around.

Forget that somber picture. Take advantage of the tools available to you in Mint.com to stay on top of your finances.

## Getting Accustomed to Online Banking

To get the most out of Mint.com, it's necessary to bank online. If you haven't experimented with banking online, you might be wary. After all, banking is supposed to be a private matter, and banking on the Internet seems so exposed.

# Why online banking is so cool

Following are some reasons why online banking is not your enemy:

- **Banking when you want it.** In the good old days, people used the phrase "bankers' hours" to describe the allegedly short workday that went along with banking. Traditionally, banks opened around 9 and closed around 4 p.m. Get real! We live in a 24/7 world and want to bank from our PDA at 3 in the morning.

- **No more standing in line.** Another fun thing about dealing with real banks is the velvet rope that herds bank customers into snaky lines. The lines are longest at lunchtime, when you're trying to get back to work before your break ends. Forget lines. Bank from the coffee shop on your laptop.

- **You can see it all.** After you make it through the line at the bank and get the attention of a teller, you can ask specific questions about your account, such as did a particular check clear, did a paycheck get deposited yet, or did I get hit with a finance charge this month? But each answer has to be looked up by the teller, who is getting more and more irritated with you for holding up the line. Instead, pull up your bank account online and see all your transactions at once.

- **Choose your bank.** You are no longer limited to banking at the neighborhood bank. Go to Chapter 3 and find out how easy it is to choose from banks all over the country, searching for the bank that gives you what you want in terms of interest, perks, and fees (or lack thereof).

- **Stay on top of your bank balance.** Between your bank's Web site and your Mint.com account, you have no excuse for not knowing exactly how much money you have in the bank. No more scratching out errors in your check register or trying to calculate the balance in your head. Now you can see your balance and be completely up to date.

But think about this. Would banks still be in the business of offering online services if they didn't get the bugs out of the system long ago? Electronic banking has been around for more than 20 years, and some banks exist only online.

Chances are good that you already do electronic banking without even realizing it. When you charge a purchase with a credit card, no currency changes hands, yet you relinquish ownership to some of your money. When you use an automated teller machine (ATM) to transfer money from savings to checking, no one at the bank moves cash from one pile to another, yet the money now belongs to a different account. When your employer gives you a receipt indicating that your paycheck has been deposited in your checking account, don't think for a minute that a basket of cash has arrived at the doorstep of your bank — the transfer was electronic. And if you hand the cashier at the grocery store a check, no money appears in the cash register, but in many cases the money has been taken from your account before you get out the door.

Still worried? Start small. If online banking is new to you and you aren't ready to transfer all your banking activities to cyberspace, open a new account and use it sparingly while you get your online banking feet wet. Put a bit of money in there, write some checks, see how they appear online, use the ATM to withdraw some cash, pay a bill or two. We're betting that once you see how easy and painless online banking is, you'll soon be conducting all your trans-actions online.

Online banking has opened up great opportunities for accuracy and timeli-ness, but there are imperfections, too. We think it's important to have a relationship with a banker, a real person whom you can call when you have questions or when something turns up on your bank statement that you don't understand. And there's no substitute for having a banker in your court when you're trying to get the best deal on a loan. Our recommendation is to get the best of both worlds: Find a local bank where you can meet the people who work there, but make sure the bank has online services, too.

# Paying Bills Online

The Internet has made bill paying a new experience. Iconic phrases like, "The check's in the mail" have little meaning when you're transferring money electronically (although many banks still issue checks when you initiate an electronic payment). Here are some of the many reasons why you might want to pay your bills online:

- **Speed:** The online payment process is almost faster than a speeding bullet. Click the payee, enter an amount, click Send, and you're finished.

- **Accuracy:** Assuming that you don't mistype the numbers yourself, there's no room for misinterpretation of the amount you're sending with your online payment. Handwritten checks rely on, well, handwriting, and we all know that doctors and others have serious problems with legibil-ity. Numbers typed on keyboards are easy to read.

- **Timing:** Suppose you're getting ready to go on vacation and your mort-gage will be due while you're away. Go online, schedule the payment to be made while you're floating on a raft down the Colorado River, and stop worrying.

- **Scheduling:** Say your car payment is due on the 5th of the month, every month. Set up an automatic payment to occur on the 5th of every month until the loan is paid off. You never have to worry again about missing your payment.

- **24/7 availability:** If you like to pay your bills at midnight or 4 in the morning, no one will stop you. The online banking bank never closes.

✔ **Bad weather:** If you're snowed in, rained in, fogged in, or just plain don't feel like going out to the post office or even the mailbox, you can still pay your bills when you use online bill payment.

✔ **Traveling:** Your bank knows no boundaries. If you're on business in London or hiking in Peru, you can still get yourself online and pay those bills.

✔ **Savings:** No more stamps, envelopes, checks. All this stuff adds up. Let the post office raise the letter rate to 50 cents. You don't care because you're paying bills electronically.

# Getting — and Staying — Out of Debt

By the time some people start using Mint.com to organize their finances and manage their budgeting, they're already deep in debt and trying to dig out of a financial hole.

Mint.com does a great job of telling you how much you've spent in the past months and guiding you toward a sound budget for the future. But what about making some progress toward retiring your debt?

Set up a budget category in Mint.com (see Chapter 8) for your debt payments. Rather than paying the minimum payment on your credit card bills each month, budget for a higher amount so you can start making some progress toward retiring the debt in full.

## Tips for reducing the dreaded credit card APR

APR, or annual percentage rate, translates into finance charges on outstanding credit card balances. It seems the more you owe, the higher this rate. You might even feel like all you're doing is paying the finance charge, not whittling away at the balance.

Sometimes, you can talk a credit card company into reducing the APR on your account. Give some of these tips a try:

✔ Call the credit card company and ask if they will lower your rate. If they won't lower your rate the first time you ask, ask them what you need to do to get the rate lowered. They might suggest making your payments earlier in the month or paying more than the minimum. Or they might tell you to ask again in a few months.

✔ Consider transferring your credit card balance to another card with a lower rate for transferred balances. However, make sure that the lower rate stays in place long enough for you to make a dent in your debt.

✔ Before moving your credit card debt to another card, call the credit card company that you use currently and tell them you're getting ready to transfer your balance to another company. They might match the deal that the other company is giving you.

If you have extra cash on hand one month — perhaps it's April and you just received a tax refund — make an extra payment toward your debt.

Paying off debt is a great investment. You reduce not only the amount you owe but also the amount on which finance charges will be assessed in the future.

# Avoiding Overdrafts

One reason to use Mint.com is that you can check your bank balances in real time. When you can look at Mint.com at any time from your computer or PDA, or even text a balance request from your cell phone, you run out of excuses for having overdrafts. The following options show you how easy it is to check your bank balance on-screen or on your cell phone:

- ✔ Log in to Mint.com, and your balances are displayed on the Overview page.
- ✔ Click the Update option on the top of your account list to send Mint.com to the bank and make sure all the amounts are up to date.
- ✔ Text *Bal* to MyMint (696468) from your cell phone and get the balances sent to your screen. To set up phone service, click Your Accounts at the top of the Mint.com screen, click Email & Alerts, and enter your mobile number in the field shown in Figure 13-1.

**Figure 13-1:**
You can
check
account
balances
from your
cell phone.

# Analyzing Bank Fees

No one likes to get a bank statement that includes fees. It seems reasonable to expect fee-less banking in exchange for letting the bank use your money. Nevertheless, banks inflict many charges on customers, and recent legislation opens the door for banks to charge fees more liberally.

The good news is that most fees are avoidable, and Mint.com can help you find bank accounts with low or even no fees, as shown in Figure 13-2.

**Figure 13-2:** Get info about minimum balance fees and monthly fees in Mint. com's bank account suggestions.

Following is a sampling of the types of bank fees you might run across:

✔ **Monthly service charge:** Some banks charge a flat fee for the privilege of having an account. Other banks let you avoid a monthly service charge if you do other banking with them. For example, if you have a mortgage or car loan through the bank, you might qualify for a free account. Sometimes arranging to have your paycheck directly deposited into your bank account is grounds for avoiding a monthly service charge.

- ✔ **Minimum balance charge:** Your bank might charge a fee if your balance goes below a certain amount or if the account is inactive. Find out what that amount is and keep your balance above the threshold so you can avoid the charge. Can't keep your balance high enough? Consider shopping for another bank (see Chapter 3), or ask your bank if you can switch to a different type of account that doesn't include charges.

- ✔ **Overdraft charge:** Spend more money than you have and you're essentially taking out a loan from the bank. For this service, the bank charges a fee that can be hefty. Check your bank balance regularly at Mint.com or look for a bank that provides free overdraft protection.

- ✔ **ATM fees:** Many banks charge for the use of their ATM. Fees ranging from 50 cents to as high as $5.00 for the right to take your own money out of your own account cause surprise and frustration. One way to avoid such fees is to use only ATM machines associated with your own bank instead of universal ATM machines. Before getting a bank account, ask about the fees at the bank's machines and at other machines in the bank's network.

If you need cash in a hurry, consider using your debit card instead of making a withdrawal from an ATM. When you make a debit card purchase, you can often also get cash back without paying a fee.

# Chapter 14

# Accounting for Health Care

· · · · · · · · · · · · · · · · · · · · · · · · · · · · · · · · · · · · · · · · · · · · · · ·

## In This Chapter

▶ Selecting health insurance

▶ Contributing to a cafeteria plan

▶ Understanding health savings accounts

▶ Finding ways to pay for noncovered health costs

▶ Participating in COBRA

▶ Staying current with health care legislation

· · · · · · · · · · · · · · · · · · · · · · · · · · · · · · · · · · · · · · · · · · · · · · ·

*I*n a perfect world, no one would ever get sick, so you wouldn't have to worry about how to pay for health care. Instead, we live in a world where medical costs continue to rise, so we get less medicine and less care for our money.

More likely than not, you make some payments for your health care. You might be covered by a health insurance plan at work but pay for some expenses or for a portion of your insurance cost. Or you might not have health insurance at all.

In this chapter, you find out how Mint.com helps you keep an eye on health expenses. The more you know about how much health care really costs you and your family, the more control you can take over those costs.

## Choosing a Health Insurance Plan

Many people who have jobs are faced with an annual decision about their health insurance coverage. Employers who offer health insurance often provide employees with a choice of policies, and the decision about which type of policy to get can be daunting. You wish you knew a fortune teller who could let you know the medical situations you and your family will face in the year ahead.

But because you don't have a line on that fortune teller, here are some questions you should ask yourself when getting ready to make your health care decision:

✔ **Are you planning on staying at your job all year?** If the answer is no, the issue of which health care coverage to choose is not as important as it would be if you were not going to change jobs. Presumably, whatever you choose will be replaced when you move to a new job.

✔ **How much did you spend last year on medical expenses?** Because you can't see into the future, the next best thing is to look at the past. Add all your medical expenses for the past year or two and determine how much you would have paid out-of-pocket if you had each type of health insurance policy being offered. Work out which insurance plan would have been the most economical.

✔ **Do you need extra coverage for vision and dental care?** This type of care is often included in separate policies, so these are additional decisions you have to make. Look at your expenses in previous years and weigh those against the cost of the care. Also look at the value of the dental and vision care insurance. Sometimes the coverage isn't all that great compared to the cost of the policy. If you're not a family of eyeglass wearers, vision care insurance probably isn't important to you. If you're not sure of the value of dental insurance, call your dentist and find out the going rate on exams and x-rays, and then do the math to see how much you'll save with the insurance and how that savings compares to the cost of the insurance.

✔ **What types of medical expenses can you anticipate having in the year ahead?** You don't know when a family member is going to get sick or hurt, but some types of medical events can be planned. For example, will anyone in your family need orthodontic work? Are you planning on starting a smoking-cessation or weight-loss program? Are you considering elective surgery? Determine which of these issues apply to you and your family, and then examine the health insurance options to figure out which policy would give you the best coverage.

# *Paying for Health Insurance*

Some people are lucky enough that their employers pay for all their health insurance. Others get to share in the joy of paying for insurance.

Whether you pay all or a portion of your health insurance cost, if you get your health insurance at work, the amount you pay is typically withheld from your paycheck on a *pretax basis*. This means that no tax is withheld on the amount of money you earn that is directed toward health care costs.

If you receive pretax health care benefits from your employer and itemize your deductions on your tax return, those health care benefits don't count as a medical deduction. Because you've already received the benefit tax-free, it's as if you've already taken a deduction for your share of the health care costs. Deducting them again would be double-dipping.

If you purchase health insurance outside your job and don't pay for the insurance with a payroll deduction, you need to track the cost of this insurance in your Mint.com transactions.

When an insurance payment appears in your Mint.com transaction list, make sure the amount is charged to the correct category as follows:

1. **Click the Transactions tab to display a list of your transactions.**

2. **Select your health insurance payment.**

   Scroll through the list until you find your health insurance payment and then click the payment. An Edit Details tab appears below the payment.

3. **Select the proper category.**

   In the Category field, select Health & Fitness and then select Health Insurance.

# Using a Cafeteria Plan

A cafeteria plan, in the context of this chapter, has to do with medicine and doctor visits, not extra trips to the pasta bar. Companies that offer a cafeteria plan, sometimes called a *flexible spending account (FSA), flex plan,* or a *Section 125 plan,* give their employees the option of paying for medical spending on a pretax basis, much like the health insurance discussed earlier in the chapter.

These plans are called *cafeteria plans* because you select which medical expenses you spend your money on. First, you decide how much of your money you want your employer to withhold from your paycheck. To get the money from your employer, you fill out a form explaining that you have some medical expenses that you've already paid for out of your own pocket or that your doctor has billed you for. This convoluted plan has both advantages and disadvantages.

## Things we like about cafeteria plans

Here are the things that make cafeteria plans a good investment:

✔ **You can lower your taxes**. The cafeteria plan money that you leave with your employer is not taxed. For example, if you agree to let your employer withhold $1,000 during the year for your Section 125 plan, and you normally pay Federal income tax at a rate of 15 percent, you've just saved $150 (1,000 × .15). Not bad!

✔ **You can lower your taxes even more.** With a cafeteria plan, you can save up to about 5 percent state income tax, depending on where you live. And in most cases, this money is not subject to FICA and Medicare tax. You might save up to 6.2 percent, or $62 on your $1,000. Altogether, you've easily saved more than $200 on that $1,000.

✔ **You can pay for noncovered expenses with your flex plan money.** Use the money in your flex plan to cover the amount of your deductibles and copay amounts on your regular health insurance plan. Cool.

✔ **You select the type of medical expenses for which you use this money.** Unlike pesky health insurance plans that tell you what types of medical expenses you can and can't get coverage for, a flex plan provides more opportunities to use the money to pay for medical-related items that your regular health insurance might not cover, such as transportation related to health care, mental health care, laser eye surgery, and orthodontics.

✔ **You can spend money you don't have.** One of the more interesting features of the flex plan is that your employer is required to let you spend all the money you have agreed to have withheld from your pay for the entire year, even if you haven't yet had that full amount withheld. For example, suppose you run up $1,000 of unreimbursed medical expenses in February and are planning on having $1,000 in flex plan money withheld by the end of the year. You can request the full $1,000 from your employer to cover the expenses; your employer is paid back over the course of the year with the rest of your pre-agreed-upon withholding.

## Things we don't like about cafeteria plans

Sometimes you have to take the bad with the good. Here's the lowdown on the undesirable side of cafeteria plans:

✔ **Starting January 1, thanks to our friends in Congress, you can no longer use your flex plan to pay for over-the-counter medicine.** You either have to have a prescription for your medicine or a note from your doctor (no kidding) saying that you are supposed to take a particular over-the-counter medicine. Otherwise, you bear the cost yourself out of non-flex-plan money. Medicine such as acne medication, allergy drugs, cough, cold, and flu medicine, eye drops, and pain relievers can no longer be purchased with your flex plan money. Contact lens solution and reading glasses still qualify as flex plan purchases. You might be in pain, but at least you can focus. Go figure.

✔ **Use it or lose it.** If you don't use the money in the plan by the end of the year (and by *end of the year* most employers mean March 15 in the next year or two-and-a-half months after the company's year-end), you don't get the money back. So that $1,000 you let your employer hold onto and on which you saved more than $200 in tax is now money your employer gets to keep, so you lose big time.

# Keeping your cafeteria plan money

If you have a cafeteria plan, the goal is to use all the money in your plan and not leave any with your employer at the end of the year. So you need to control how much money you put in the plan and then you need to make sure you use the money.

Follow these steps to set up a flex plan goal in Mint.com to help you keep track of how much money is deposited in your flex plan and how much you have left to spend:

1. **Make sure you don't put more money in the plan than you expect to spend.**

   Look at your medical expenses for previous years and determine how much you typically spend out of pocket.

2. **Set up a Flex Plan goal in Mint.com to help track your money.**

   Click Goals and then click the Create a Custom Goal button. If you don't see this button, click the Add a Goal button, and then click the Create a Custom Goal button.

3. **In the Give It a Title field, name your goal.**

   Enter a description for this plan: FSA, Flex Plan, Cafeteria Plan, Section 125 Plan, Use-It-or-Lose-It Health Expenses, or whatever description fits your mood.

4. **Enter the goal information:**

   a. **In the Set a Goal Amount field, enter the total amount you want to have withheld during the year.**

   b. **In the Goal Category field, choose Other.**

   c. **In the When Do you Want to Reach This? field, enter the last month of your company's year.**

This date is when your plan year ends. Many companies work on a fiscal year, which is a fancy way of saying that the company has declared a date different from December 31 as the last day of the company's year. (Companies get to choose their own year-end date to save on their taxes.) The information you get with your flex plan should indicate the last month of your company's year, but you can ask your employer if you're not sure. Mint.com does the math and determines how much you're expected to contribute each month, as shown in Figure 14-1.

   d. **Upload an image if you want.**

   Mint.com displays a piggy bank image to go along with this goal. If you want to customize the look of your flex plan goal, you can click the Upload link under the piggy bank and choose an image from the files on your computer.

   e. **Click Next.**

5. **Select I'll Choose an Account Later and then click Save Goal.**

   No bank account is associated with this goal because your employer is holding the money, so choose the third option, and the goal will not be linked to one of your own accounts.

The goal appears in the Goals section of the Overview tab and as a Custom Savings Goal on the Goals page as a reminder that you are using a flex account and need to keep track of the amounts added to and subtracted from the account monthly.

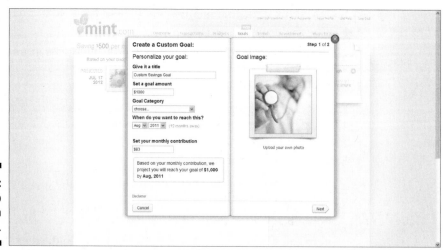

**Figure 14-1:**
Setting up
a flex plan
goal.

We recommend creating a spreadsheet in a spreadsheet program or on paper, recording how much is available in your cafeteria plan and your usage of the funds. (Remember that the full amount is available to you as of the beginning of the year, even though you will be funding the plan for the entire year.)

As you approach the end of the plan year, compare your account balance to your spending. If you haven't used all the money, find a way to incur some qualifying medical expenses before the end of the year or the end of the grace period (usually two-and-a-half months after the plan year-end) so that you don't lose the money. Get extra contact lenses, eyeglasses, or prescription sunglasses, have your teeth cleaned, get a checkup, join a doctor-recommended weight-loss program, get a flu shot, or sign on for some psychotherapy or psychology sessions. It may seem wasteful to incur nonemergency medical expenses, but it's more wasteful to lose that money.

# Using a Health Savings Account

A *health savings account (HSA)* is a savings account that works similarly to the cafeteria plan, with the following notable exceptions:

✔ An HSA has no use-it-or-lose-it provision. The money belongs to you, and there is no time frame in which you must use the money.

✔ The money in the HSA is invested in a fund that earns interest income.

✔ You have to be insured with a high deductible health plan (HDHP) to have an HSA. Specific guidelines regard what constitutes an HDHP, the deductible, and the maximum out-of-pocket expenses.

✔ The annual contribution limit is set by statute instead of by the employer. For 2010, the contribution limit is $3,050 for a single taxpayer, $6,150 for a family, and an additional $1,000 for a single taxpayer or family when the account holder is 55 or older.

The money you contribute to an HSA is tax-free as long as you spend it on medical expenses. You set up an HSA in Mint.com in the same way that you set up a bank account or a mutual fund account. For more information, see Chapter 2.

# Paying for Noncovered Health Costs

Most health insurance plans don't cover all your costs. First you have a *deductible,* or the amount of money you pay up front before your health insurance kicks in. Then you have a copay, or your share of any doctor visit, prescription, or other medical care. Next is stuff that the insurance won't cover at all, such as certain cosmetic surgeries or a second pair of glasses.

Some years you might not have much in the way of medical costs. Other years these costs will really add up. If you do have substantial medical costs, you might qualify for a tax deduction on your income tax return. For that reason, you should keep track of your medical expenses so you can easily total them at the end of the year and see whether you qualify for a deduction.

## Creating a tag to track particular expenses

It makes sense to track all health-related expenses in one place. Doing so not only helps with budgeting in future years but also saves time if you're entitled to a medical expense deduction on your income tax return.

The Health & Fitness category in Mint.com includes gym fees and sports expenses, as well as other health and fitness expenses you might add. These expenses generally aren't tax deductible. However, you can create custom tags for grouping expenses into different categories.

In the following example, you can create a tag for health expenses that are eligible for a tax deduction:

1. **Click the Transactions tab in Mint.com.**

   Tags appear on the left.

2. **Click Edit.**

   The Manage Your Tags window appears.

3. **Click Add a New Tag and enter the name of the new tag.**

   We entered *Health Expenses,* as shown in Figure 14-2. The tag name can be no more than 20 characters.

4. **Click Save It to make your tag a permanent part of your tag list.**

5. **Click Okay to close the window.**

When you have a transaction that includes a health expense, click Edit Details for the transaction and then click the Health Expenses tag.

Mint.com applies tags to an entire transaction, so if you split a transaction, you can't apply a tag to just a split part. However, you can tag the entire transaction and then put a comment in the transaction's Notes field, explaining how much of the transaction relates to medical expenses.

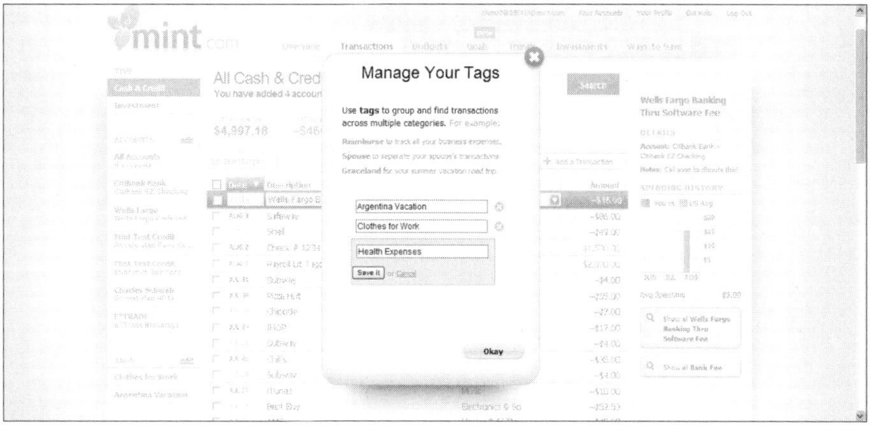

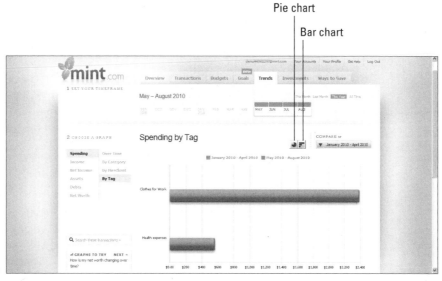

**Figure 14-2:**
We have
tags!

# Viewing your tagged expenses

At any time, you can click one of your tags on the Transactions tab and see
a list of all transactions associated with that tag. In addition, you can see a
graphic rendition of your tagged expenses: Click the Trends tab and then
click By Tag in the Choose a Graph area. You see a chart displaying spending
in all your tagged areas, as shown in Figure 14-3.

Pie chart

Bar chart

**Figure 14-3:**
Tags
displayed in
chart mode.

Change from a bar chart to a pie chart by clicking the pie chart icon (labeled in Figure 14-3). Mouse over any section of the chart, as shown in Figure 14-4, to see how much you spent on an item and what percent of your total tagged items that item represents.

**Figure 14-4:** Get the statistics.

# Participating in a COBRA Arrangement

If you leave your job for any reason, either by your choice or the decision of your employer, and you participated in a health plan at your place of employment, by law your employer must offer you the opportunity to continue to participate in its health plan for up to 18 months after your termination date.

Wow! Free health care for 18 months! Okay, not really. You can stay on the company health insurance policy, but you have to pay the cost of your share of the policy. This policy, called COBRA (Consolidated Omnibus Budget Reconciliation Act), has been around for more than 20 years.

Obamacare to the rescue! If you left your job between December 2008 and March 2010, U.S. taxpayers are picking up the tab for 65 percent of the cost of your health insurance under the COBRA plan.

If you're a member of the COBRA club, you're paying for health insurance through your former employer's plan. Your health insurance payments show up in your transaction list along with other payments that you make.

Make sure your payments are categorized in Health Insurance (check the category of a typical transaction). If you've tagged health expenses for tax purposes in addition to categorizing these as health insurance, make sure that these transactions are getting the proper tag.

For more information on tracking your tax deductions in Mint.com, see Chapter 21.

# Staying on Top of Health Care Legislation

The health care legislation passed in 2010 — officially called the Patient Protection and Affordable Care Act, but generally referred to as Obamacare — provides sweeping changes to the health care system. The text of the legislation is more than 2,000 pages, so obviously most of the bill's contents are omitted here. However, we do include some features of the law that will affect most individuals and businesses:

- Starting in 2013, individuals not covered by Medicare or Medicaid will be required to purchase health care insurance or pay a penalty. The penalties will go into a pool to fund the cost of health care insurance for certain lower income people.

- Starting in 2014, employers with 50 or more employees are required to offer minimum health care insurance to eligible full-time employees or pay a penalty. A federal subsidy will reimburse some or all health care costs to employers with fewer than 25 employees who keep wages under a certain threshold, thus providing an incentive for small employers to not increase wages for employees.

- Beginning in 2013, the most an employee can contribute to a flexible spending account is $2,500 per year (indexed for inflation).

- Beginning in 2011, the penalty for withdrawing HSA funds and using the money for nonqualified medical purposes is increased from 10 percent to 20 percent.

- Under current law, taxpayers are allowed to take an itemized tax deduction for medical expenses that exceed 7.5 percent of adjusted gross income. Starting in 2013, the deduction is allowed only for medical expenses that exceed 10 percent of adjusted gross income, Note that taxpayers over age 65 are exempt from this change until 2017, at which time the new law applies to everyone.

- Effective for health insurance plan years beginning after September 23, 2010, insurers won't be able to deny coverage for adult children up to the age of 26 if the policy covers dependent children.

- Starting in 2018, all health insurance plans must include coverage for preventive care and checkups without a copayment.

# Chapter 15

# Navigating the School Daze Maze

*Y*ou might think that the hardest part of college is all the tests, from entrance exams to finals and term papers. But for many college-bound students and their parents, the toughest part of higher education is finding a way to pay for it.

College costs continue to skyrocket to the point where a degree is almost prohibitively expensive for many. Meanwhile, the U.S. economy continues to morph in such a way that many top-paying jobs demand higher degrees from applicants. All this means that college is not only more expensive than ever but also more important.

Don't be discouraged by the fact that paying for college is one of the biggest financial challenges you'll face. In this chapter, you find out about investment accounts that make it much easier to save and accumulate the money you need to pay for college. And with enough planning, you might be able to save enough for college without taking on huge student loans. But if you do find that you need to borrow, Mint.com can help you monitor how much you owe.

## Planning for Education Costs

You can put off saving for some financial obligations. For example, you might be eyeing a new set of wheels, but if your current car runs, you can hold off your purchase until you've saved enough money. And even if you'd like to buy a home, you can keep renting until you have enough for a down payment.

College is a different situation. Many high school students prefer to start college right after graduation so they can get their career underway. But without proper planning, you'll be stunned at how high the tab will be when you or your children are ready to enroll.

Meanwhile, saving for college ahead of time reaps big benefits. If you're a parent and start saving when your child is very young, you'll have many years to stockpile your money. Starting early reduces the financial sacrifice you have to make each year. And if you are a student and are successful saving enough money to pay for college, you can enter the workforce free and clear of student loans and start accumulating money for future goals.

## The soaring price of college

One factor that makes saving for college a challenge is the rate of tuition increases. As shown in Table 15-1, tuition and fees for four years is $32,600 at a public university and $121,800 at a private college. That $32,600 number may sound manageable, but here's the rub: Tuition and fees are expected to increase by 6 percent a year, which means the price for college is growing much faster than the roughly 3 percent annual increase for the price of other products, called *inflation*. And college costs are rising much faster than personal income and far outstrip the roughly 2 percent interest you'd get if you put your college fund in a savings account.

| Table 15-1 | College Tuition Costs | |
|---|---|---|
| *Institution* | *Four-Year Tuition and Fees in 2010* | *Four-Year Tuition and Fees in 2028* |
| Private college | $121,800 | $347,700 |
| Public university | $32,600 | $92,900 |

*Source: Savingforcollege.com, assuming a 6% annual increase in costs*

Although four years of a public college cost $32,600 in 2010, that bill will be $92,900 for a student enrolling 18 years later, in 2028. Now you know why some parents say they gave up their Porsche 911 to send their kid through college.

The costs listed in Table 15-1 don't include the expensive extras that go along with getting a college degree, such as books, housing, food, and transportation. You should plan for these expenses as well when thinking about the total cost of college.

# The payback from college

While saving and paying for college is a big-time sacrifice while you're doing it, the rewards can be enormous. Statistics show that education usually more than pays for itself. Perhaps the best evidence of how college is worth the cost is revealed in the government statistics in Table 15-2. The median worker over the age of 25 with a bachelor's degree earned a salary of $1,024 a week during the first quarter of 2010. That's well above the $787 median weekly salary of all workers above 25 years old and the $448 median weekly salary of workers lacking a high school diploma.

| Table 15-2 | College Pays for Itself |
|---|---|
| *Education* | *Median Weekly Salary of Workers 25 Years Old and Older* |
| Less than high school | $448 |
| High school graduate, no college | $624 |
| Some college or associate degree | $738 |
| Bachelor's degree only | $1,024 |
| Advanced degree | $1,361 |
| All workers | $787 |

*Source: Bureau of Labor Statistics based on data from the first quarter of 2010, www.bls.gov/news.release/archives/wkyeng_04152010.pdf*

If you need any more proof that college is worthwhile, consider that Aaron Patzer, the founder of Mint.com, holds degrees from Princeton University and Duke University.

# Tax breaks when saving for college

To get a tax break on college savings, you don't need a high-powered CPA who knows every trick in the IRS code. Investment accounts are available expressly for helping you save for college.

You can use several types of investment accounts to save money for college, but the one that makes sense for most people is a 529 plan. This type of plan, which is administered by the state, gives college savers the following huge benefits:

✔ **Tax breaks:** If you're looking for an easy way to cut your tax bill, it's hard to beat a college savings plan. These accounts let you sock away money and then withdraw it tax-free as long as you use it for qualified education expenses, such as tuition, fees, books, and supplies.

Money you take out of a 529 plan to pay for college costs is tax-free. If you save in a regular taxable account instead, you'll need to save even more to pay the tax bill.

It's impossible to know what *capital gains rates*, or tax rates applied to investment gains, will be in the future. Failing to take advantage of the tax breaks of a 529 plan will make it even harder to save for college. For example, to afford a four-year college tab of $92,900 in 18 years, you'll need to save $3,302 a year, or a total of $59,400, assuming you get a 5 percent annual return on your money. But if you instead use a regular, taxable brokerage account, you'll need to save $3,490 a year, or a total of $62,820.

✔ **Oversight over the dough:** Unlike other ways of saving money for your children's college, the 529 plan lets you maintain control. You can name your child the beneficiary of the money but retain ownership. And if your child gets a scholarship and doesn't need the money, you can change the beneficiary to anyone, including yourself. You can monitor your 529 using Mint.com even if you're not the beneficiary.

✔ **Availability:** 529 plans are offered by the states, and most states have several flavors of plans for you to choose from. You can also use another state's 529 plan, even if your child plans to go to school in your home state. So if you want to save in Utah's 529 plan, you can still use the proceeds to pay for your child to go to a university in, say, California. Mint.com helps you keep track of just about every state's 529 plan.

If you withdraw money from a 529 plan that's not used for qualified higher-education expenses, you must pay a 10 percent penalty.

# Building College Savings with 529 Plans

In addition to letting you escape taxes, a 529 plan, unlike other tax-advantaged savings plans, doesn't have all sorts of confusing rules and limits. Setting up a 529 plan is easy, as you see in this section.

# *Setting up a 529 plan*

Before you can connect Mint.com to a shiny new 529 plan, you need to set up the plan. If you've already opened a 529 account, you can skip this section and head to the next section, which shows you how to import your 529 information into Mint.com.

Opening a 529 plan is surprisingly simple:

1. **Check into your state's 529 plan.**

   Check your home state's 529 plan first because you might be able to get a state tax deduction or credit. For details about your state's plan, visit www.savingforcollege.com.

2. **Expand your search.**

   If your state doesn't provide a deduction or credit for using its 529 plan, look at other states' plans. You can find comparisons of all the states' plans at www.savingforcollege.com.

3. **Open your account.**

   After you settle on a state's 529 plan, create the account and get a user ID and password. You'll need this information to pull your information into Mint.com. Enter your name, name the person who will be using the money, and move money into the 529 by writing a check or setting up an electronic transfer. The process to open an account and get sign on information is different for every 529 plan, but the plan's Web site should have clear instructions.

4. **Choose your investments.**

   Most 529 plans let you choose from a menu of various *mutual funds,* which are pools of shareholder money used to invest in a broad array of securities. (Read more about mutual funds in Chapter 18.) Some 529 plans allow you to split your savings between mutual funds that put their money in different sorts of investments such as large U.S. company stock, small U.S. company stock, international stocks, and bonds. Other 529 plans just ask you to indicate when your child will be going to college, and the mutual funds are selected for you. The plans select more conservative funds as your child nears college enrollment.

# Adding your 529 plan

After you establish a 529 plan, all that's left to do is to add the account to Mint.com, just like you add your checking and savings accounts.

Check the Web site for the 529 plan to find the plan's official name before trying to enter it into Mint.com. You'll save some frustration that way.

Simply follow these steps to connect your 529 plan to Mint.com:

1. **Log into Mint.com and click the Your Accounts link.**

   The link is located in the upper-right corner.

2. **Click the Add button on the screen that pops up.**

   The Add button is blue and sports a plus sign.

3. **Start typing the name of the 529 plan and then click the Search button, as shown in Figure 15-1.**

   This step is the tricky part of the process. Some 529 plan names aren't what you'd expect. For instance, the name of California's 529 plan doesn't contain the word *California*: it's Golden State ScholarShare 529 College Savings Plan.

4. **After you find the name of your 529 plan, click it.**

5. **Enter the user ID and password of the account.**

   The 529 plan is added to the Investments category of your accounts.

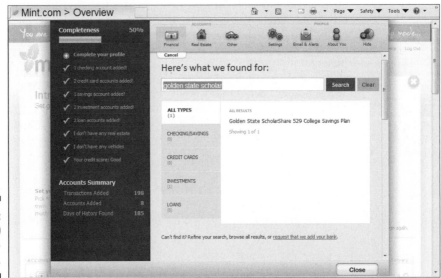

**Figure 15-1:**
Find a 529 college savings plan.

# *Adding a 529 plan created by someone else*

Another great feature of a 529 plan is that anyone can create a 529 for anyone. In other words, your parents can create a 529 plan and name your child, or even you, as the beneficiary.

You can track 529 plans that others have set up on your children's behalf. Get the user ID and password for the account, and then add the plan to your Mint.com account using the directions in the preceding section.

# *Monitoring 529 plan investments*

Because Mint.com sees your 529 plan as an investment account, you can track it as you would any brokerage or mutual fund account. After logging into Mint.com, click the Investments tab at the top of the page. Next, click the name of the 529 plan on the left, below All Investments.

After selecting your 529 plan, you can view it in several ways by clicking tabs that appear below the name of the plan. You can see how your investments are doing in the following areas:

✔ **Performance:** When it comes to investing for college, you're definitely counting on getting some decent performance from your 529. As mentioned, you need a 6 percent return on your money simply to keep up with the cost of school. The grey line on Mint.com's performance chart shows how much you invested. A green bar above the grey line indicates that you're making money on your 529 plan investments. A red bar below the grey line means you're losing money.

Change the time periods from a day, five days, one month, six months, one year, and all time using the 1d, 5d, 1m, 3m, 6m, 1yr, and Max links, respectively, at the upper right of the performance chart.

If you scroll down the page that displays the performance chart, you'll see a list of all the mutual funds and investments you hold in your 529 plan. Use the display to see the best and worst performers.

✔ **Value:** The Value tab shows you how much your 529 plan is worth at the end of various months. If all is going well, each bar in the chart, which indicates how much money is in the 529 account, marches higher as it approaches the sum needed for college. If you scroll down the page, you can see which mutual funds in your 529 plan account for the biggest chunk of the overall portfolio.

✔ **Allocation:** Mint.com helps you determine how well you're spreading around your risk by classifying each mutual fund you've invested in based on its *asset class*, or the type of investments it holds. Common asset classes include stocks and bonds. If you click the Asset Type button, Mint.com displays a pie chart that shows which asset classes make up most of your 529 plan. Putting your college funds into different types of asset classes is one way to control your level of risk. If you click the Symbol button, Mint.com displays a pie chart with the relative size of the mutual funds in your 529 plan.

Mint.com downloads asset class information from your 529 plan provider. If the plan provider doesn't provide this information to Mint.com, the chart in the Allocation area might be blank.

✔ **Comparison:** The comparison shows you how your 529 plan is performing relative to major *market indexes*, such as the Dow Jones Industrial Average, Standard & Poor's 500, and the Nasdaq composite index. Market indexes are benchmarks that tell you how stocks are doing. When the Dow rises, for instance, stocks are generally up.

When watching your investments, keep performance in perspective. If the stock market is down, don't be surprised if your 529 plan has lost value, too. But if the market is rising, and your 529 isn't keeping up or is even losing ground, that's a red flag that something might be wrong with the plan's management.

## Budgeting for 529 plan contributions

Saving for college is like saving for any financial goal, except the amount is larger. Because the numbers are so big, you should have a solid plan and start early. Resources on the Goals tab help you come up with a logical plan and keep yourself on track. For example, the Save for College feature estimates how much you need to save to obtain your goal.

To create a college savings goal in Mint.com, follow these steps:

1. **Click the Goals tab.**

2. **Select a goal.**

   If you haven't yet created a goal, you'll see the Save for College goal labeled with a picture of a stack of books. If you've created goals, you'll see the Add a Goal button; click that button and then click the Save for College icon.

3. **Enter the type of college.**

Decide whether you are saving for a public in-state school, a public out-of-state school, a private school, or a community college.

4. **Tweak the assumptions.**

Mint.com estimates annual college cost increases and the age at which the student is expected to enroll in college, as shown in Figure 15-2. You can change these to fit your expectations.

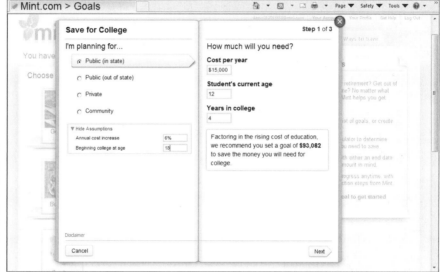

**Figure 15-2:** Examine the assumptions that the Save for College tool makes.

Mint.com defaults to an annual cost increase assumption of 4 percent. Bumping that up to 6 percent is a good idea — it's better to overestimate the annual cost increase of college and end up saving too much money rather than not enough. If it looks like you're saving too much as your child nears college enrollment, you can always lower your savings amount at that time. You can also reassign excess savings to someone else who might want to go to school, including yourself.

5. **Estimate the costs.**

Mint.com provides a rough idea of how much college will cost per year, but you may want to modify this amount. Check the college's Web site for the yearly cost. You also need to enter the current age of the student you're saving for and how many years the student plans to attend college. Based on your inputs, Mint.com tells you the amount you need to save in total and monthly, as shown in Figure 15-3.

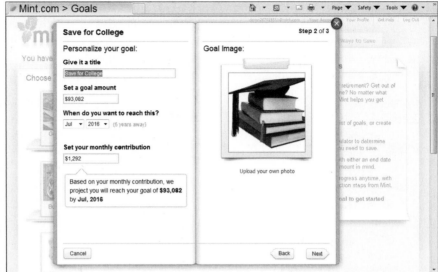

**Figure 15-3:**
Track your
progress
toward your
college
fund.

After you set up your college savings plan, click the Goals tab and see how much you've saved for college so far and how much more you have to go. Note that the Save for College Goal feature overlooks one major factor regarding college savings: Your money may grow while you're saving. Often when you save money for college, including in a 529 plan, your cash is invested so that it can grow. If the money you're saving and investing is growing at 6 percent a year, for instance, Mint.com doesn't include such returns in its calculation.

If this shortcoming bothers you, a simple workaround is to lower the annual college cost increase percentage by roughly the amount you expect your money to grow each year. So if you expect your money to grow by 2 percent a year, and college costs to increase by 6 percent a year, you might consider putting 4 percent in the annual college cost increase field, as described in Step 4. Remember, however, that the market can work against you, too. If stock prices fall, that could erode the value of your savings and require you to save even more to meet your goal.

# Borrowing Your Way to School

Mint.com helps you create a plan to have enough savings to pay for college. But you might find yourself falling a little short for any of the following reasons:

✔ **You didn't save enough:** Although Mint.com can tell you how much you should save, it can't make you save the money. You might not have had enough income to satisfy the monthly savings goal Mint.com set for you, or perhaps you just didn't get started on the plan soon enough.

✔ **College costs increased more than expected:** College costs are expected to grow by 6 percent a year, but even that estimate could prove to be too low. Your estimate for future increases in college costs is critical to Mint.com's calculation on your savings goal. If you assume a 6 percent increase in college costs, but costs actually rise by 7 percent a year, you'll find yourself short.

✔ **Financial hardship tripped up your college savings plan:** A job loss that disrupts income could derail your college savings plan. Or you might suffer a financial hardship and decide to tap your college savings plan, despite the 10 percent penalty of doing so.

If your savings won't be adequate to pay for school, you don't have to shelve your goal of higher education. But you'll probably have to think about paying the bills by going into debt.

Debt gets a bad name. And in many cases, such as with credit-card debt, borrowing can certainly ruin a well-laid financial plan. But sometimes borrowing makes sense, and paying for college if you don't have adequate savings is one of those times. Interest rates on student loans are much lower than on other forms of debt. And by borrowing to go to school, you're investing in your career, which should pay back in the future.

As you can see in Table 15-3, nearly 70 percent of bachelor's degree recipients graduated with debt, according to The College Board. And more than half graduated with a crushing load of $10,000 or more.

| Table 15-3 | Bachelor's Degree Recipients Swimming in Debt | | | | |
| --- | --- | --- | --- | --- | --- |
| *No Debt* | *Less Than $10,000* | *$10,000– $19,999* | *$20,000– $29,999* | *$30,000– $39,999* | *$40,000 and over* |
| 34% | 14% | 19% | 15% | 9% | 10% |

*Source: College Board, citing statistics from National Postsecondary Student Aid Study based on data from 2007–2008 school year, www.collegeboard.com/parents/repository/cb-policy-brief-college-stu-borrowing-aug-2009.pdf*

You can consider many types of loans when financing a college education. Which loan is best for you depends on a variety of factors. The most popular type of college loan is the Federal Stafford Loan. For other options, check with the college admissions department or visit `www.savingforcollege.com/student_loans`. Click the What Are My Student Loan Options? link located near the middle of the page.

## Setting up your loan

After you get a loan, it's time to sign away your first-born child to the lender. Just kidding. If you plan well and squirrel away money to pay down your debts, with some discipline you can be debt-free.

Mint.com can help you deal with your college loans, but first you first have to connect your student loan to your Mint.com account. You add your student loan to Mint.com just as you add any loan:

1. **Log in to Mint.com and click the Your Accounts link at the top of the page.**

2. **Click the Add icon.**

    The Add icon is the blue button with a plus sign.

3. **Identify your lender.**

    Enter the name of your lender in the Enter Your Bank's Name or URL field.

4. **Enter security information.**

    Mint.com will find your lender and prompt you to enter your user ID and password. Depending on your lender, you might be asked to provide additional information to identify yourself.

Adding some student loans may require that you to enter more information than you'd expect. For instance, to add a loan from lender Sallie Mae, you enter your Social Security number and account number, as shown in Figure 15-4. You can read Chapter 7 for a review of keeping your personal information secure with Mint.com.

Mint.com adds the student loan to the list of accounts under the Loans heading, on the left side of the Overview tab.

## Paying off your loan

If you have to borrow to go to school, you're not alone. Focus on school and get good grades. After you graduate and get a job, it's time to plan how to pay down the loan.

**Figure 15-4:**
You may
be asked
to enter
your Social
Security
number.

The Goals tab contains lots of features to help you pay down debts, such as the Get Out of Debt goal. But at press time, this goal only provided assistance to help you reduce car loans and credit card balances, not pay down student loans. Users have asked about this on the online customer-support message boards, and Mint.com employees have said that the company is considering adding other loan types to the Get Out of Debt goal.

In the meantime, just start paying off your loan. Mint.com automatically reduces the loan balance that appears in the account list on the left side of the Overview tab as you make payments.

## Dealing with school loan deferrals

When you borrow money, you're making a deal with the lender that you intend on paying them back. No one likes it when someone reneges on a deal, and that's especially the case when it comes to borrowing money.

Mint.com help you monitor all your debts and will even help you prioritize which ones to pay back first. You can find out more about how Mint.com helps you tackle what seems like a crushing debt load in Chapter 12.

One important caveat to student loans is worth mentioning. Unlike most other forms of debt, student loans can be put off, or *deferred*, in extreme cases. If you're dealing with an extreme financial hardship, you may be able to postpone paying your student loans so you can continue to pay your other debts.

Mint.com doesn't yet have a feature that helps you manage a student loan deferral. But you can read about the process at `www.nolo.com/legal-encyclopedia/article-29791.html`.

# Chapter 16

# Preparing for Retirement

. . . . . . . . . . . . . . . . . . . . . . . . . . . . . . . . . . . . . . . . . . . . .

## In This Chapter

▶ Deciding your retirement needs

▶ Tracking a 401(k)

▶ Tracking an IRA

▶ Making withdrawals

▶ Receiving Social Security

. . . . . . . . . . . . . . . . . . . . . . . . . . . . . . . . . . . . . . . . . . . . .

**D**oes your image of retirement involve Florida, shuffleboard games, and wrinkled people living on a company pension with the bonus of Social Security payments? Probably not. Today, most people are too busy thinking about keeping their jobs, hanging onto their homes, and staying ahead of day-to-day expenses to daydream about retirement. In this chapter, you find out how the retirement tools in Mint.com can help you figure out how to take care of yourself when you're no longer working.

## Determining What You Need for Retirement

Figuring out how much money you need to sock away for retirement involves a lot of speculation. Here's a simple example. Assume that you earn $50,000 a year, are 40 years old, and want to quit working when you're 70. How long do you think you'll live? The experts say you need at least 80 percent of your working income to keep you happy in retirement, but is this reasonable?

Using Mint.com, you can create a savings plan for retirement and then monitor your progress as follows:

1. **Open the Retirement goal in Mint.com.**

   Click the Goals tab and then click Save for Retirement. Or if you've previously added goals, click the Add a Goal button and then click Save for Retirement.

2. **Enter the required information.**

   Enter your age today, the age when you want to retire, and the annual income you want to receive during retirement. In the example shown in Figure 16-1, we set up a fund for a 40-year-old person that will provide $20,000 in annual income for 20 years during retirement, beginning at age 70. Any other income this person needs will come from other sources. Based on the criteria entered in this example, this person needs to save $197,375, and the earnings on the savings will take care of the balance of the income needed in the retirement fund.

**Figure 16-1:**
Enter your retirement savings plan.

When planning a retirement savings account, remember that you don't need to save all the money yourself. Before you proceed with filling out this savings form, think about the sources of your retirement income. You can expect to receive Social Security payments, maybe a company pension, income from a tax-deferred plan such as a 401(k) or an IRA, and maybe an inheritance. You might also have some money saved. In other words, you don't have to assume that you have to fund the entire amount of your retirement income from money you set aside each month. A good resource for experimenting with retirement planning is available from Fidelity at http://personal.fidelity.com/planning/investment.

3. **Enter your assumptions.**

Click Show Assumptions and enter **3** percent as the inflation rate and **20** as the number of years in retirement. (During the past 20 years, inflation has remained below 5 percent, so 3 percent seems like a reasonable estimate of future inflation.) As you monitor your savings over the decades, keep an eye on inflation and the predictions of economists, and make adjustments to your savings plan as needed.

4. **Describe your investment style.**

   Drag the lever to indicate how you expect to invest and what rate of return you want to receive. As you slide the lever, you see the amount you need to have saved by age 70.

   Analysts suggest that the longer you have to save, the more aggressive your savings plan should be. If you are in your 20s or early 30s and willing to take some risk with your investment (stock market and riskier mutual funds) in exchange for a higher rate of return, move the lever to a more aggressive level. As you get closer to your retirement age, you should take less risk with your money and invest in safer investments (savings account, bonds, Treasury bills, money market funds, and mutual funds that invest more heavily in bonds and Treasury bills), so move the lever toward the short-term and conservative end of the spectrum. This sample investor is 40, at the middle of his investing life, and so is investing in the middle of the spectrum.

5. **Click Next.**

6. **Name your retirement savings plan.**

   Go on, give it a fun name such as *Geezer Club.* Based on the information you enter, Mint.com calculates how much you need to save monthly. In the example in Figure 16-2, this person needs to save $549 a month for the next 30 years. He might need a raise.

**Figure 16-2:** Mint.com calculates your monthly required savings.

7. **Designate a savings account.**

Click Next, and the final Save for Retirement screen appears so you can select an account for tracking your retirement savings. Mint.com makes some recommendations if you need to open a new account, as shown in Figure 16-3, or you can use an existing account. If you select the third option, I'll Choose an Account Later, Mint.com stores your retirement savings information but doesn't start tracking your savings. Note that Mint.com lets you associate only one account with this savings goal. If you want to use multiple accounts for your retirement savings, you must set up each savings goal individually.

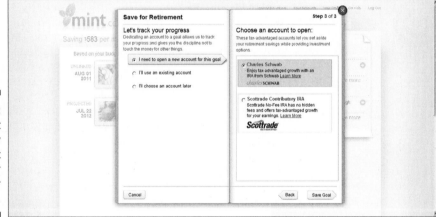

**Figure 16-3:**
Select
a new
retirement
account or
use your
own.

# *Tracking Your 401(k) Investment*

Many employers provide a 401(k) tax-deferred retirement fund for their employees. A 401(k) plan is an important part of your overall retirement plan. You can track the activity in your 401(k) through Mint.com the same way you track activity in your bank accounts and investment accounts:

1. **Click the Investments tab and then click Add Account.**

    You see a screen for adding a new account.

2. **In the Enter a Bank Name or URL field, enter the name of the invest-ment company that holds your 401(k) account and then click Search.**

3. **In the search results, select the name of the investment company.**

4. **Enter your user name and password.**

Mint.com determines what login information the financial institution requires and presents you with fields to enter that information.

5. **Click the Add It! button.**

The account is added to your other investment accounts.

Mint.com links the account Web site in the account description. In this way, you get quick access to the account so that you can monitor your investments and make changes if necessary.

## Making contributions to your 401(k)

With a 401(k), 403(b), or similarly named retirement account, you get to put money in the account and not pay tax on that money, at least not for awhile. So, if you contribute $2,000 a year to your 401(k) and are normally taxed at a 15 percent marginal income tax rate, you save $300 in taxes. And if you live in a state with an income tax, you save more because the state doesn't tax your contribution amount either.

The tax savings is one of many great things about a 401(k) account. Here are some more benefits:

- ✔ **You save without feeling the pain.** Amounts that you contribute to a 401(k) are automatically taken from your pay before you ever get your hands on the money.

- ✔ **You get free money from your boss.** Most employers offer a matching program, whereby if you contribute to your 401(k) plan, the employer kicks in an extra amount based on a percentage of your salary. You should contribute enough to your 401(k) plan so that you can get the maximum match from your employer.

- ✔ **The more you save in your 401(k), the less you have to put aside in additional savings.** The 401(k) might not give you all the money you need for retirement, but it can help you reach your goal.

- ✔ **The money you put in your 401(k) plan and all its earnings are tax-deferred.** The interest, dividends, and capital gains earned by the investments in your 401(k) plan are not taxed until you withdraw the money.

- ✔ **You can keep your money in a tax-deferred plan even if you change jobs.** If you have at least $5,000 in your 401(k) plan when you leave a job, you can keep the plan in place with your former employer. But no matter what the plan balance, you can roll over the money in your 401(k) plan to an IRA account when you leave your job. The IRA has the same tax-deferred status as the 401(k) plan. (See "Rolling over your 401(k) plan," later in the chapter.)

The name *401(k)* comes from the section of the Internal Revenue Code that gives special tax-deferred status to a certain type of retirement fund.

## Tracking your 401(k) investments

One of the biggest mistakes people make regarding their 401(k) is ignoring the plan. Typically, your 401(k) plan allows you to make choices about how to invest your money. You can select from a variety of mutual funds with different levels of risk. Just like with any investment, you should monitor the fund's performance and make regular decisions about how your money is invested. See Chapter 18 for more information about analyzing your mutual fund investments.

Here are some general tips for keeping tabs on your 401(k) plan investments:

- ✔ **Know the rules.** Find out how often you are allowed to change your 401(k) investments. The documentation that comes with your plan explains how frequently you have the right to make changes. Some plans let you change as often as you like; other plans let you change investments only at particular times.

- ✔ **Read about the investments.** Research online and study your investment options. Find out what you can about the past performance of the funds you have chosen or are considering.

- ✔ **Know the contribution limits.** For 2010, you are allowed to contribute up to $16,500 to your 401(k), plus an additional $5,500 if you're over age 50. However, your company might have lower and stricter contribution limits based on your pay level and other factors, so check out the actual limits with your employer. Annual contribution limits are indexed for inflation and are announced at the end of the year for the upcoming year.

- ✔ **Diversify your investments.** Don't put all your eggs in one basket. Remember what happened to investors who had all their retirement money in Enron or with Bernie Madoff. Your 401(k) plan has several investment options for a reason. You can probably choose from a mix of conservative, aggressive, and in-between investments. Split your account balance among multiple accounts so that you don't lose everything if one goes south.

- ✔ **Keep your hands out of the cookie jar.** It's difficult but not impossible to get your hands on your 401(k) money. Don't do it! The cost of withdrawing money from your plan when you leave your job is ridiculous when you factor in the Federal income tax, the state income tax, the penalty, and the lost earning power. Don't invest money in your 401(k) plan that you need in the short term.

## Rolling over a 401(k)

When you leave a job, whether or not your termination is voluntary, you have to make some decisions about the money in your 401(k) plan. Keep the following general rules in mind:

- ✔ If the balance in your 401(k) is at least $5,000, you can leave the money right where it is, in your former employer's 401(k) plan.

- ✔ You can roll over the balance to an Individual Retirement Arrangement (IRA), which you control. Read all the rules that accompany your 401(k) plan documentation to make the rollover tax-free.

- ✔ You might be able to transfer the balance to a new 401(k) plan with your new employer. Check the rules associated with both plans to find out if you can do this and how it should be done so that you aren't taxed.

- ✔ You can take the money out of your 401(k) plan. You pay a penalty of 10 percent plus income tax on the amount you withdraw. For example, if you withdraw $4,000 and are in a 15 percent tax bracket, you pay $1,000 for the privilege of getting the money before you reach retirement age. State taxes are additional. If you're in a 28 percent Federal tax bracket, you can quickly lose 45 percent of your money by withdrawing it early.

The paperwork you get with your 401(k) plan explains which of these options will happen if you do nothing. In the most likely scenario, the money is distributed to you unless you request a transfer or rollover. A tax of 20 percent will be withheld on the 401(k) balance before you receive your distribution.

Before making a decision about your 401(k) plan, read the plan documentation. The information presented in this book is generalized and doesn't necessarily apply to every 401(k) plan. Your plan has its own rules, and you need to know what they are to make an informed decision.

# Tracking Your IRA Investment

An individual retirement account (IRA) is a savings plan that allows you to put aside money for retirement in an account that you manage yourself. You get to choose how the money is invested, and you get to decide how much you want to contribute each year. The earnings in the fund accumulate on a tax-deferred basis, just like the earnings in a 401(k) plan.

For 2010, the maximum you can contribute to an IRA is $5,000, plus an additional $1,000 if you're over age 50. Here's the scoop on how IRAs work:

✔ **You get to select your own investments**. With a 401(k), you're limited to the investment choices your employer gives you. With an IRA, you can choose from all investment options, including stocks, mutual funds, and real estate, and you can spread your investment choices over as many different selections as you want.

✔ **You may or may not get a tax deduction for your IRA contribution.** Contributions to 401(k) plans are always tax-deferred. The tax-deferral opportunities for contributions to IRAs depend on several factors, including your income, whether you participate in a retirement plan at work, and your spouse's income and retirement participation.

✔ **It's easier to get your hands on IRA money**. If you absolutely must take money out of your retirement savings, you can do so more easily with an IRA than with a 401(k). However, steep penalties are associated with withdrawing money early from an IRA.

✔ **You can't borrow from your IRA**. Unlike a 401(k) plan, which might provide the capability to establish a loan program, either money stays in the IRA or it doesn't.

✔ **An IRA has no matching program.** Alas, the cool matching program that an employer offers with a 401(k) plan doesn't exist when you make contributions to an IRA.

✔ **You can create a spousal IRA for a nonworking spouse**. Typically, you have to earn income to make IRA contributions. However, the spouse of someone who qualifies to make IRA contributions can set up an IRA, even if the spouse doesn't have income to offset the contributions.

To set up a new IRA account in Mint.com, see the instructions in the "Determining What You Need for Retirement" section, at the beginning of this chapter. If you have an existing IRA account, set it up in Mint.com as follows:

1. **Click Your Accounts at the top of the Mint.com screen.**

   The accounts you've already entered in Mint.com are displayed.

2. **Click the Financial tab.**

3. **Click the Add button, and enter the name of the broker or fund where your IRA money is held, as shown in Figure 16-4.**

4. **Enter login information.**

   Enter your user ID and password for online access to your IRA account. If your login access requires additional information, answer the privacy questions provided.

5. **Click Add It! to add your IRA to the collection of accounts that you track in Mint.com.**

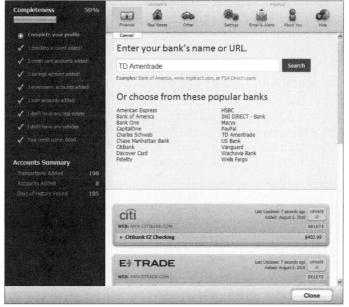

**Figure 16-4:**
Enter the
name of
your IRA
broker or
mutual fund.

# Traditional versus Roth IRA

A traditional IRA is a tax-deferred account in which you make tax-deductible deposits and the earnings are not subject to tax until you withdraw the money. Rules restrict your access to the money as well as require minimum withdrawals starting at a particular age. Although anyone is entitled to make a nondeductible contribution to a traditional IRA, assuming the person has earned income at least equal to the contribution amount, income limits prevent certain taxpayers from making a deductible contribution to an IRA. Both types of contributions have benefits. It's wise to consult with a tax accountant or financial planner before making any retirement savings choices.

Alternatively, a Roth IRA is a tax-free option for those who don't qualify for or prefer not to make tax-deductible contributions to a tax-deferred account. The money you contribute is taxed when you earn it and you receive no deduction for your contributions, but the earnings in the Roth are not taxed, even when you withdraw them. Note, however, that only taxpayers with income below certain levels are entitled to contribute to a Roth IRA. For 2010, individual taxpayers with income greater than $120,000 and married taxpayers filing a joint return with income greater than $177,000 cannot contribute to a Roth. These amounts are indexed for inflation and change each year. Married taxpayers filing separately are not allowed to contribute to a Roth IRA.

You set up a Roth in Mint.com in the same way you set up a traditional IRA. However, if you are making tax-deductible contributions to a traditional IRA, you should tag the transactions as tax-related.

## Making required withdrawals

You've reached retirement and it's time to bust out that money. After you reach age 59½, you can start pulling money out of your IRA or 401(k) without penalty. You still have to pay income tax on the money from a traditional IRA or a 401(k), but there is no penalty.

You're not required to start pulling out the money just because you turned 59½. In fact, the longer you leave your money in your retirement accounts, the more the money will grow, thanks to compounding.

 You are required to take your first mandatory withdrawal from your traditional IRA by April 1 of the year after the year in which you turn 70½. If your 70th birthday is on August 1, 2011, you'll be 70½ in 2012 and your first mandatory IRA withdrawal must be made by April 1, 2013.

When you begin withdrawing from your IRA, you can choose between withdrawing the entire balance or receiving periodic distributions. You make this choice on the date on which your distribution begins. However, even after receiving periodic distributions, you can still withdraw your entire balance. The mandatory withdrawal rules are tricky, and how they are implemented can affect how much you have available for your retirement years and how much is left for your heirs. Talk to a financial advisor to make sure you're making the best withdrawal decisions for you and your family.

The IRA mandatory withdrawal rules apply to traditional IRAs, not Roth IRAs. You are not required to ever withdraw the money from your Roth IRA.

The money you withdraw from your IRA is recorded as a transaction in Mint. com, assuming you've added your IRA accounts to your Mint.com file.

## Receiving Social Security Payments

Part of today's retirement income package includes Social Security income. Social Security payments are available to anyone who worked for at least 10 years during his or her life.

---

# When it's time to start receiving Social Security

When you think you're old, wise, or can- retire to apply for benefits online.
tankerous enough to start receiving Social Alternatively, you can call the Social Security
Security benefits, you can go to the Social Administration at 800-772-1213 and tell them
Security Administration's Web site at www. you're ready to apply for benefits.
socialsecurity.gov/applyto

---

Although you can start receiving Social Security benefits at age 62, you receive more money if you wait until you're somewhere between the ages of 65 and 67, depending on the year you were born.

You can calculate your retirement benefits by visiting the Social Security Administration's Web site at www.ssa.gov/planners/calculators.htm. Or you can download Form SSA-7004 at www.ssa.gov/online/ssa-7004. html, fill it out, and mail it to the following address:

Social Security Administration
Wilkes-Barre Data Operations Center
P.O. Box 7004
Wilkes-Barre, PA 18767-7004

When you start receiving your Social Security benefits, the amounts appear in your Mint.com transactions, just like a deposit that appears in your bank account.

Social Security is part of your complete package of retirement income. When planning for your future needs, incorporate your anticipated Social Security benefits into the total amount you plan on saving for your retirement. However, legislation in the coming years as well as other factors relating to current economic conditions might affect how much Social Security you have in the future. Your age, how long you work, how much you make, and the condition of the Social Security system when you retire will all determine how much money you'll receive from this source.

The Social Security benefits you receive are based on the average monthly earnings during the 35 years in which you earned the most money. A secret formula is applied to the average to come up with your actual earnings.

# Part IV
# Borrowing and Investing

The 5th Wave                    By Rich Tennant

"Annuities? Equity income? Tax-free municipals? I say we stick the money in the ground like always, and then feed this guy to the sharks."

## In this part . . .

Nearly every sport or activity has a few moves that are extremely difficult to master. Figure skaters face the triple Axel, basketball has its windmill dunk, and baseball batters shoot for the grand slam.

Part IV helps you determine which aspects of your financial life are the most challenging and then conquer them. Planning for big-ticket purchases, such as buying a car and a house, can be a huge financial objective that might seem insurmountable at first. But with Mint.com and some wise planning as discussed in this part, you can achieve these financial goals.

In addition, designing a portfolio of stocks, bonds, mutual funds, and other investments might seem out of reach. But using Mint.com, you can find out how to design a portfolio of investments that will help your money grow so you can achieve long-term financial success.

# Chapter 17

# Managing Car Loans and Mortgages

*A* CEO brought in to revive a company that filed for bankruptcy protection was asked if the heavy load of debt piled onto the firm killed it. He wisely responded that it wasn't the debt that did the company in but the fact that they couldn't afford to pay it back.

A little bit of financial gallows humor might seem like a strange way to kick off a chapter about auto and home loans. But the point raised by the CEO is exactly what gets consumers into trouble when it comes to borrowing. When you take that brand-new car for a test drive or see your dream home for sale, it's easy to talk yourself into the fiction that you can take on the debt. Mint. com can help you navigate these large and important purchases by showing you how much car or home you can actually afford. And after you sign on the dotted line and assume the debt, Mint.com helps you put that debt to work for you rather than the other way around.

## Setting Realistic Goals

The biggest forms of debt that consumers deal with are the loans, or *long-term debt*, used to pay for assets they will use over an extended period of time. The two most common types of long-term debt are car loans and home loans, or *mortgages*. How you manage these two types of long-term debt will have a gargantuan influence on how much money you'll be able to save to reach your other financial goals.

Because car and home loans are so important to your financial health, Mint. com dedicates quite a few resources to helping you manage them. Although this chapter shows you how to use these resources, we don't cover all aspects of the purchases. For more details on home buying, check out *Home Buying For Dummies,* 4th Edition, by Eric Tyson and Ray Brown. Also remember that Mint.com doesn't know all the details of your financial situation, so don't take its financial advice blindly.

## Long-term debt is a double-edged sword

If you've read the story of Cinderella, you might have wished that you had a fairy godmother, too. Wouldn't it be great if all the material things you'd ever wanted appeared in your driveway or on your lawn at the snap of your finger? Well, you do have a fairy godmother of sorts. But instead of wearing a flowing gown and waving a magic wand, your fairy godmother is a green-eyeshade-wearing banker wielding a financial calculator.

Your bank can sprinkle around some financial magic and put you in the castle and coach of your dreams. But just as with Cinderella's deal with her fairy godmother, your deal with your debt godmother has a deadline, too. If you don't repay your debts on time, you get a "repossessed" sign in your front lawn or a tow truck yanking the car out of the driveway.

When used responsibly, debt can help you put your financial life on track. After all, if you don't have a car, it might be difficult to have a job. And if you waited to save enough money to buy a house with cash, you'd probably be unable to enjoy it very long. Debt lets you get these important *assets*, or financial items that you own, much faster than you would if you paid cash. However, taking on too much debt can be a big problem when it comes time to repay.

## Getting a car you can afford

You've probably heard that it's a bad idea to go grocery shopping when you're hungry. And it's an equally bad idea to show up at the car dealership before you know what you can afford to spend on a car. If you know ahead of time what kind of car payment your budget can accommodate, thanks to insights from Mint.com, you'll be less of a target for a persuasive salesperson.

First, though, you should understand a few auto loan terms:

   ✔ **Loan term:** When you borrow money, you pay a portion back each month as a *payment*, for a preset number of months. The length of time that you pay back money is the *loan term*.

✔ **Interest rate:** When you borrow money, you have to pay back not only the money you borrowed but also *interest*, or a charge applied to the loan that you pay in exchange for getting the money. Interest rates are expressed as a percentage of the amount you borrowed, or the *principal*. The *interest rate* is usually the amount of interest you pay per year divided by the amount you're borrowing. So if you pay $5 per year to borrow $100, you're paying a 5 percent interest rate.

✔ **Desired monthly payment:** Mint.com bases much of its analysis on how much you are prepared to cough up each month to pay interest on your loan and to repay principal. This is the *monthly payment.*

### Finding the car's actual cost

One of Mint.com's most powerful tools for car buyers is its capability to give you a good idea of how much the car you think you want will cost before you even fire up that seat-warmer during a test drive. Simply follow these steps:

1. **Click the Goals tab.**

2. **Click the Buy a Car link or the Add a Goal button.**

   If you don't have any goals set up yet, you'll see the Buy a Car link. Otherwise, you see the Add a Goal button.

3. **Select the I Need Help Estimating My Cost option.**

4. **Set the sales tax rate in your state.**

   Click the Show Assumptions link to change the sales tax rate, if necessary.

5. **Enter the kind of car you're thinking about and then click Next.**

   Decide whether you're interested in a new or used car, as well as the year, make, and model. Mint.com accesses the Kelley Blue Book database to see what the car would cost, as shown in Figure 17-1.

6. **Select the I Need Financing for This Purchase option.**

   You see an estimate of what the car will cost.

7. **(Optional) Modify the amount if desired.**

   If you disagree with the price that Mint.com estimates for the car, you can change the estimate. For instance, if you're a good negotiator and think you can get a better deal for the car, feel free to override the estimate.

8. **Enter your desired monthly payment.**

   Provide a monthly payment you think will fit into your budget. Don't worry about being exact yet. You find out how to change this information later in the chapter.

   As a general rule, make sure your monthly car expenses are less than 20 percent of your *net pay*, or take-home pay. Don't forget to factor in vehicle maintenance costs such as oil changes, repairs, and auto insurance.

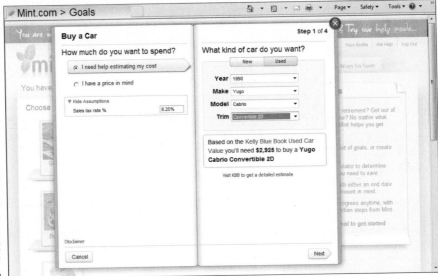

Figure 17-1:
What kind
of car are
you thinking
about
buying?

9. **Select a loan term and interest rate.**

   You can customize the type of car loan by borrowing for 36 to 60 months and changing the interest rate.

10. **Indicate whether you're trading in a car.**

    If you're trading a car, enter its estimated trade-in value. You see a summary of the car costs, complete with the purchase price with tax, the monthly payment, and the interest rate, as shown in Figure 17-2.

11. **Click the Next button.**

    When it comes to seeing what you can really afford to drive, assume that you can't borrow at all. Select the I Will Pay in Full option, and you see how much the car will cost, including tax. If you can't afford to save up enough money to buy your desired car with cash within a reasonable time, that might be a warning to scale back your expectations.

12. **Review your needed monthly contribution and then click Next.**

    You see how much you need to save per month to accumulate your down payment as well as when you'll have the money.

13. **Track the progress of your saving.**

    Open a new savings account for the car savings fund, use an existing account, or choose the account later.

## Finding whether the car fits your budget

After you find out the cost of the car you want, you can find out whether or not you can afford it. The easiest way to see if the car you've described will fit into your budget is to consult the Budgets tab. Here's how:

**Figure 17-2:**
Determine
how much
you need to
save to pay
for the car
you want.

1. **Click the Budgets tab.**

   If you entered all your bank accounts and credit card accounts following the instructions in Chapter 2, you see how much you make and spend each month as well as how much is left after saving for goals, including your car fund, as shown in Figure 17-3.

2. **Interpret the findings.**

   If you have money left after your spending and budgeting for goals, Mint.com will suggest that you can use that money to speed up your goals. If that's the case, congrats: That car you're eyeing appears to fit into your budget. But if you're coming up short, you may need to lower your expectations.

3. **(Optional) Adjust your expectations.**

   If you have a deficit in your budget after adding your car goal, you'll need to scale back your car plans. Click the Goals link on the right, below the You've Budgeted heading. Repeat the steps in the "Finding the car's actual cost" section using a different car until the numbers work out.

You can review and change any goal. On the Goals tab, select the goal that you want to revisit. A pop-up window displays the goal's information, including how much you've saved toward your down payment for a house or car. To change the details of the goal, click the small Edit button at the top of the pop-up window.

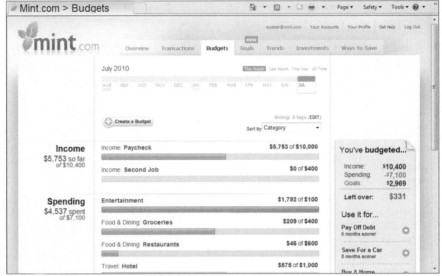

**Figure 17-3:**
See how much you have after paying for your expenses and goals.

# Putting a roof over your head

Consumers let their eyes get larger than their wallets during the financial crisis that began in 2007. The entire U.S. financial system almost fell to its knees as mortgage lenders and banks were hammered by *defaults,* or loans that went bad as borrowers couldn't afford to repay them.

The debt-triggered financial crisis of 2007 is a reminder that it's up to you to determine how much you can afford to borrow to buy a house — if you can afford to buy a house at all. Relying on the advice of real-estate brokers or bankers can be dangerous because they can benefit if you increase the amount you spend on a home.

Instead, use the tools in Mint.com to help figure out what you can afford. First, though, you should be familiar with the following home-buying terms:

- **Mortgage rate:** When you take on a mortgage, you have to pay back not only the money you borrowed but also a fee on that money, or *interest.* The amount of interest you pay is measured as a percentage of what you borrowed. The interest rate on a home loan is called your *mortgage rate.* If you pay $5,000 a year in interest to borrow $100,000, you're paying a 10% mortgage rate.

- **Down payment:** Lenders usually want you to have a *down payment,* or some of your own money on the line when you take on a mortgage. A typical amount is 20% or the home's purchase price. If you can't put down 20%, you may not be able to get the loan or you may have to pay a higher rate of interest or pay for private mortgage insurance (PMI) to protect the bank against loss.

✔ **Mortgage term:** When you borrow money to buy a home, you must agree to pay the lender back within a set amount of time, called the *mortgage term*. The traditional mortgage term is 30 years, but you can find terms of all lengths, including 7 or 15 years. Because lenders are taking less risk when you borrow for less time, interest rates are usually lower when the term is shorter.

✔ **Homeowner's insurance:** Because your home is such a big asset, you'll want to purchase *homeowner's insurance* each year to cover your house against perils such as fire. Also, when you buy a house with a mortgage, the bank has quite a bit of money on the line and will most likely require you to have homeowner's insurance. Mint.com refers to homeowner's insurance as *annual insurance*.

✔ **Mortgage type:** With a mortgage that has a *fixed interest rate*, you're locked into an interest rate with a preset rate of interest. Fixed-rate mortgages are considered the most conservative because you're protected if interest rates rise. *Variable rate* mortgages usually have a brief period at the start of the loan when interest rates don't change, but after that, they change to reflect the ups and downs of the going market rate.

It's easy to get seduced by variable rates because they tend to be lower than fixed rates at the time you sign the loan. However, if the economy heats up and interest rates rise, the rate on your variable rate mortgage will rise, too — and you could find that you can no longer afford your monthly mortgage payment. Strongly consider a fixed rate on your mortgage. Even if you have a fixed rate mortgage, you can *refinance,* or get a new loan with the lower rates, if mortgage rates fall.

✔ **Annual property tax:** Don't think your mortgage and insurance payments are the only bills you need to pay to be a homeowner. You'll most likely need to pay the local government a tax based on a percentage of the value of your home. Different localities handle this tax in different ways.

✔ **Debt-to-income ratio:** Lenders decide how much mortgage you can afford by looking at the *debt-to-income ratio,* or the relationship between the amount of debt you have — including car loans, student loans, credit-card bills, and mortgage-related costs — and how much you earn. For example, if you have $19,800 in debt payments a year, including costs you'd incur if you bought a house (such as insurance and property taxes), and income of $60,000, your debt-to-income ratio is 33% (or $19,800 divided by $60,000). As a general rule, your debt-to-income ratio should be 33% or lower. That means $1,650 of your monthly gross pay of $5,000 should cover your monthly debt payments.

## Seeing how much house you can afford

The question that stops many potential home buyers in their tracks is one of the most important ones, "How much can I afford?" As we mentioned, you should figure this out yourself because some of the people you'll be working with during the home-buying process would be happy if you spent more.

You can determine how much you should spend on a house without becoming financially strapped. Here's how it works:

1. **Click the Goals tab and then click the Buy a Home goal.**

2. **Review your annual income.**

   Mint.com estimates your annual income based on everything it knows about you, but you can customize this number, as shown in Figure 17-4.

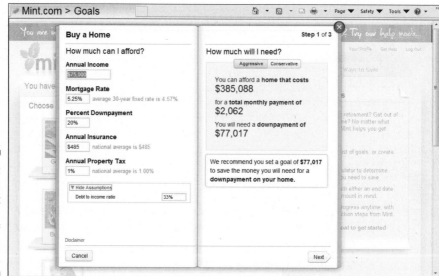

**Figure 17-4:**
The important considerations of becoming a homeowner.

If you're married, Mint.com includes your spouse's income in its annual income estimate. However, you might try basing the Buy a Home goal on a single income, in case one of you decides to stop working or loses a job.

3. **Enter the mortgage rate.**

   The mortgage rate is the interest rate the lender charges you to borrow money to buy a home. Be careful with this number because even a seemingly small change in the mortgage rate can dramatically alter what you can afford. Mint.com suggests the average rate on a 30-year mortgage, but you may need to adjust this if lenders are quoting a different rate or you're looking at a mortgage with a different term.

4. **Provide the percent down payment.**

   Enter how much of the purchase price you're providing as a down payment.

5. **Estimate the annual insurance.**

   Enter the amount you need to pay each year to insure the home against peril. Mint.com suggests a national average, which you'll likely want to modify based on where you live. Contact the company where you buy other insurance for an estimate.

6. **Input the annual property tax.**

   Enter the property tax rate. Mint.com provides a national average, but you can get the actual amount by checking the Web site of your local property assessment office.

7. **Review the debt-to-income ratio assumption.**

   Click the Show Assumptions link to see whether the debt-to-income ratio is appropriate. Mint.com automatically sets the assumed debt-to-income ratio at 33 percent, meaning your debt payments should be less than a third of your income.

8. **See what Mint.com says you can afford and then click Next.**

   You see how much of a house you can afford, with an estimate of your monthly payment and down payment.

   Click the Aggressive and Conservative buttons and decide if you want to stretch or take a more cautious approach to how much you spend. Err on the side of caution. And again, be sure to consult a specialty book such as *Home Buying For Dummies* to double-check Mint.com's conclusions.

9. **Set a goal and then click Next.**

   On the screen shown in Figure 17-5, you design the goal and set a date by which to meet it.

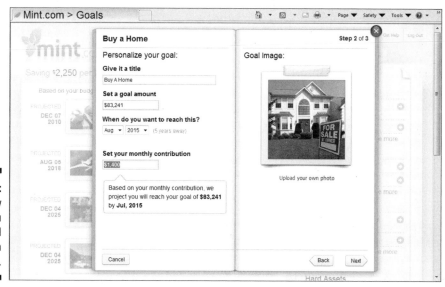

**Figure 17-5:** See how much you can afford to spend on a house.

10. **Decide where you'll save and then click the Save Goal button.**

    Decide whether you want to create a new savings account, use an existing account, or choose an account later for saving your down payment.

### Seeing how the house fits into your budget

After you enter all the home-buying variables, you see how this purchase would fit into your budget and alter your financial situation. To see how the goal fits in your budget, click the Budgets tab. On the right side of the screen, you see your income and spending, including the cost of goals such as a home purchase plan. If you have enough money to save for those goals, you see a green dollar amount next to the Left Over line.

If you have money left over after paying all your expenses and funding your goals, consider saving more toward your Buying a Home goal to see if you can scrounge up the down payment more quickly.

# Setting Up Auto and Home Loans

You've used Mint.com to see how much of a car or house you can afford and made sure it fits into your budget. Would you believe it if we told you that's the fun part? Because after you buy the car or house, it's time to repay the money. Mint.com can help you keep track of repaying loans, but first you need to make sure all the necessary information is added to your account.

## Getting behind the wheel

You can add your auto loan to your Mint.com account just like you add any other financial account or loan. But adding a car and house is a little different from adding other loans because with cars and homes, an asset is attached to the loan. To make all this work in Mint.com, you need to enter not only how much you owe but also what you own.

The easiest way to get your car and car loan set up with Mint.com is by first attaching your car loan to your Mint.com account. Follow these steps:

1. **Log into Mint.com and click the Overview tab.**

2. **Click the Your Accounts link at the upper-right corner.**

    The Your Accounts window appears.

3. **Click the blue Add button.**

4. **Enter the name of the lender and then click the Search button.**

5. **Click the lender's name in the list.**

6. **Add your account number and password.**

   You are given these numbers when you first access your loan information on the lender's Web site.

7. **Click the Add it button.**

Now, when you return to the Overview tab, you'll see the name of your lender on the left, under the Loans heading.

After adding your loan, it's time to tell Mint.com about the car you bought with the loan. Follow these steps:

1. **Go back to the Your Accounts page.**

   Click the Overview tab and then click the Your Accounts link.

2. **Click the Other tab.**

3. **Click Vehicle, select Automobile and then click Next.**

   The screen shown in Figure 17-6 appears.

4. **Give the car a name and enter its value.**

   You can get a realistic estimate of your car's value at automotive Web sites such as www.kbb.com (Kelley Blue Book) or www.edmunds.com.

5. **Connect the car asset to the car loan.**

   Click the Yes option and then select the option next to the car loan.

6. **Click the Add it button.**

When you've completed these steps, you've added the car loan and car asset to your account. Now you're ready to start tracking your progress in paying back the loan, which is something you discover later in the chapter.

## Setting up a mortgage

Even before you kick out the last guest from your housewarming party, it's time to invite your home loan and asset information into your Mint.com account. Linking both the mortgage loan and the house asset is important in helping you manage your *cash flow*, or the timing between when you receive cash income and when you must pay your mortgage. Also, adding both the mortgage and the house to Mint.com will help you track your *net worth*, which is your financial value. Tracking your net worth is covered briefly in this chapter and in more detail in Chapter 12.

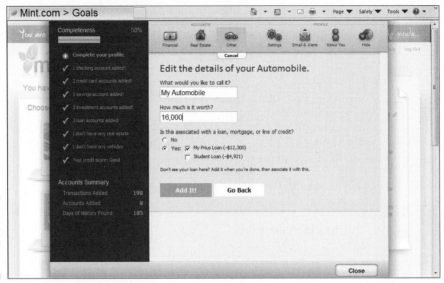

**Figure 17-6:** Enter the value of your car.

The easiest way to import your housing data into Mint.com is by starting with your mortgage. You add the mortgage to your account just as you add any financial account. Follow the steps in the preceding section on adding a car loan to your account. You just need the name of your mortgage lender, the account number, and the password.

Next, you need to add your home to your Mint.com account as an asset. Doing so takes just a few steps, as outlined next:

1. **Go to the Your Accounts page.**

   Click the Overview tab and then click the Your Accounts link.

2. **Click the Real Estate tab below the Accounts heading.**

3. **Type the street address and zip code of the home you bought.**

   Mint.com attempts to find your home and estimate its value. If you see your home in the list, click it.

4. **Modify the home's details.**

   Mint.com takes a good stab at the property's value, as shown in Figure 17-7, but you might want to tweak it based on what you paid and the selling prices of similar homes. You can double-check the value Mint.com assigns at real estate Web sites such as www.zillow.com or www.homegain.com.

5. **Link the home asset with the mortgage.**

   Select the Yes option and then select the option next to the mortgage loan.

**6. Click the Add it button.**

The home and the associated mortgage loan are listed on the left side of the Overview tab.

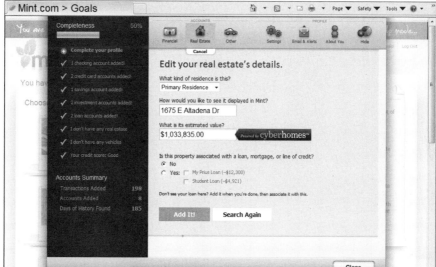

**Figure 17-7:**
Review the
estimate of
your home's
worth.

# Looking to improve your home

Talk to most homeowners, and you'll quickly find that buying a house is just the beginning of the expenses. You might want to remodel your living room and get rid of the funky seventies-style shag carpet. Or maybe you want to update the kitchen or bath. Mint.com assumes you will pay for home improvements in one of two ways:

- ✔ **From savings:** You can set up a financial savings goal. Enter how much the improvement will cost and the date by which you want to have the money. The site then estimates how much you need to save each month to reach your goal.

- ✔ **Using a home equity loan or line of credit:** After you buy a home and pay down the mortgage, your ownership stake in the home increases. Banks allow you to tap this ownership, or *home equity*, in the form of a loan. Such loans can be used to help finance home improvements.

If your financial goal is to own your home, be careful about tapping home equity loans. Although these loans can make sense when improving your home, they prolong the time it takes to own your home, free and clear.

Setting up a goal to improve your home takes just a few steps:

1. **Click the Goals tab and then click the Improve My Home goal.**

   The screen shown in Figure 17-8 appears.

**Figure 17-8:**
Mint.com
helps you
save for
home-
improve-
ment
projects.

2. **Enter how you plan to pay for the improvements.**

   You can pay using savings or several pools of cash, including savings and a home equity line.

3. **Indicate the type of improvement you're planning and how much it will cost.**

4. **If you indicated that you will borrow, enter the loan amount and then click Next.**

   In the field below Amount to Be Financed, enter the size of the loan you intend to take out.

5. **Set an amount of the savings goal.**

   This is the project's cost that you plan to pay for out of pocket.

6. **Indicate the date by which you want to save the money.**

7. **Review the results and then click Next.**

   You see how much money you need to save each month to reach your savings goal.

8. **Tell Mint.com whether you want to set up a new savings account or use an existing one.**

After entering your home-improvement goal, Mint.com adds it to your list of goals. When you click the Budgets tab, you can see whether the goal you've set leaves you with any money left over. If not, go back to the goal and lower your expectations.

# Managing Long-Term Loans

You've come a long way in a short time using Mint.com to set your long-term goals for a car and house. Now it's time to find out how Mint.com can help you not only plan for big, long-term financial goals but also keep on track paying for them.

## The cruel way loan payments work

Your car or mortgage payment is typically the same amount each month, but not all payments are equal. Part of the payment you make on your car loan or mortgage goes to interest, and the other part goes to paying down the amount you borrowed, or the *principal*. This process is called *amortization*.

But here's the most important part of how loan payments work. The portion of the payment that goes to paying the interest and principal changes over time as you make more payments. When you first take out a loan, a vast majority of your money goes to paying interest. But over time, the balance shifts, and most of your payment starts to be applied to paying down the principal. Table 17-1 shows a sample $200,000, 30-year fixed mortgage ($1,074 a month), detailing the shift over time of the part of the payment that applies to interest and principal. You can calculate your own amortization schedule using Bankrate's free tool at `www.bankrate.com/calculators/mortgages/amortization-calculator.aspx`.

| Table 17-1 | | Sample Amortization Schedule | |
|---|---|---|---|
| *Year* | *Total Payment* | *Payment Applied to Principal* | *Payment Applied to Interest* |
| 1 | $12,884 | $2,951 | $9,933 |
| 10 | $12,884 | $4,623 | $8,260 |
| 20 | $12,884 | $7,615 | $5,269 |
| 30 | $12,884 | $12,537 | $342 |

*Based on a $200,000 30-year loan at 5% interest*

Understanding how most of your payments go toward paying interest during the early part of your loan's life is critical, especially when it comes to refinancing. You can save money by refinancing, but remember that if the new loan has the same original term as your old loan, you're starting over, and your interest payments again go to mostly interest. You can manage this setback, however, by refinancing to a loan with a shorter term or by paying extra each month toward the principal.

## Keeping on top of debt: Making payments

If you've ever gone mountain biking, you know that one of the worst things to do before climbing a giant mountain is to look at the peak. If you fixate on how much of a challenge lies ahead of you, it's easy to get frustrated. Instead, just focus on keeping the pedals churning.

The same is true for big, long-term bills such as a car loan and mortgage. If you look at the massive principal amount you owe, the debt can be intimidating. Instead, focus on each individual payment and make sure you keep the wheels of payment turning.

When you make a payment to your loan company, the transaction shows up in your Mint.com account in two ways:

✔ **Your payment account:** If you paid your car or mortgage payment with your bank's online bill-pay service or wrote a check and the account is set up in Mint.com, the transaction will appear in the account you used to make the payment. Review Chapter 2 for a refresher on adding your financial accounts to Mint.com.

Make sure that the payment transaction is in the correct category. Mint.com usually places car payments in the Car Payment subcategory of the Auto & Transport category and mortgage payments in the Mortgage & Rent subcategory of the Home category.

If Mint.com doesn't place your car or mortgage payment transaction in the correct category, fret not. To reclassify the payments, click the Transactions tab and then click the payment account listed on the left. Find the payment in the transaction list, click the Category field, and then select the correct category.

✔ **Your loan account:** You get credit for your payments. Mint.com automatically subtracts the amount of your payment that applies toward the loan principal. The updated number is reflected in the loan balance shown on the left side of the Overview tab.

## Tracking how much you've paid

After you've been paying your loans for awhile, it's only natural to become curious about how much of a dent you've made in the loan. On the Transactions tab, click the most recent car or mortgage payment in the transaction list. On the right side of the page, you find several helpful pieces of information:

- ✔ **Spending history:** This small chart shows how much you've paid to your mortgage or auto loan lender. You see also how your spending compares with the U.S. average.

- ✔ **All spending with the lender:** Click the Show All button and then click the name of the lender. You see a list of all your payments to that lender.

- ✔ **All loan payments:** If you're looking at a car payment, click the Show All Auto Payments button to see all the auto payments you've made.

The Show All Auto Payment button is especially handy if you have several car loans. You can see how much you're paying on all your vehicles in one place.

## Seeing the big picture

Do you suspect that your long-term loans are eating up a big portion of your budget? Want to see exactly how much? Click the Trends tab to see all your spending by category. Click the Auto & Transport or Home category, and drill down to see how the payments fit into your overall spending in those categories.

You can change the time frame you're interested in examining on the Trends tab. Click and drag the abbreviations of the months at the top of the page to select the months you want to check out. Or select a preset time frame: This Month, Last Month, This Year, and All Time.

## The lowdown on your net worth

Your car and home have a profound influence on your net worth. They are likely some of your largest assets, while your car loans and mortgage are some of your biggest bills. Mint.com has some comprehensive tools to examine your net worth, including your car and home. Just scroll down the Overview tab to see your net worth. For details, flip to Chapter 12, which covers net worth in more detail.

# Chapter 18

# Your Mutual Fund Guide

*I*f you've been using Mint.com to manage your finances, you may have hunted down areas where you've been wasting money. You might have even created a budget. These two things put you miles ahead of many others who are trying to make ends meet and living paycheck to paycheck.

By being financially savvy with your day-to-day expenses, however, you have a new — but good — problem: excess savings. Having cash you don't need for immediate needs is the basis for paying for long-term goals, such as buying a car or a house or preparing for retirement.

With a mounting pile of savings, though, comes the problem of knowing what to do with the money so it can grow. If you just stuff your savings under your mattress, you'll actually erode your cash. Your savings sit still while the prices of goods you want to buy increase with inflation.

The answer to battling inflation and the secret to financial success is putting your savings to work in the form of investments, to make your money grow.

For many people, mutual funds are a great way to invest, as you discover in this chapter. We also show you how Mint.com helps you monitor your mutual fund investments so you can take advantage of your financial head start.

# You and Mint.com Have a Mutual Friend: Mutual Funds

Mint.com is all about helping make the complicated process of managing your money more simple. And in many ways, mutual funds aim to bring the same idea of simplification to investing. Unlike other types of investments that require you to pore over tons of research, mutual funds are designed so you can just hand over your money to a mutual fund company and let it take care of everything.

What are mutual funds? *Mutual funds* are pools of cash gathered from many people that are used to buy a basket of investments. Mutual funds aim to give individual investors some of the clout usually reserved by bigger professional investors. Individual investors may not have enough money to buy the best investment research or hire accountants, but when mutual fund investors put their money together, they can hire people to manage their money and get cost savings.

When you buy mutual funds, you're taking a risk that you could lose money. Taking on the risk of a loss is the only way to get a shot at a higher return than you would get by putting your money in a bank account or burying it in your backyard.

But don't let this fact cause you to make the same mistake many others commit. Some think that by not investing and just keeping money in a savings account, they aren't taking any risk and will be better off than if they took a chance on investing. Nothing could be further from the truth. On average, prices generally rise about 3 percent a year. That means if you put all your money in a savings account paying 2 percent a year in interest, your money is losing roughly 1 percentage point of value each year.

Suppose you bury in your backyard $15,000, which is just enough to buy an economy car. And let's say that in 30 years, you decide to buy your grandchild an economy car. You run outside and dig up the $15,000. But guess what? The economy car that was $15,000 in 2010 costs $36,409 in 2040, assuming 3 percent annual inflation. You've lost nearly 60 percent of your purchasing power over the 30 years due to inflation. Protection from the erosion of the value of money is a big reason why you need to invest in financial instruments that increase in value over time, like mutual funds.

## Advantages of mutual funds

You can invest your savings in many ways. Mutual funds are designed primarily for people looking to offload their investment chores. Following are some of the advantages of mutual funds:

✔ **Simplicity:** You just choose a mutual fund and transmit your money to the investment company, and you're all set. The mutual fund handles most of the details, such as buying and selling securities, choosing investments, handling tax and other bookkeeping, and monitoring the stock market. You don't even need to open a brokerage account to invest in mutual funds.

✔ **Diversification:** By investing in just one mutual fund, you may be spreading your investment over hundreds or thousands of individual stocks, bonds, and other investments. Spreading your money around into different investments is called *diversification* and allows you to protect your portfolio from disaster in case a single investment goes bad. You can buy a single mutual fund, and that mutual fund diversifies your money by investing in different types of investments, or *asset classes*, such as bonds and stocks. Spreading your money into different asset classes is a fundamental rule of investing because it helps increase returns while reducing risk.

✔ **Track record:** Before you invest in a mutual fund, you can see how the fund has performed over time. While past performance isn't indicative of how the fund will do in the future, you at least can see whether it's been a solid performer in the past.

✔ **Reasonable fees:** Mutual funds charge a bevy of fees, many of which are summarized in the next section. But if you look around, you can find mutual funds that charge extremely low fees, much less than you'd have to pay a professional money manager to perform a similar job.

Given the advantages of mutual funds, it may not be surprising to find out that they're popular. Mutual funds are one of the most common ways individual investors own stocks and bonds. Mutual funds are so popular that by the end of 2009, there were 7,691 mutual funds, according to the Investment Company Institute, outnumbering the number of stocks that trade on major stock market exchanges.

The number of mutual funds in the United States has been growing rapidly since their earliest days in the 1940s, as you can see in Table 18-1.

| Table 18-1 | Mutual Funds Continue to Be Popular | |
|---|---|---|
| *Year* | *Net Assets (in $ Billions)* | *Number of Mutual Funds* |
| 1940 | $0.5 | 68 |
| 1950 | $2.5 | 98 |
| 1960 | $17.0 | 161 |
| 1970 | $47.6 | 361 |
| 1980 | $134.8 | 564 |
| 1990 | $1065.2 | 3,079 |
| 2000 | $6,965 | 8,155 |
| 2009 | $11,120.7 | 7,691 |

*Source: Investment Company Institute,* www.icifactbook.org/pdf/10_fb_table01.pdf

## Disadvantages of mutual funds

Despite the advantages of mutual funds, they're not the perfect investment for everyone. Mutual funds have several serious drawbacks, some of which Mint.com can help you spot and avoid. Following are the downsides of mutual funds:

- **Outlandish fees:** Didn't you just read that mutual funds have low fees? That's right. But some mutual funds charge astronomical fees and provide little in return. Mint.com can help you spot these types of mutual funds.

- **Lack of control:** When you invest in a mutual fund, you're trusting the mutual fund and its boss, the *portfolio manager*, to invest in the types of investments it's supposed to. You can't opt out of investments you disagree with.

- **Tax inefficiencies:** Mutual funds can hit you with nasty tax bills that can spoil your tax-planning strategy. When a mutual fund sells a winning stock, for instance, it may incur a *capital gain*. As an owner of a mutual fund, you're responsible for paying the tax on your portion of that gain. Making things worse, sometimes mutual funds can't manage taxes effectively. If a number of mutual fund investors sell, or *redeem*, their shares, the mutual fund may need to sell investments to raise enough money to cash out the departing investors. If this selling occurs and you still own the mutual fund, you might be left with the tax bill if investments held by the fund were sold for a gain.

- **Index shadowing:** Some mutual funds may be charging you a relatively high fee but not giving you anything in return. The classic example of this bad deal for investors is called *index shadowing*, where you hire a mutual fund manager to select winning stocks but the manager instead simply buys commonly held stocks. You can buy baskets of commonly held stocks at extremely low fees instead of hiring an expensive portfolio manager to do the same thing. Mint.com can help you spot index-shadowing mutual funds that are charging you for no added value.

# Choosing Mutual Funds

Now that you're onboard with the idea of owning mutual funds, it's time to get started. First you need to choose a mutual fund and set up an account with a mutual fund company.

## Knowing the types of mutual funds

There are nearly as many types and stripes of mutual funds as there are animals in the zoo. The catch-all term *mutual fund* masks a diverse jungle of all types of investments that pool investors' money.

This chapter focuses on giving you everything you need to know about mutual funds to use Mint.com. If you want to find out more about the nitty-gritty of mutual fund investing, we suggest *Mutual Funds For Dummies,* 6th Edition, by Eric Tyson.

Most mutual funds are in one or several of the following categories. You'll encounter these terms when shopping for mutual funds, so it's a good idea to know what they mean:

- **Open-end:** *Open-end mutual funds,* which are by far the most common type, use the money gathered from investors to buy and sell stocks, bonds, and other investments. The price of each share of an open-end mutual fund is set at the end of the day, when the company adds the value of all the investments in its portfolio. This end-of-day tally is the mutual fund's *net asset value,* or NAV. The NAV is how much the fund company would pay you if you redeemed, or sold, your shares in the mutual fund.

- **Closed-end:** *Closed-end mutual funds* share some traits of mutual funds and some traits of stocks. Like open-end mutual funds, closed-end funds buy portfolios of investments. But closed-end funds don't cash out investors who redeem by selling investments held in their portfolio. Instead, owners of closed-end funds buy and sell shares of the fund with each other on the stock market. Prices of shares of closed-end funds rise and fall during the day as investors assess the value of the portfolio owned by the fund. You own closed-end funds through a brokerage, not a mutual fund company; see Chapter 18 to find out how to track them.

Don't confuse closed-end mutual funds with *exchange-traded funds* (ETFs), which are increasingly popular. ETFs allow you to invest in a basket of investment by buying a single stock. For more on ETFs, see Chapter 19.

- **Actively managed:** Many managers of mutual funds try to beat the market, or generate better returns than average, by selecting stocks they think will do the best in the future and by getting in and out of the market by selling and buying at times they think are ideal. *Actively managed mutual fund*s hire professional investors to decide what investments to buy, and when to buy and sell them. Actively managed funds usually have the highest fees because you're paying the portfolio manager's salary.

A vast majority of actively managed funds fail to beat the market over the long term. While some funds go on hot streaks from time to time, usually those streaks don't last long enough to profit from them.

- **Index funds:** Index funds have become increasingly popular alternatives for mutual fund investors who don't want to pay a professional portfolio manager. *Index funds* robotically own all the stocks in popular market indexes, such as the Dow Jones Industrial Average and Standard & Poor's 500. If you buy an index fund that owns the S&P 500, your investment rises and falls along with the value of that index, which tracks the collective stock prices of 500 of the biggest U.S. stocks. Index funds have a huge advantage over actively managed funds in that their fees are much lower because they don't have to pay an expensive portfolio manager to select investments. Mint.com can help you track both actively managed mutual funds and index funds.

✔ **Stock:** Mutual funds can invest in all sorts of asset classes. *Stocks,* or shares of ownership in companies that trade on major market exchanges, are a common investment for mutual funds. Other subsets of stock mutual funds include those that invest in stocks that meet the classifications in Table 18-2. Mint.com can track all common types of stock mutual funds.

✔ **Bond:** Companies not only sell stock but also raise money by borrowing. Governments can also raise money by borrowing. Governments and companies borrow by selling investments called *bonds,* which are promises by companies or governments to repay a set amount of money by a certain time in the future at a predetermined interest rate. The *interest rate* is the fee the borrower pays to borrow the money. Because investors know what they're likely going to get when they buy a bond, some types of bonds can be less risky than stocks. Mutual funds can buy bonds sold by governments and by companies with shakier finances, called *high-yield,* or *junk,* bonds. Such bonds are called high-yield because the interest rates tend to be higher than on safer types of debt, such as government debt. With high-yield bonds, investors are taking more risk that they might not get repaid if the company cannot afford to pay interest, or *defaults.* Mutual funds can also buy bonds sold by solid companies, called *investment-grade* bonds, which tend to be less risky because they're more likely to be repaid.

✔ **Hybrid:** Some mutual funds don't fit neatly into a category because they buy both stocks and bonds. A common form of *hybrid mutual fund,* called a *balanced fund*, spreads its investments more or less equally between stocks and bonds. In addition, *target date funds* reduce their risk as you get closer to a financial goal by reducing their exposure to stocks and increasing their exposure to bonds over time.

| Table 18-2 | Common Types of Stock Mutual Funds |
|---|---|
| *Stock Fund* | *Invests In* |
| Growth | Companies that are more expensive relative to other stocks because they're expected to increase revenue and earnings more rapidly |
| Value | Bargain-priced stocks ignored by investors due to less-desirable characteristics, such as being mature, slower growing, or in a declining industry |
| Income | Companies that tend to return large portions of their profits to investors in periodic payments called *dividends* |
| International | Companies located outside the United States |
| Global | Companies located in any part of the world, including the United States |
| Sector | Companies in specific industries, such as technology, energy, or finance |

## Examining mutual fund fees

Mint.com is your wingman when it comes to spotting mutual funds that might not be worth the fees you're paying. But first, you must understand all the types of fees mutual funds charge, so you can better use the information you get from Mint.com. The most common forms of mutual fund fees follow:

- **Front-end loads:** Fees charged to you when you first buy a mutual fund. These fees averaged about 0.99 percent in 2009, according to the Investment Company Institute.

- **Back-end loads:** Fees charged when you sell a mutual fund. These fees are often waived if you keep your money in a mutual fund for a certain period of time. These back-end loads are often intended to discourage investors from buying and selling mutual funds too often.

- **Redemption fees:** Fees charged when you sell a mutual fund that help the mutual fund cover expenses associated with you selling.

- **Management fees:** Ongoing charges the mutual fund hits you with as its payment for handling your money.

## Finding more info about mutual funds

By now, you've probably gained an appreciation for how difficult it can be to sift through all the possible mutual funds. Thousands of mutual funds with different structures, objectives, investment philosophies, and fees are available.

Mint.com isn't designed to help you prospect for individual mutual funds. However, free online resources can help you sift through the thousands of mutual funds to find the best ones for you. Morningstar (www.morningstar. com) and Lipper (www.lipperleaders.com) are top Web sites that let you explore the massive world of mutual funds and choose the funds that make the most sense in your situation. You can also read more about how to use such online resources to find mutual funds in *Investing Online For Dummies,* 7th Edition, by Matt Krantz.

# Tracking Mutual Funds

In this section, we show you how to open a mutual fund account and link that account to your Mint.com account. Then you can log into Mint.com, view your mutual fund portfolio, see how you're doing, and decide whether you're getting the kinds of performance you're paying for.

# Opening a mutual fund account

If you already have an account with a mutual fund company, you can skip to the next section, "Adding your mutual fund account." Mutual fund companies make it simple to give them your money. The steps differ slightly depending on the mutual fund company. In the following example, we use Vanguard:

1. **Visit the mutual fund company's Web site.**

   You can get the Web address of most mutual fund companies by using a search engine such as Bing or by using Morningstar and Lipper, the mutual fund databases listed previously.

2. **Click the button to open an account.**

   Most mutual fund companies have a prominent open an account button on their sites. Click that button and you are prompted to set up an account. Figure 18-1 shows the open an account screen at Vanguard.

3. **Choose the mutual fund you'd like to buy.**

   You tell the mutual fund's Web site which individual mutual funds you'd like to invest in and how much you'd like to invest.

4. **Fund the mutual fund account.**

   You can usually either mail a check to the mutual fund company or establish a link with your checking or savings account and move the money electronically.

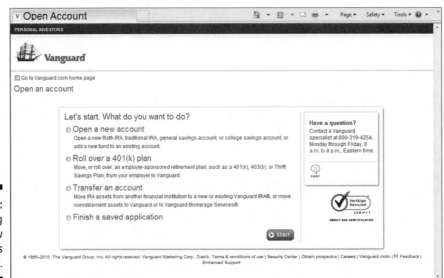

**Figure 18-1:**
Setting
up a new
account is
easy.

5. **Get your user ID and password.**

   After opening your mutual fund account, you get a user ID and password so you can view your account at the mutual fund company's Web site. Some mutual funds also require that you choose a *challenge question*, or a piece of trivia about yourself that strangers would have difficulty guessing, such as your mother's maiden name. Mint.com uses this same information to connect to your mutual fund account.

## Adding your mutual fund account

You add your mutual fund account to Mint.com in the same way you add just about any financial account, including investment accounts. Follow these steps:

1. **Log in to Mint.com and select the Your Accounts link.**

   The Your Accounts screen appears.

2. **Click the blue Add button to add an account.**

3. **Enter the name of the mutual fund company and then click Search.**

   Type as much of the mutual fund company's name as you know.

4. **Select the name of the mutual fund company.**

5. **Enter your user ID and password.**

   You might also be asked to answer the challenge question you created when you opened the mutual fund account.

6. **Click the Add it button.**

   Mint.com adds the mutual fund account to the Overview tab, under the Investments heading.

## Examining your mutual fund transactions

You're on your way to becoming a Mint.com-powered mutual fund investor. To see your mutual fund *transactions,* or the funds that have been bought and sold, click the Transactions tab. Scroll down the list on the left and click the name of your mutual fund account. You see a summary of all the transactions taking place in your mutual fund account, as shown in Figure 18-2.

The Transactions tab gives you the following details about each transaction in your mutual fund account:

- ✔ **Date:** This is the month, day, and year on which the mutual fund transaction occurred.

- ✔ **Description:** This line of text tells you what the mutual fund transaction was for. Typically, a transaction might be a deposit into the mutual fund account, a redemption, a sale of a mutual fund, or a purchase of a mutual fund. If any of your mutual funds owned an investment that paid a dividend, the transaction will be described as a dividend.

- ✔ **Category:** Movement in your account is organized in one of five subcategories of the Investments category. These subcategories are

  - • Deposit: Put money in the mutual fund account

  - • Withdrawal: Redeem mutual fund shares

  - • Buy: Purchase a mutual fund

  - • Sell: Sell a mutual fund

  - • Dividend & Cap Gains: Receive a dividend or other payment from the mutual fund.

- ✔ **Amount:** This is the dollar value of the transaction.

If Mint.com places a transaction in an incorrect category, you should fix it manually. Click the misclassified mutual fund transaction, click the arrow in the Category blank, and select the transaction's category.

**Figure 18-2:**
See the cash in your mutual fund account, plus the funds being bought or sold.

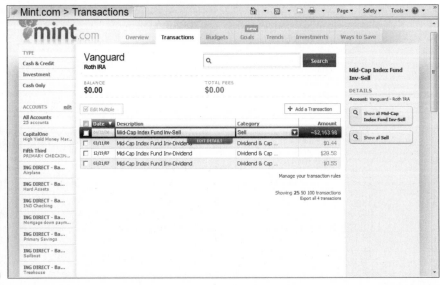

# Putting your mutual fund under the microscope

Mutual funds are often the investment of choice for people who don't want to be troubled with watching their portfolios daily. You can invest in mutual funds and then largely put them on autopilot.

Unfortunately, because mutual funds are so easy to just forget about, that's exactly what many investors do. They toss aside any e-mails or printed statements regarding their investments. You can make sure that your portfolio is on track without digging into the minutiae of money management by using the Investments tab.

 Even if you're paying someone to manage your money, you still have a responsibility to keep tabs on your investments to make sure things are going the way they should.

### Sizing up your fund's performance

Expect the value of your mutual funds to move up and down in the short term. But over time, you'll likely see the value of your mutual fund portfolio rise above the amount you invested, or your *price paid,* as Mint.com calls it.

To see how your mutual funds are doing, click the Transactions tab and then click the Performance tab. Next, select the name of the mutual fund account listed on the left. You see the Investment Performance chart for your mutual fund account displaying three important pieces of mutual fund information over time:

- ✔ The gray line in the middle is the amount you paid to buy all the investments in your mutual fund account.

- ✔ Green sections indicate when the value of your mutual fund account exceeds the price you paid, called an *unrealized capital gain.*

- ✔ Red sections indicate when the value of your mutual fund portfolio fell below the value you paid, called an *unrealized capital loss,* or simply losing money.

The term *unrealized* might seem scary, but it just means that the capital gain, or capital loss, is on paper. You don't realize capital gains or losses until you sell the mutual funds. If the chart is green, you're making money on your mutual fund investments.

 You can evaluate how your mutual fund account has performed over various time frames. Click the 1d, 5d, 1m, 6m, 1yr, and Max links at the top of the chart to see how your account has performed the past day, five days, one month, six months, one year, and over the entire time you've had the mutual fund account, respectively.

If you scroll down this chart, you can see a list of all the individual mutual funds in your mutual fund account. Remember that one mutual fund account may hold many individual mutual funds. The chart shows you if you're making money or losing money on each individual mutual fund in the mutual fund account. You see the price you paid for each mutual fund and its worth now, or *market value*. Mint.com also calculates the *percent change,* which is how much you've gained or lost from the price you paid for each mutual fund.

The Investment Performance chart can be helpful at tax time, too. If you have green in your chart, you might have a taxable realized capital gain if you sell the mutual fund. Similarly, if you sell when you have red on the chart, you have a realized capital loss. Realized capital gains and losses can affect your tax situation; to find out more, see Chapter 21.

### Tracking the value of your mutual fund account

To see how much your mutual fund account is worth over time, click the Investments tab and then click the Value tab. Select the name of your mutual fund account on the left. You want to see the bars getting bigger over time because that shows you're making money. You can look at the value of your account during different time frames.

### Spreading your mutual fund dollars

When you buy mutual funds, you're leaving much of the work to the portfolio managers. One aspect of mutual fund investing that is up to you, though, is *asset allocation,* or the way your mutual fund portfolio is spread between different mutual funds. A typical asset allocation might spread your investments over mutual funds that invest in different asset classes. If you have $10,000 in your mutual fund account, and $6,000 is invested in stock mutual funds and $4,000 in bond mutual funds, you have a *60-40* stocks-to-bonds asset allocation.

Keep an eye on your mutual fund account's asset allocation. If your bond mutual funds are doing better than your stock mutual funds, your asset allocation might shift and you'll have a 50-50 stocks-to-bonds asset allocation, not the 60-40 mix you were targeting. Your asset allocation determines in large part how risky your mutual fund portfolio is and what returns you'll get.

To monitor your asset allocation and make sure it remains in balance, click the Investments tab and then click the Allocation tab. Select the name of your mutual fund account on the left.

Your asset allocation is displayed in the following two ways:

- **Asset type:** Click the Asset Type button below the pie chart, and the chart is updated to show you how your money is spread out between different asset classes, such as stocks and bonds.
- **Symbol:** Click the Symbol button below the pie chart to see how many individual mutual funds you hold in your mutual fund account. You can also see the size of each individual fund.

Mint.com relies on the mutual fund company to provide the correct asset class information for all the mutual funds you own. If the mutual fund doesn't provide the allocation data or provides incorrect data, the chart in Mint.com will not be accurate. Verify this information at a mutual fund tracking site such as Morningstar by searching for your specific mutual fund.

### Keeping an eye out for laggard mutual funds

When you invest in a mutual fund, you're paying part of the portfolio manager's salary, so you're the boss. And as the boss, you want to make sure that your hired hand is delivering the results you expect.

To check up on your portfolio manager, click the Transactions tab and then click the Comparison tab. Select your mutual fund account on the left. You see a chart containing information some mutual fund managers might prefer you didn't know. Mint.com sizes up your mutual fund account's performance relative to other major stock market indexes. When you see green, the mutual fund account is beating the market, and the managers are delivering better than average returns. If you see red, the mutual fund account is lagging the market, meaning you're paying fees for subpar performance.

You can size up your mutual fund account against various market indexes, including the S&P 500, which is a popular measure of the biggest U.S. stocks, the Dow Jones Industrial Average, a widely watched gauge of the market, or the tech-heavy Nasdaq composite index. To change the benchmark that you're comparing your mutual fund account against, just click the option next to the index's name. You can also change the time period in which you evaluate your mutual fund accounts performance.

If your mutual fund account is consistently lagging the market, and the chart on the Comparison tab is usually red, it might be time to find another mutual fund. Index mutual funds are often great alternatives to actively managed funds because of their low fees. And because index mutual funds own the stocks in a major index, such as the S&P 500, you never have to worry about lagging the market.

# Chapter 19

# Buying and Selling Stocks

*Y*ou don't have to be a famous investor like Warren Buffett or Peter Lynch to buy and sell stocks. You don't even need a high-powered broker. Thanks to the stock market, you, too, can own pieces of some of the best-known companies in the world.

The costs of buying and selling stocks have plummeted, and these lower costs make investing accessible to more people than ever before. You can buy stocks indirectly by investing in a stock mutual fund (the topic of Chapter 18), or you can select individual stocks, the topic of this chapter. You discover some of the traits to look for when investing in companies and find out how to get started investing in stocks by opening a brokerage account and linking your account to Mint.com.

# Deciding Whether to Buy Stocks

You might be surprised at how often you interact with companies you can invest in. A spin through the grocery store presents you with goods from companies ranging from ConAgra to Kraft and Starbucks. Driving down the street might bring you in contact with companies such as Ford, ExxonMobil, and Federal Signal. Even Mint.com's parent company, Intuit, has stock.

You're surrounded by goods and services sold by companies that are *publicly traded*, which means they have shares that anyone can buy or sell. These *shares* are small pieces of ownership in the company. With just a few mouse clicks, you can become a partial owner of some of the world's biggest companies.

As companies grow and expand, many of them must raise money. A company can borrow from a bank or investors, but then the company is on the hook to repay the money with interest at a set point in the future. A less costly and more flexible way to raise money is to sell stock.

When you buy stock in a company, you're hoping that the value of your shares will increase over time as the company generates revenue and earnings by selling goods and services. Typically, stock investors make money on stock in the following ways:

- **Dividends:** Sometimes companies make so much profit that they don't know what to do with it. When this situation occurs, companies may decide to pay out cash to their shareholders in periodic payouts called *dividends*. The size of the dividend is usually expressed as a percentage of the price of a stock, or its *dividend yield*. If a company pays $1 a year in dividends and its stock price is $20 a share, it has a dividend yield of 5 percent. So if you invested $1,000 in the company, you would receive $50 in dividends during the year.

- **Changes in the stock price:** If the company you own a piece of becomes more valuable to other investors, the stock price rises. You can sell your shares at any time because investors are free to buy and sell shares of publicly traded companies on marketplaces called *exchanges*. Trading on exchanges such as the New York Stock Exchange and Nasdaq determines a *market value*, or a tally of what the shares of the company are worth.

Don't think that dividends are only for risk-adverse investors. Dividends are a critical piece of your *total return* on a stock, or the ultimate profit you make from both dividends and stock price changes. Dividends can account for a third or more of your total return or even be the only money you make if the value of your stocks falls, as you can see in Table 19-1.

| Table 19-1 | Dividends Are a Big Source of Stock Gains | | |
|---|---|---|---|
| **Year** | **Stock Price Change** | **Dividend Yield** | **Total Return from Dividend** |
| 2009 | 23.5% | 3.0% | 11.4% |
| 2008 | -37.0% | 1.5% | n/a |
| 2007 | 3.5% | 2.0% | 35.8% |
| 2006 | 13.6% | 2.2% | 13.8% |
| 2005 | 3.0% | 1.9% | 38.9% |

*Source: Standard & Poor's, based on the S&P 500 market index*

## Owning stock versus other investments

With so many investment and savings instruments competing for your cash, you might wonder why you would want to bother with stocks. After all, if you just want to invest your money, you could just buy a mutual fund, as described in Chapter 18. And if you're looking to park your money in a safe place, you can put it in a savings account.

But stocks are worthwhile for several reasons:

- ✔ **Superior historic returns:** When it comes to places where your money can grow, it's tough to top stocks. Over the long term, stocks have posted total returns of 9.8 percent a year on average since 1926, according to Morningstar. That return blows away the 5.9 percent return of bonds issued by companies. *Bonds,* or financial instruments that pay interest in exchange for you lending your money, are investments that often compete with stocks. And stocks certainly trounce the interest paid by savings accounts, where you get 2 percent a year in interest if you're lucky.

  The past 10 years haven't been good for stocks, as you can see in Table 19-1. But don't make the mistake of thinking stocks are a bum investment because they've been disappointing lately. When you buy stock, you're investing in companies, and over time, stock prices will catch up to a company's revenue and profit.

- ✔ **Control:** When you buy individual stocks, you're the boss. You decide when you buy and sell stocks, and which companies you'll invest in. This added control can be beneficial if you think you have the ability to find companies with the best prospects and know how to buy stocks at the right time and for a good price. And at tax time, you decide when to sell winning stocks, which may result in *capital gains* that you must pay tax on, or sell losing stocks, which may reduce your tax bill. Investments such as mutual funds put most of the control of timing in the hands of a portfolio manager, who determines when stocks are bought or sold. Mutual funds can cause unfavorable tax situations, as described in Chapter 18.

- ✔ **Priced during the day:** Stocks constantly trade on exchanges, so you see exactly what a stock is worth, or its *market value,* at any time. The constant availability of market values of stocks is a big difference with mutual funds, whose value is known only at the end of trading.

## *Downsides to investing in individual stocks*

Stocks have great advantages over other investments, which probably explains why some people spend so much time thinking about which stocks to buy and dreaming of that big trade that will make them millions. But unlike Warren Buffett, we don't always know which stocks to buy and sell. Investing in individual stocks has the following drawbacks:

✔ **Higher risk:** When you invest in an individual company, you're placing great trust in the management team and the company's future. If the company makes a mistake or, worse yet, commits a fraud, your money is at risk. For instance, stock investors lost practically all their money when dozens of banks failed in the wake of the mortgage crisis that began in 2007. Stocks tend to be riskier than other investments, including bonds. The prices of stocks can fluctuate wildly as investors react to news about a company's financials. Extreme volatility and exposure to nasty bear markets can cause investors to lose their heads and make big mistakes.

If you choose the wrong stock or pay too much, you can lose all your money. This extra risk you're taking is the tradeoff to getting a shot at the superior returns generated by stocks. If you're not willing to accept the risk of stocks, you have to accept the lower returns from bonds or a savings account.

✔ **Time consuming:** You can't just buy individual stocks and forget about them, as people tend to do with mutual fund investments. You're an owner of the company, so it's up to you to monitor the company's management team and profit forecasts. You also have to be prepared to sell the stock if you're wrong.

✔ **Requires expertise:** When you invest in individual stocks, you need to research companies and investments. You must be familiar with a company's financial statements, including its income statement and balance sheet. You also need to understand how much to pay for a stock, which is its *valuation*. The following section gives you a rundown of some of the things to consider when investing in individual stocks. For details on selecting stocks, see *Fundamental Analysis For Dummies* by Matt Krantz.

# Are exchange-traded funds the best of both worlds?

Stocks or mutual funds? Individual stocks give you control and real-time market value information but require more work and increase your exposure to company-specific issues. Mutual funds require less work than stocks because you're paying a portfolio manager to handle your money, but mutual funds take away control.

If you're having trouble deciding between stocks and mutual funds, *exchange-traded funds*, or ETFs, might be perfect for you. Like shares of individual stock, ETFs constantly trade on market exchanges. You buy ETFs in the same way you buy shares of any stock, such as General Electric or Microsoft. However, ETFs have a big edge over individual stocks because they resemble mutual funds. ETFs may trade like an individual stock, but they own a basket of individual investments much like mutual funds do. You can buy one ETF, for instance, that owns all 500 stocks in the S&P 500 index.

It gets better. Many of the top brokerage firms, including Vanguard, Fidelity, and Schwab, allow investors to buy and sell select ETFs without paying trading fees, or *commissions*. ETFs charge annual fees to investors, but these fees are usually much less than those charged by similar mutual funds. In many ways, ETFs have become a dream investment for investors. And yes, Mint.com can track all your ETFs so that you can stay on top of your portfolio online.

# Types of Investors

Famous athletes often say they visualize what success will look like. Basketball stars, for instance, might imagine a perfect shot that wins the championship. Leading surfers dream about the perfect wave.

The same power of visualization goes on in the mind of investors, minus the cheering crowd or beautiful beach. Before you set up a brokerage account or buy your first stock, it's worthwhile to think about what kind of investor you want to be. The first distinction is between a buy-and-hold investor or an active trader:

- **Buy-and-hold investor:** This type of investor chooses individual stocks, or even ETFs, and holds on no matter what. Even if the world appears to be coming to an end, buy-and-hold investors don't sell; in fact, they might even buy more shares at the lower price. Buy-and-hold investors don't worry about trading commissions because they don't trade frequently.

- **Active trader:** This type of investor is constantly reacting to news and developments with individual stocks. Active traders attempt to get a leg up on other investors by looking for patterns in the ways stocks have been trading so they can guess at the future. Other active traders might look at a company's financial reports and try to predict whether the profit will be better or worse than expected in the near future. Active traders care quite a bit about commissions because they trade so much.

After you think about what kind of investor you want to be, you need to decide what kind of brokerage account to use. When you sign up for a brokerage account, you're asked if you want a taxable account or a retirement account:

- **Taxable account:** This type of account is the standard brokerage account that has tax considerations. If a stock you own is worth more than the price you paid, you have an *unrealized capital gain.* If you sell that stock, the profit is a realized *capital gain,* which is taxable. Similarly, if a stock you own is worth less than the price you paid, you have an *unrealized capital loss.* If you sell that stock, you have a *realized capital loss,* which you may be able to use to offset realized capital gains at tax time.

- **Retirement account:** The government gives this type of account special tax treatment. Retirement brokerage accounts are established to give you a tax break when saving for retirement. When you buy and sell stocks in a retirement account, you likely won't trigger any tax events. Many types of retirement accounts are available; see Chapter 16 for more information.

# Finding a Brokerage

Mint.com analyzes your portfolio by pulling in stock information from your brokerage firm. Note that you can't buy or sell stocks through Mint.com.

You first need to choose a brokerage firm. Dozens are available, each catering to a different type of investor. Choosing a brokerage firm is an important decision because that firm will be your partner in managing your money. Most brokerages are in one of three main categories:

- ✔ **Deep discounters:** The bargain players among brokers, deep discounters offer the lowest commissions to buy and sell stock, often charging $5 or less. These low commissions can save you money if you trade frequently. Examples of deep discounters are BUYandHOLD, FolioInvesting, Sharebuilder, SogoTrade, and Zecco.

  Not all brokerage firms support Mint.com, such as TradeKing, a popular deep discounter. Before signing up with a broker, check to see whether the brokerage account will link up with Mint.com. Click the Your Accounts link, click the Add button, type the firm's name, and then click the Search button. If the brokerage doesn't appear, Mint.com doesn't support it.

- ✔ **Discounters:** This category represents the sweet spot of reasonable commissions in addition to amenities not offered by the deep discounters. With most discounters, trades cost less than $10, and you often get access to physical branch locations as well as human financial advisors or unique online tools. Leading discounters include Charles Schwab, E*TRADE, Fidelity, OptionsXpress, Scottrade, TD Ameritrade, and Vanguard.

- ✔ **Premium discounters:** This type of brokerage charges the highest commission but offers a broad array of other financial services, such as savings accounts, insurance, and estate planning. Premium discounters charge more than $10 a trade for most customers but might offer deals for investors who have established relationships with the brokerage. Ameriprise, Banc of America, and Wells Fargo are premium discounters. Banc of America and Wells Fargo, however, offer some free trades to investors with balances of $25,000 or more.

Choosing the right brokerage hinges on a variety of variables. The major considerations when evaluating brokers include commissions and other fees, availability of financial advice, and quality of the Web site. Try out an online brokerage's site before committing to it.

Mint.com can help you decide which brokerage to choose. Click the Ways to Save tab and then click the Brokerage tab. You see a screen like the one in Figure 19-1, where you can step though many of the important considerations when choosing a broker. You are asked how many times a year you buy or sell stocks and mutual funds, and the commission you pay. If you don't have a brokerage, use the default values.

You can also enter any fees you pay, how much cash you have in your account, and the interest rate on that cash. Mint.com then displays various brokerages and how much you could save if you opened an account. You can limit the search results using the options on the left. And if you click the Show Savings Calculations link under the broker's name, you can see all the fees the broker charges.

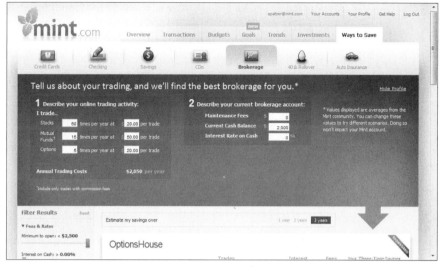

**Figure 19-1:**
A list of
brokerages
and
promotional
offers.

Be skeptical of the brokerages you see listed because the ones labeled *spon-sored* pay to appear on the site. The information is useful, but be sure you expand your search to include deep discounters, discounters, and premium discounters who don't pay to be included.

# Understanding Key Traits of Stocks

Mint.com is designed to help you analyze your portfolio after you've selected stocks, not to help you prospect for stocks. For more information on choosing stocks, see *Investing Online For Dummies,* 7th Edition, by Matt Krantz; *Stock Investing For Dummies,* 3rd Edition, by Paul Mladjenovic; and *Fundamental Analysis For Dummies* by Matt Krantz.

Choosing the right stocks is no small undertaking, and you can evaluate stocks in countless ways. Following are a few of the basic stock investing terms you should be familiar with:

- ✔ **Stock or ticker symbol:** All publicly traded stocks that are bought and sold on exchanges are given descriptive abbreviations called *stock symbols* or *ticker symbols*. These symbols, which are usually three or four letters, make it easy for investors and traders to refer to particular stocks. Mint.com uses stock symbols to show the stocks you own.

- ✔ **Shares outstanding:** Companies usually issue thousands or millions of shares of stock. These shares are then held by the public and traded. The *shares outstanding* is the total number of shares in the public's hands.

✔ **Stock price:** The rapid-fire buying and selling of a company's stock creates a going price for the shares called the stock price. The *stock price* is the value investors place on owning one of a company's outstanding shares.

✔ **Style:** Stocks are frequently classified by whether their style is growth or value. *Growth stocks,* which tend to command high stock prices relative to their profits, are also described as stocks with a high *valuation.* Growth stocks get lots of media attention because they're in a fast-growing industry or are leaders in their markets. *Value stocks* tend to be the ones with low stock prices relative to their financial performance. Value stocks usually come from slow-growing industries or have seemingly poor prospects.

✔ **Market value:** The price tag investors put on an entire company is called its *market value.* Market value is simply a stock's price multiplied by the number of its outstanding shares. Investors use market value to determine whether a company is small, midsized, or large, as shown in Table 19-2.

| Table 19-2 | What's Big and What's Small? |
|---|---|
| *Asset Class* | *Market Value* |
| Large | Greater than $8.2 billion |
| Medium | Greater than $975 million but less than $8.2 billion |
| Small | Greater than $140 million but less than $975 million |
| Micro | Less than $140 million |

*Source: Standard & Poor's*

# Tracking Your Stocks

Before you can track your stock with Mint.com, you must first open an online brokerage account. Nearly all online brokerages make signing up for an account straightforward:

1. **Visit the brokerage's Web site.**

2. **Click the Open an Account link.**

   You find this link or something similar on the front page of every broker's Web site. Figure 19-2 shows you Fidelity's open an account page.

3. **Select the type of brokerage account you want.**

   Typically, the account will be a taxable account or a retirement account, such as an individual retirement account, or IRA.

4. **Enter your personal information.**

   Most brokerages ask for your name, address, birth date, and Social Security number.

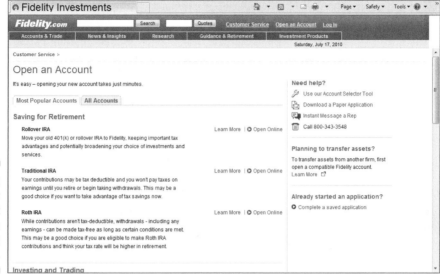

**Figure 19-2:**
Fidelity
makes it
easy to
open an
account.

5. **Select a user ID and password.**

   This information allows you to access your broker's Web site. You use your user ID and password to link your brokerage account to your Mint. com account.

6. **Fund your account.**

   To trade, you need to put money in your brokerage account. You can transmit money electronically from a savings or checking account or mail a check.

## Adding your brokerage account

Next, you need to link your brokerage account to your Mint.com account. Mint.com reads your brokerage account just as it reads your other financial accounts, such as your savings or checking accounts.

To connect your brokerage account to Mint.com, follow these steps:

1. **Click the Your Accounts link.**

2. **Click the blue Add button.**

   The Add button is designated with a plus sign.

3. **Type your brokerage's name and then click Search.**

   Type as much of the brokerage's name as possible in the Enter Your Bank's Name or URL field.

4. **Select the name of your brokerage.**

   If your broker doesn't appear, try Step 3 again but type fewer letters. If your broker still doesn't appear in the list, Mint.com might not support the firm.

5. **Enter your user ID and password.**

   You received your user ID and password when you signed up for the account; you use this information to log in to the broker's Web site. Mint.com connects with your brokerage firm, imports your financial information, and lists the brokerage account on the Overview tab under the Investments heading, as shown in Figure 19-3.

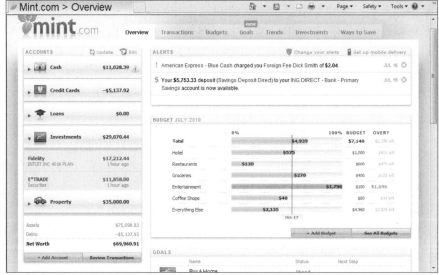

**Figure 19-3:**
Accounts are displayed on the left side of the Overview tab.

If you simply want to see the value of your stock portfolio, you're finished. The balances of your brokerage accounts are displayed on the left side of the screen.

## Understanding the nitty-gritty of transactions

You probably have your own method for selecting stocks. You might pore over companies' financial statements, including their income statement or balance sheet. You might analyze the patterns in historical stock price changes. Heck, you might even check with your astrologer for stock picks.

Mint.com doesn't concern itself with how you pick stocks. And it doesn't pass judgment on the stocks you do decide to buy.

You can use Mint.com to track your every move and record every significant event that occurs in your brokerage account. Mint.com calls these events *transactions*. When it comes to your brokerage account, Mint.com concerns itself with the following types of transactions:

- ✔ **Buys:** When you click the buy button on your broker's Web site, congrats! You're now the proud owner of stock. After you buy stock, Mint. com tracks the symbol of the stock you bought, the number of shares you bought, and the price you paid.

- ✔ **Sells:** So that investment in Enron stock didn't work out so well? When you finally sell a stock, either because it didn't pan out or you want to lock in gains, Mint.com, records the price you sold at and the number of shares that you sold.

- ✔ **Dividends:** Many companies pay *dividends,* or periodic payments of cash to shareholders. Mint.com tallies all your dividends.

- ✔ **Deposits:** You have to have money to make money, right? You might add money to your brokerage account from time to time as you save excess cash. Mint.com makes sure the money you're sending to your brokerage firm appears in your brokerage account.

- ✔ **Withdrawals:** Brokerage accounts are good places to stuff money that you don't need right away. But you might need to yank cash out of your brokerage account to pay for a big bill or to shift money to a retirement account. Mint.com tracks these withdrawals.

You could always log in to your brokerage's Web site to see all your transactions. But if you use Mint.com, you can view all your transactions and easily compare the size of your checking and savings accounts to the size of your brokerage account.

Accessing your investment transactions is Mint.com is just a matter of following a few steps:

1. **Click the Transactions tab.**

   This tab is Grand Central Station when it comes to looking for movement in your investment accounts.

2. **Click the Investment option.**

   You see all transactions in all your investment accounts.

3. **Zero in on a specific investment account.**

   If you want to look at just the transactions in a single investment account, scroll down the Transactions tab. On the left, you see a list of your individual brokerage accounts. Select the name of the individual brokerage account, and you see just the transactions from that account, as shown in Figure 19-4.

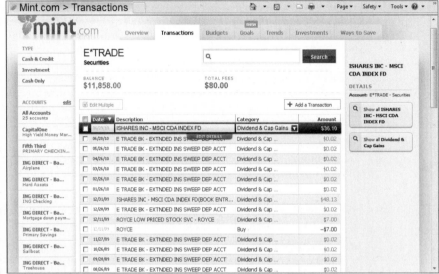

Figure 19-4:
See the
comings
and goings
in your
brokerage
accounts.

Now that you've accessed your brokerage transactions, it's time to see what Mint.com tells you about them. For each transaction, Mint.com displays four pieces of data:

✔ **Date:** This is the date on which the transaction occurred.

✔ **Description:** Your brokerage provides an abbreviated summary of what the transaction was, such as a stock buy or sell. The description also contains the identification of the stock that was bought or sold, although it might not provide the stock's symbol.

✔ **Category:** Every investment transaction is grouped according to its type, or *category*. Mint.com has one Investments category broken into five subcategories: Buy, Sell, Withdrawal, Deposit, and Dividend & Cap Gains. Cap Gains, short for capital gains, in this case refers to the periodic payments that you may get from investments, often mutual funds, when assets are sold for a profit.

Sometimes Mint.com puts transactions in the wrong subcategories, so take a spin through your transactions and make sure they're grouped correctly. If they're not, you can change them manually by selecting the correct subcategory from the drop-down list.

✔ **Amount:** This is the dollar value of the transaction. Suppose you buy 100 shares of a stock for $10 a share. The amount of the transaction is $1,000.

On the Transactions tab, you can do more than just look at your transactions. With just a few mouse clicks, the Transactions tab lets you see where your money is coming or going in the brokerage account.

Just click any transaction in the list. On the right side of the screen, you see two useful buttons. Click the first Show All button to see all transactions pertaining to the stock you've selected. The second Show All button is even more useful. Click it to see all transactions in the same category. For instance, if you click the button after clicking a buy transaction, you see a list of all your stock buys.

## Taking stock

With just a few mouse clicks, you can see if all the effort you're putting into choosing stocks is paying off. This kind of stock analysis is called *performance*.

To see how your portfolio is doing, click the Investments tab and then click the Performance tab. You see a chart that tells you whether you're making or losing money, as shown in Figure 19-5.

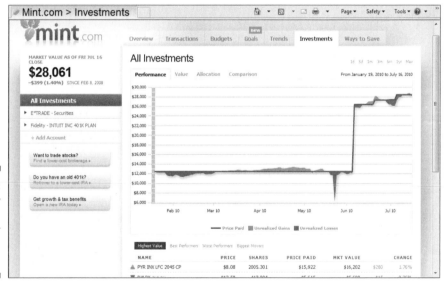

**Figure 19-5:** See how much money your stocks are making.

The Performance chart shows three key pieces of information:

- **Price you paid for the stocks:** The grey line in the middle of the chart is the price you've paid to buy all the stocks in your portfolio.

  If a brokerage account you added to your Mint.com account already contained stocks, mutual funds, and other investments, Mint.com will likely record the price as the value the day you added the brokerage account to Mint.com. This may or may not be the actual amount you paid for the stock or mutual fund and is an important consideration when looking at an investment's overall performance.

✔ **Times you're making money:** Above and below the grey line are areas of green and red. If you see green, the value of your stocks are worth more than the price you paid. In other words, you're making money. Hover your cursor over the green patches on the chart to see your exact unrealized gain at that point in time. If you have unrealized gains, selling these stocks could incur a tax bill.

Mint.com provides a useful guide when it comes to managing your potential tax hit when it comes to investments, but the site isn't powerful enough to rely on. For instance, Mint.com does not keep track of *tax lots*, which is something the Internal Revenue Service requires. Suppose you buy 100 shares of stock ABC in January for $10 a share. This is your first lot. In March, you buy another 100 shares of ABC for $15 a share. This is your second lot. A few months later, you sell 100 shares for $15. Did you have a gain or a loss on the stock sale? That depends on which lot you say you sold. If you say you sold the first lot, you have a realized capital gain of $5 a share, which is taxable. If you say you sold the second lot, there's no gain and therefore no tax. If you're a serious investor, you'll need to track your tax lots. Most brokers' Web sites will track your tax lots for you. You might also consider using Intuit's Quicken personal finance software to track your portfolio because it contains many more investment features than Mint.com, including tax lot accounting. For instance, Quicken can measure your portfolio's total return, which is something Mint.com may not be able to do for all your investments.

✔ **Times you're losing money:** If you're like most people, you're not always in the green with your stocks. Red areas in the chart indicate periods where your portfolio is worth less than what you paid, or an unrealized loss. Again, you can mouse over the red sections of the chart to see exactly how much you're down.

If you have unrealized losses, consider selling them. Realized capital losses can be used to reduce your tax liability from winning stocks you've sold.

Below the chart is a listing of all the stocks in your portfolio, including the stock's current price, the number of shares you own, the price you paid, the current market value, and the dollar amount you're up or down. You can sort the list to show the individual stocks that are your biggest winners or your biggest dogs.

Mint.com lets you evaluate the performance of your portfolio for several different time frames if you click the 1d, 5d, 1m, 3m, 6m, 1yr, and Max links in the upper-right corner. Those links show the performance for the past day, five days, one month, three months, six months, year, and lifetime of your account, respectively.

You can view the performance of all your investment accounts as a whole or drill down to study how one stock is doing. You can control how specific or general Mint.com is by using the links on the left. Click the name of the brokerage to see only the performance of that particular brokerage account. If you click the arrow next to the name of the brokerage firm, you can drill down even further to see how specific stocks in the brokerage account are doing, as shown in Figure 19-6.

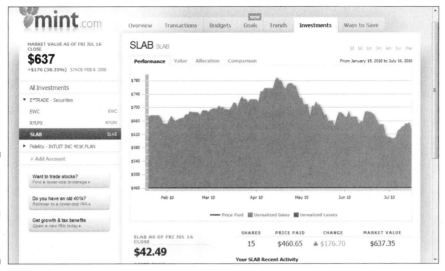

**Figure 19-6:**
Examine
the perfor-
mance of
individual
stocks.

## *Measuring your stock portfolio growth*

If you just want to know whether your stock portfolio is increasing in value
and are not concerned about performance, Mint.com has a simpler chart you
might like. Click the Value option under the Transactions tab to see a series
of bars that indicate how much your brokerage account is worth over time,
as shown in Figure 19-7.

You can analyze the value of your holdings by different time periods, and you
can look at all your investment accounts or just individual stocks by clicking
the selections on the left side of the page.

## *Investigating your portfolio allocation*

If you've been buying many stocks and other investments, your brokerage
account can become a jumble. You might even buy mutual funds using a brokerage firm. And as you deposit money to your brokerage account and buy
investments, things can get somewhat cluttered.

The Allocation option on the Investments tab makes sense of even the most
chaotic brokerage account. From the Allocation screen, you can view the
types of investments that make up your portfolio in terms of the following:

✔ **The types of investments you own:** Click the Asset Type button under
 the chart to see a pie chart that breaks down your investment accounts
 into cash, stocks, and mutual funds, as shown in Figure 19-8.

✔ **Big holdings in individual stocks:** Click the Symbol button under the chart to see a pie chart with the skinny on which individual stocks and mutual funds have the largest weighting in your account.

**Figure 19-7:**
See how much your portfolio is worth at different times.

If one stock makes up a big slice of your brokerage account, your portfolio might not be properly *diversified*, or spread over different types of investments. Not being diversified exposes you to risk if one of your big holdings doesn't work out well.

## Making sure you're a good stock picker

You wouldn't drive your car blindfolded. But many investors do the financial equivalent of driving with their eyes closed. It's common for investors to go on buying and selling investments, assuming that they're doing a great job, without knowing for sure.

Prepare to meet your most honest critic: Mint.com. The Transactions tab contains a Comparison option that sizes up the performance of your portfolio next to major *stock market indexes*. Stock market indexes are statistical measures that tell you how the market is doing. Mint.com can compare your performance against several popular indexes, including

✔ **Dow Jones Industrial Average:** The Dow is a popular measure of how the stock market is doing based on the performance of 30 large and widely held stocks.

✔ **S&P 500:** The S&P 500 is a widely accepted gauge of how large companies are doing, based on the performance of 500 stocks. Stocks that have the largest market values are given greater weight in the S&P 500's value.

✔ **Nasdaq composite index:** The Nasdaq measures how the top stocks on the Nasdaq exchange are faring. Because the Nasdaq is home to many smaller companies and technology stocks, it tends to be more volatile than the Dow and S&P 500.

If your portfolio is consistently lagging the S&P 500, it might be time to take a hint and hang up this stock-picking thing. If you're not beating the S&P 500, you're much better off buying an index mutual fund or ETF that invests in all the stocks in the S&P 500. You'll save time and money buying and holding an investment that invests in an index rather than trying to beat the market.

**Figure 19-8:** The stocks, mutual funds, and other investments in your account.

# Chapter 20

# Exploring Alternatives for Your Money

. . . . . . . . . . . . . . . . . . . . . . . . . . . . . . . . . . . . . . . . . . . . . . . . . . . .

## In This Chapter

▶ Tracking savings and banking products

▶ Finding bank accounts that fit your needs

▶ Getting up to speed with bonds

▶ Evaluating and monitoring commodities

▶ Valuing tangible assets

. . . . . . . . . . . . . . . . . . . . . . . . . . . . . . . . . . . . . . . . . . . . . . . . . . . .

*E*ver been to a cocktail party where people were bragging about the 0.01 percent interest they're collecting on their checking accounts? Didn't think so. Bank accounts aren't exciting. Stocks and mutual funds tend to get most of the attention because they're usually the most volatile and exciting parts of your financial portfolio to watch. However, don't make the mistake of overlooking other kinds of accounts or investments just because they aren't as glamorous as stocks.

In this chapter, you examine ways to put your cash to use with better bank accounts. You also see how bonds can bolster your portfolio. Finally, you consider various tangible assets as possible alternative investments and see how your collectibles contribute to your overall financial wealth.

## Taking It to the Bank

Cowboys in the Wild West had low expectations from their banks. They'd put money on deposit in a bank in a dusty town, figuring that leaving it there was safer than taking a chance of losing it all in a hold-up.

You might have similar expectations from your bank. Banks, especially ones with physical branches, are infamous for paying low interest rates on money you put on deposit with them. The interest that banks pay you on your money is the *APY*, or *annual percentage yield.* Don't write off bank accounts, though. Bank deposits are safe if the institution is a member of the Federal Deposit Insurance Corp., or FDIC. Your money — up to $250,000 per person per bank — is safe even if your bank goes kaput.

Never put your money in a bank that does not have FDIC insurance. Check www.fdic.gov to make sure your bank is covered. If your bank isn't covered, get another bank.

## Getting better bank deals

Mint.com does quite a bit of the legwork required to make sure your bank accounts are pulling their financial weight. But before you can search to see whether another bank account might be better, you need to know the ins and outs of what you're getting from your bank accounts right now. You should know the following details about your bank accounts:

- **Account type:** The variety of account you have with the bank. Mint.com tracks savings accounts, checking accounts, money market accounts, and certificates of deposit. *Checking accounts* are pools of money you primarily use for paying your bills. Checking accounts typically pay you very little interest or no interest. *Savings accounts* are holding tanks for money you don't need immediately but can tap quickly if needed. Savings accounts usually pay more interest than checking accounts. *Money market accounts* restrict your access to cash, often requiring that you write no more than a particular number of checks a month, but sometimes pay higher interest rates than savings accounts. *Certificates of deposit,* or *CDs,* are bank savings instruments that pay the highest rates of interest. But CDs usually lock up your money for a set period of time, and if you take the money out before the CD matures, you may be hit with a penalty. You can compare interest rates on different account types at www.bankrate.com.

Be sure that you know what you're getting when you put cash into a money market account. Some money market deposit accounts offered by banks are insured by the FDIC, but other popular money market mutual funds are not insured by the FDIC. Know what you're buying.

- **APY:** The annual percentage yield, or the rate of interest the bank is paying you to borrow your money. The APY is perhaps the most important factor when evaluating your bank accounts. APY is measured by dividing the amount of interest you're paid a year by the amount you've deposited. If you receive $10 a year from your $1,000 deposit, your APY is 1 percent.

- **Total balance:** The amount of money you have on deposit with the bank.

- **Length of deposit:** If you're willing to buy a certificate of deposit and leave your money untouched for months or years, you're likely to get a higher APY compared with a regular savings account you can tap anytime. Just know that for a higher APY, you're giving up some of your money's availability.

✔ **Monthly fee:** The charge a bank hits you with to have an account.

✔ **Minimum no fee balance:** How much money you must keep in your account to avoid paying a monthly fee or other service fee.

When sizing up your bank, Mint.com doesn't ask whether you need access to a physical branch. You may not need access to a bank branch if your paychecks are deposited electronically and your bank provides free access to ATMs to withdraw cash. Many banks that don't have physical branches may reimburse fees you're charged when you use other banks' ATMs. But if you routinely deposit checks or cash, a bank branch will be handy.

To evaluate your bank situation, you need to add your existing financial accounts to Mint.com. See Chapter 2 for information on adding your bank account. Then take a quick spin through your accounts and make sure the critical information is entered and correct:

1. **Click the Overview tab and then click the Your Accounts link.**

   The Your Accounts window appears.

2. **Click the Financial tab.**

   The Financial tab contains a list of all your bank accounts.

3. **Select each bank account.**

   For any account you hold with a bank, hover your mouse over the name of the account in the list. Select the Edit Details option when it appears.

4. **Review the account details.**

   Make sure the information is correct, paying special attention to the bank account's APY, as shown in Figure 20-1. You might need to visit the bank's Web site to make sure the information in Mint.com is current and accurate.

   Mint.com often has zeroes in the fields, so don't overlook this step. If the numbers in the Edit Details screen are not updated, Mint.com's recommendations will not be helpful.

# Getting smarter with the lowly savings account

When it comes to saving your money, few options are less glamorous than the savings account. You've probably had a savings account since you were a kid. Savings accounts have a common shortcoming: They often pay low interest rates relative to other financial accounts or investments. But that doesn't mean you have to settle for a savings account that pays the lowest interest rate. Mint.com can help you see whether you can do better.

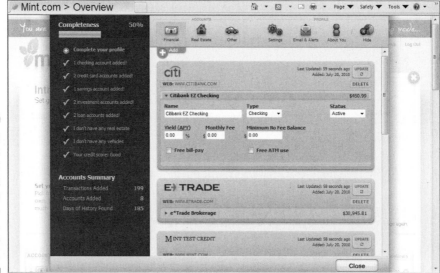

**Figure 20-1:**
Check the
details of all
your bank
accounts
before rely-
ing on Mint.
com's sug-
gestions.

Finding a savings account with a higher APY isn't going to make you rich. Let's say you have $5,000 deposited with your bank and your bank pays you 0.5 percent a year in interest. That's equal to $25 a year in interest. If you're lucky, Mint.com will find a savings account paying 1.25 percent a year, which is $62.50 a year. Sure, extra cash is always welcome, but we're not talking about a huge bonanza here.

Evaluating your savings account and looking for a better alternative is simple:

1. **Log in to Mint.com.**

2. **Click the Ways to Save tab.**

   The tab is located at the top of all pages in Mint.com.

3. **Select the Savings tab.**

   This tab is labeled with an icon that looks like a sack of money.

4. **Double-check the assumptions.**

   You see the average total balance and current APY on your current savings accounts. If these numbers aren't correct, refer to the steps in the preceding section to adjust the details.

5. **If you want to change Mint.com's assumptions without revising your account details, type new numbers for the average total balance and current APY.**

   You can adjust the assumptions also by using the sliders.

6. **Limit the results.**

   You see various savings accounts and how much you could save by switching to a new account. Use the sliders shown in Figure 20-2 to eliminate banks or savings accounts that don't offer features you need, such as free ATM withdrawals.

7. **Dig into the numbers.**

   Click a bank's Show Savings Calculations tab to see the considerations Mint.com makes to estimate how much this savings account could save you.

**Figure 20-2:** See if you'll save by switching your savings account to another bank.

Savings accounts are especially well-suited for your *emergency fund*, or a pool of cash you can tap in case your financial situation takes a turn for the worse. If you're curious how much money you should have in an emergency fund, check out the Save for an Emergency goal in the Goals tab. For details on starting an Emergency fund, see Chapter 11.

## Checking in on your checking accounts

The term *checking account* is a misnomer because many consumers don't write paper checks out of their checking accounts. Most banks attach online bill payment services to checking accounts, so you can pay all your bills without writing a check or using your debit or ATM card.

To see whether you have the best checking account, log into Mint.com, click the Ways to Save tab and then click the Checking tab. You see a list of checking account offers that you might want to consider, as shown in Figure 20-3. Again, be sure to check the assumptions Mint.com makes about your current checking account before relying on the results.

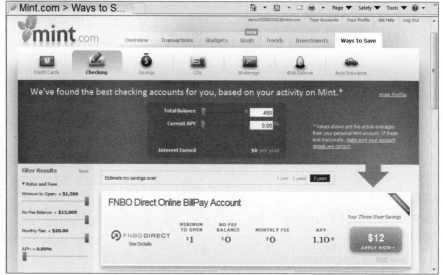

**Figure 20-3:** See if you're getting the best deal on your checking account.

# You don't need a CD player for these CDs

Certificates of deposit, or CDs, typically offer much higher APYs than savings accounts and come with FDIC protection, if the bank offering them is covered. But CDs have a serious downside, too. When you buy a CD, you're agreeing to not touch the money until a set time in the future, called the *maturity date.* If something comes up and you need the money sooner, you'll probably pay an early withdrawal penalty.

To evaluate whether it's worthwhile to move money from a savings or checking account into a CD and to find which CDs might be the best deal for you, follow these steps:

1. **Log in to Mint.com.**

2. **Click the Ways to Save tab and then click the CDs tab.**

3. **Provide your saving timeline.**

   Using the How Long Do You Plan to Invest? drop-down menu, select how long you'd be comfortable leaving your money locked in a CD, from three months to five years.

**4. Indicate where the money will come from.**

Select the bank accounts that you will use to fund the CD.

**5. Review the results.**

You see a list of all bank CD offers that might help you earn more on your money, as shown in Figure 20-4. You can limit the results to certain banks or only CDs offering APYs above certain levels by using the filters on the left.

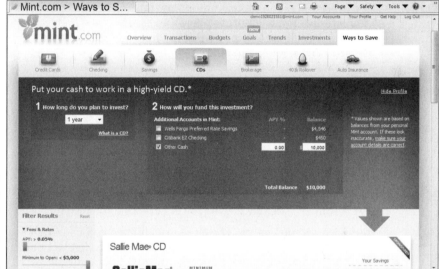

**Figure 20-4:** Parsing through CD offers is simple.

When Mint.com is paid to present a savings account, checking account, or CD on the Ways to Save page, it adds a *Sponsored* banner in the corner of the offer's description. Just because an offer is sponsored doesn't mean it's a bad deal, but you should be aware that the bank is paying Mint.com to advertise to you.

# *Finding Financial Freedom with Bonds*

Savings accounts, checking accounts, and CDs are all fine places to park your money. It's tough to beat the safety of a good, old-fashioned FDIC-insured bank account. But when it comes to generating decent returns or paybacks for lending your money, bank accounts can be lacking.

If you're looking for a better return than you can get from a bank, you'll need to invest rather than save. You're investing when you buy a financial asset with the hope that it will be worth more in the future when it comes time to sell. Investing is riskier than saving: You can lose the money you've invested, but savings are insured.

## What is a bond, anyway?

Mutual funds and stocks might come to mind when you hear the word *invest,* but bonds are another viable investment option. If you've stuffed your savings accounts and are looking for a bigger return and willing to take on some extra risk, bonds might be for you.

*Bonds* are financial obligations sold by governments and companies when they borrow money. When you buy a bond, you receive a promise from the borrower that it will repay your money in full at a preset time with a preset interest rate. The guarantees offered by bonds make them safer investments than stocks historically. And because bonds are riskier than savings accounts and aren't insured by the FDIC, bonds have better returns than bank deposit accounts historically.

## Getting up to speed with bonds

We can't spell out everything you need to know about bonds in a single chapter. But you should know the following key terms if bonds sound like something you want to try out and track in your Mint.com account:

- ✔ **Maturity:** The day the borrower promises to give your principal back.

- ✔ **Face (or par) value:** The amount of money you can expect to get back when the bond reaches maturity. The face value of a bond is typically the amount of money the person who first bought the bond lent, or the *principal*.

- ✔ **Interest rate:** The percentage the borrower agreed to pay to the lender for borrowing the money. If you buy a $1,000 bond that pays a 4 percent interest rate, you would be paid $40 a year or $20 twice a year. You also get the $1,000 initial investment back when the bond matures.

- ✔ **Price:** How much you would have to pay to buy a bond now. Bond prices rise and fall as investors buy and sell them amongst themselves. Mint.com calls the current price of your entire holding of a bond investment *market value*.

- ✔ **Price paid:** How much you paid to buy a bond or bond holding.

- ✔ **Current yield:** The interest rate you receive based on the price you paid for a bond. Let's say you paid $900 for a bond with a $1,000 face value that pays 4 percent interest. Your current yield is 4.4 percent, which is the $40 a year in interest you receive, divided by the price you paid, or $900.

- ✔ **Total return:** The sum of all your profits from buying a bond. You can make money from a bond when the price rises or as you collect interest payments.

When you lend money, the most important consideration is who you're loaning cash to. The same goes for bonds. The leading sellers of bonds are

- ✔ **The U.S. government:** Bonds sold by the U.S. government are called *Treasuries*. Treasuries are some of the most popular investments in the world because they're backed by the full faith and credit of the U.S. government. Because Treasuries are considered safe investments, they typically have yields that are lower than similar bonds sold by other borrowers.

- ✔ **Companies:** Companies of all sizes typically borrow money so they can grow and expand. Bonds sold by rock-solid companies with high credit ratings are called *investment grade*. Investment grade bonds tend to have lower yields than Treasuries. Investment grade bonds, though, tend to have higher yields than bonds sold by companies with shaky finances, called *junk,* or *high-yield, bonds.*

- ✔ **Cities and municipalities:** Local governments often borrow money to pay for schools, libraries, and other facilities. Such municipal bonds are attractive to many investors in higher tax brackets because their interest is usually not taxable by the Federal government.

Bonds are complicated financial instruments. Reading this chapter will in no way make you an expert on bond investing. If you'd like to find more about bond investing, check out InvestingInBonds.com or *Bond Investing For Dummies* by Russell Wild.

## Monitoring bonds

If you want to add your bond holdings to your Mint.com account so you can monitor them, you have to buy your bonds in one of the following ways:

- ✔ **Through a brokerage firm that supports Mint.com:** Many discount and premium discount brokerage firms as well as some deep-discount brokerage firms allow you to buy and sell individual bonds. If the brokerage you choose is supported by Mint.com, the program may be able to display the total value of your account, including your bond holdings. Mint.com may also display the value of bond holdings on the Investments tab. If you want help finding a brokerage, review Chapter 19, which digs into the topic at length.

- ✔ **Bond mutual funds:** Just as you can invest in stocks by buying a stock mutual fund, you can invest in bonds with a bond mutual fund. You can buy bond mutual funds through a brokerage firm or directly through a mutual fund company. Either way, you can display your bond mutual fund holdings on the Investments tab. Review Chapter 18 for more on buying and tracking mutual funds.

- ✔ **Bond ETFs:** *Exchange-traded funds* are mutual-fund-like investments that trade like stocks. You can buy a bond ETF using a broker, and instantly, you'll own an investment that has positions in many bonds. Best of all, you can easily add bonds to your portfolio by buying bond ETFs through your existing broker. Mint.com displays your bond ETF holdings in the same way it shows your holdings in all stocks. Because bond ETFs are considered stocks for accounting purposes, you can track them in Mint.com just as you would track your stocks. Review Chapter 19 for a refresher on monitoring your stock portfolio.

Click the Investments tab to see how the value of your brokerage or mutual fund account containing individual bonds, bond mutual funds, or bond ETFs has changed over time. When it comes to measuring the performance of individual bond investments, though, Mint.com has its shortcomings. The program is designed to compare the price you paid for a bond with the current value of the bond, which is a notable limitation in tracking bond performance. Most of the gain you achieve by holding a bond is the *total return*, or the value of the interest payments you receive plus the change in the bond's price. Not factoring in the value of interest payments omits a significant portion of the investment's performance. If you're serious about tracking the performance of individual bonds, bond ETFs, and bond mutual funds, you might want to use your broker's Web site or financial software such as Quicken.

# Investing in Tangible Assets and Commodities

When it comes to most financial accounts, you can't see or touch what you own. When you put money into a savings account or buy a bond, you're entrusting your money with a third party and hope the safeguards are in place for you to get that money when you need it. Mint.com helps you track these intangible financial assets.

Some people, though, prefer investments they can feel, touch or smell, which are called *tangible assets*. Many types of tangible assets are available, but the ones that Mint.com can help you track follow:

- ✔ **Commodities:** Physical goods deemed to have widespread value to many users. Most major commodities are traded on *exchanges,* or marketplaces where buyers and sellers haggle over the price. Common commodities that investors trade include metals such as gold and agricultural products such as corn.

- ✔ **Real estate:** Land or property you can invest in. Homes are common pieces of real estate consumers might buy, but you can invest also in commercial real estate in the form of *real estate investment trusts*, or REITs. You can read more about how to save and pay for a home in Chapter 17.

✔ **Collectibles:** Typically assets accumulated by rich folks, such as antiques, paintings, and rare cars. But collectibles come in many forms, including jewelry, expensive musical instruments, or baseball cards.

Don't confuse tangible assets that are investments with those that are not. A tangible asset is an investment you buy on the reasonable assumption that it will increase in value, or *appreciate*, and you can sell it for a profit later. Land, rare art, and collectible cars are objects that might increase in value, which is why they're sometimes considered investments. Your beat-up car, however, is not an investment because it will likely lose value, or *depreciate*, over time.

## Buying and selling tangible assets

If you're interested in buying and selling tangible assets as investments, you'll need a better understanding of how the marketplace for each asset works. Different tangible assets are bought and sold in varying ways, so before you jump in, you need to know the following:

✔ **Where the tangible assets trade:** Some tangible assets, such as commodities, have highly organized trading systems just as stocks do. Precious metals, agricultural commodities, and energy commodities trade on *futures exchanges*, such as the CME Group's Chicago Mercantile Exchange. But other tangible assets are typically bought and sold between private investors or through distributors. REITs, on the other hand, trade like stocks on stock market exchanges.

Buying tangible assets that do not actively trade on a marketplace can be risky. You could find yourself in a tough spot if you need to sell your bottle-cap collection and can't find a buyer willing to pay a fair price.

✔ **How the tangible asset is valued:** The price of gold that's still in raw form, called *bullion*, is set with active trading through the Chicago Mercantile Exchange. You can look up the price of gold bullion on financial Web sites. But gold coins are collectibles that are typically *rated*, or graded in terms of quality, to help investors determine their worth. Putting a price tag on tangible assets such as fine wine, paintings, or antique cars can be a specialized skill.

## Understanding and investing in commodities

Investing in commodities that actively trade on futures exchanges gives you several advantages over trying to invest in tangible assets that don't. If you stick with tangible assets that have investors constantly buying and selling, you benefit from an established network of competing buyers and sellers. That competition ensures that you can sell your commodities when you need to and that you'll get the highest price when you sell and the lowest price when you buy.

You can buy and sell commodities in many ways, but the two main methods that will let you easily monitor your investments in Mint.com follow:

- **Commodity mutual funds:** Some mutual funds specialize in investing in all sorts of commodities as well as in companies that produce commodities. For instance, you can find mutual funds, or pools of investors' cash used to buy investments, that own stakes in companies that mine for gold and other precious metals. You can read more about how to invest in mutual funds and track them in Chapter 18.

- **Commodity ETFs:** ETFs make it easy to invest in commodities. When you buy a commodity ETF, you purchase a piece of a commodity as easily as you'd buy a share of ExxonMobil stock. Commodity ETFs, like stocks, have ticker symbols, and you can easily buy and sell them using a brokerage account. You can track your commodity ETF holdings using Mint.com just as you monitor your stock portfolio. (For more on tracking stocks, see Chapter 19.) Table 20-1 provides examples of commodity ETFs and which commodities they let you invest in.

| Table 20-1 | | Popular Commodity ETFs |
|---|---|---|
| *Commodity ETF Name* | *Symbol* | *Commodity the ETF Tracks* |
| SPDR Gold Shares | GLD | Gold |
| iShares Silver Trust | SLV | Silver |
| iShares S&P GSCI Commodity-Indexed Trust | GSG | A basket of several commodities designed to mirror the Goldman Sachs Commodity-Index Total Return Index |
| iPath S&P GSCI Crude Oil Total Return Index ETN | OIL | Oil |

## Considering collectibles

Collectibles such as coins, antiques, jewelry, and art don't trade on formal exchanges like stocks. You can log into a stockbroker's site and buy 100 shares of Disney stock, but you can't buy a rare Walt Disney sketch the same way. Collectibles are traded in a variety of ways, including one-on-one transactions, through online auction sites such as eBay, or in live auctions.

Mint.com can't track the ongoing value of collectibles. And in some cases, you don't know what a collectible is worth until you try to sell it. The more unusual a collectible, the more difficult it is to put a price on it.

But the fact that a collectible isn't easy to value doesn't mean it has no value. A collectible might account for a large piece of your financial value, or *net worth*, so you should include it in your Mint.com account. You can add the value of the collectible as follows:

1. **Click the Your Accounts link.**

2. **Click the Other tab.**

3. **Click the blue Add button.**

   The button has a plus sign on it.

4. **Select the Other Property option.**

5. **Select the type of property you own in the list of options and then click Next.**

6. **Name the asset and place a value on it.**

7. **Click the Add It! button.**

   The collectible is added to your list of assets.

You're on the honor system when you value your collectibles and tangible assets. If you cheat, you'll cheat only yourself. If you inflate the value of your collectibles, Mint.com overestimates your net worth, which distorts many of its charts and analyses. See how much similar objects have sold for on eBay to get a better estimate of what things are worth.

# Part V
# The Part of Tens

"That reminds me — I have to figure out how to straighten out my credit report after having my charge cards stolen and used in four different states."

# In this part . . .

Mint.com is chock-full of ways to help you manage your money, and in this part we spotlight aspects of Mint.com that are especially noteworthy.

If you're like many people, you dread preparing for the taxman every spring. With Mint.com, taxes don't have to be the financial equivalent of a painful root canal. The Web site can help you keep your tax papers in order, and this part will show you ten ways to do so.

Much of Mint.com is focused on helping you get the best credit card possible. But one of the best ways to get the best credit card is having a solid credit score. You discover ten ways to boost your reputation in the eyes of credit card issuers and other lenders (not to mention possible future employers) by raising your credit score.

In the last chapter, we share ten hidden gems to using Mint.com.

# Chapter 21

# Ten Ways to Prepare for the Tax Man

**M**ost people would agree that there's no good time to start preparing your tax return. However, tax time just got a lot easier because you have Mint.com in your court. Although you can't prepare your tax return in Mint.com, you can go a long way toward getting your information organized and arranged so that the preparation process becomes relatively painless.

## Tracking Taxes You've Paid

To start preparing for your tax return, look at what you've already paid in taxes during the year. You might pay several different types of taxes, and each kind plays a different role in your income tax return:

- **Federal income tax:** The Federal income tax that is withheld on your paycheck is already in the hands of the government. You can jump through some hoops to have Mint.com keep track of how much of each paycheck went for Federal income tax, but the quickest way to find this number is to look on your W-2 form, which your employer sends you at the end of the year. If you need to know during the year how much tax you've paid, look at your pay stub, which should have a year-to-date tax column. The Federal income tax that you pay during the year is reported on IRS Form 1040 (or 1040A or 1040EZ) and offsets your Federal income tax liability.

- **State and local income tax:** Much like the Federal income tax, income tax at the state and local level is withheld from your paycheck and summarized on your W-2 form and your pay stub. Not only is the state and local income tax reported on your state (and, if applicable, local) income tax return, but taxpayers who itemize their deductions on Schedule A of their Federal income tax return get to report the state and local income tax as a deduction, thus reducing the amount of Federal income tax they owe.

- **FICA and Medicare taxes:** Your paycheck also lists withholding for FICA and Medicare taxes. The only time you need to worry about reporting this information on your income tax return is if you work more than one job and the total FICA withholding from all your jobs exceeds the maximum, which is $6,622 (6.2 percent of $106,800) for 2010. (The amount is indexed for inflation and typically increases each year.) Note that Medicare taxes withheld from your paycheck are not eligible to be claimed as a medical deduction on your tax return.

- **Real estate property tax:** If you own real estate, you probably pay property tax. If you own real estate as part of a condominium community, you still pay property tax on your share of the real estate in the community. If you don't receive a year-end statement from the condo association, ask for one so you can see how much of the condo fee represents property tax. You don't have to itemize your deductions on your tax return to claim a deduction for at least a portion of the real estate tax you paid.

- **Personal property tax:** Some people pay personal property tax and are entitled to deduct that personal property tax if they itemize their deductions on their Federal tax return. Depending on the laws in your state and community, you might pay personal property tax on your automobile, boat, livestock, tools, computers, inventory, household goods, attachments to mobile homes, and machinery. If you pay personal property tax for any reason, save that bill and include it with your tax receipts.

- **Sales tax:** If you live in a state with no state income tax and itemize your deductions, you're missing out on a deduction that people in other states get — the deduction for state and local income tax. Unlike those unfortunates in other states, you didn't have to even pay state and local income tax, but the folks in Washington decided to give you a benefit that people in taxed states don't enjoy: You get to take a deduction for the sales tax you pay. Happily, you don't have to hang onto the receipts for every purchase you made during the year. The IRS provides tables for calculating the sales tax you can deduct based on your income. If you purchased a big-ticket item, such as a vehicle, a trailer, or an airplane, keep track of the sales tax you paid on that purchase because you can add that amount to the amount you calculate based on the tables.

✔ **Foreign income tax:** If you receive income from a foreign source, you might be subject to tax on that income in the country where the income was earned. Most frequently, this situation occurs if you own shares of a mutual fund that invests overseas. You don't file a tax return in the foreign country — the thoughtful tax officials just take the tax out of your earnings before you get them. Keep this information for your U.S. tax return so you can make sure you don't pay tax twice on the same money.

Mint.com provides tags for taxes. For example, if you make a payment to your city for property tax, tag that expense as property tax. In that way, you'll remember to include the amount when summarizing information for your income tax return. Simply follow these steps:

1. **Click the Transactions tab.**

   You see your transaction list.

2. **Select the property tax transaction.**

   Scroll down until you find the transaction you want.

3. **Enter the proper category.**

   Click the arrow in the Category field, select Taxes, and then select Property Tax.

4. **Save the transaction.**

   Simply click off the transaction to save your new category.

To see whether you have other transactions of the same type to tag, click the Show All button on the right side of the screen. For example, if your property tax was paid to City Treasurer, a Show All City Treasurer button appears on the right when you click the transaction.

At any time, you can search all your transactions for a particular payee. Enter the search criteria in the Search box at the top of the Transactions page and then click Search. All transactions matching your search criteria appear.

# *Organizing Deductions*

Tags enable you to mark a transaction as a particular type and then produce a list of all tagged transactions, regardless of the category. You might have tax-related transactions in with doctor bills, tax payments, weekly donations to church, school expenses, and so on. Pull all those expenses together by tagging them as tax-related, as follows:

1. **Click a transaction on the Transactions tab and then click that transaction's Edit Details tab.**

   You see the transaction's details, including the source of the transaction, any notes you might have entered, and the tag boxes.

2. **Mark this transaction as tax-related.**

   In the Tags section, select the Tax-related option, as shown in Figure 21-1.

3. **Click I'm Done, at the bottom of the details screen, to save your change.**

**Figure 21-1:**
Organize your tax-related expenses.

# Viewing Deductions

You can view your tax-related items in several ways, as follows:

- **Display all tax-related items in your transaction list.** On the left side of your transaction list is a list of tags. Click Tax-Related to see all tax-related transactions.

- **View your tags in a chart.** Click the Trends tab. In the Choose a Graph area on the left, click Spending, and then click By Tag to display a pie chart showing how much of your spending is designated for each tag. If you prefer a bar chart, click the bar chart icon at the top of the chart. Click the hyperlinked tag description to return to the list of transactions that make up that tag.

- **Control the time period the chart covers.** On the Trends tab, while viewing a tags chart, select from the date options at the top of the screen for this month, last month, this year, all time, or specific months.

✔ **Compare your spending for the selected period to previous time periods.** Click the arrow in the Compare field and choose a time frame for comparison. Mint.com displays a bar chart comparing your tax-related spending in the current period to the previous period you selected.

# Exporting a Tax Report

Some people complain that Mint.com doesn't have an advanced reporting feature, although a plethora of reporting options are available on the Trends tab. If you want more control over the presentation of your numbers, or you want to print statements and sort and organize your numbers, you can export a trends statement to Excel. Do the following:

1. **View your report (see Figure 21-2).**

   Click the Trends tab and then select the type of report you want to display. For taxes, select a report of your tagged items, as described in the preceding section, "Viewing Deductions." When the chart appears, click the Tax-Related link to display a list of all tax-related transactions.

**Figure 21-2:**
See your
tax-related
transac-
tions.

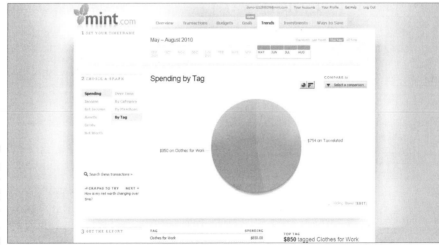

2. **Scroll below the transactions list.**

3. **Click Export all *x* Transactions, where *x* is the number of transactions in your transaction list, as shown in Figure 21-3.**

**Figure 21-3:**
Send your report to Excel.

Click to export the report

4. **Click Open to open the file in your spreadsheet program or click Save to save the file on your computer.**

   The file created from your Mint.com transactions is a CSV file. This type of file can be opened in a spreadsheet program such as Excel or in a free online spreadsheet such as Google Docs.

5. **Organize your report.**

   In the spreadsheet program, you can adjust the column widths to accommodate your information and sort, total, and display your information anyway you like.

# Looking for Deductions

You have examined all your transactions for the year and are getting ready to meet with your tax accountant. You just wish you could find some additional deductions so that you can lower your tax.

Following is a shopping list of tax deductions that people forget to claim:

- Mileage driven for charity, medical, or business
- Moving expenses
- Tools and equipment purchased for use in your job
- Medical expenses
- Long-term care insurance

- Nursing home costs
- Interest on your mortgage
- Interest on your refinanced mortgage
- Points paid with your mortgage
- Interest expense on investment property
- Casualty and theft losses
- Home office expenses
- Job hunting expenses
- Education
- Gambling losses
- Alimony
- Unreimbursed business expenses
- IRA contribution

Every person doesn't qualify to deduct all the items in the preceding list, and not all these items are 100 percent deductible. Use this list as a reminder of what to ask your accountant when you're discussing the preparation of your tax return.

# Saving Supporting Documents

Record keeping for your tax return has taken on a new meaning in our current digital age. And that, as Martha Stewart would say, is a good thing. If you plan to keep printouts of your paperwork, make sure you copy or scan any thermal paper receipts that you want to save with your tax records. Most thermal papers fade quickly and won't be of any use if your tax return is audited.

The IRS wants you to have original receipts or reproductions of original receipts to support the numbers on your tax return. Digital receipts are acceptable, so if you want to scan your receipts and save them on your computer, that's just fine with the IRS.

If you scan your receipts so you can save them digitally, don't just keep the receipts on your hard drive. Save a copy of all your receipts to a CD and then store the CD with your tax records. To be extra safe, store the CD off-premises so that it won't be harmed in the event of a fire or other catastrophe, or store your receipt file online.

The IRS recommends that you keep most records for three years from the date on which you filed your tax return. If you amend your tax return, or if the IRS changes your tax return, keep records for three years from the date on which the tax return was finalized.

If you don't pay all your income tax with your tax return (for example, if you request an installment plan for paying your tax), save your receipts for two years from the time you made the final payment (or three years after you filed the return, whichever is later).

The three-year rule is fine for post office receipts and evidence of your business mileage, but what about purchase and trading information on stocks and mutual funds, or information about the purchase of the home you're still living in? When you still own an item that will (or might) have an effect on your tax return, the IRS expects you to save records until you sell the asset.

# Preparing Your Tax Return

Estimates today put the tax code at about 70,000 pages. We have a limited space for our own version of the tax code, so we're doing some serious condensing. Here's the tax code in a nutshell:

- **Income:** If you received money or any other item of value except amounts received as a gift or an inheritance, put the amount on your tax return. If you received goods or services in the form of a barter, put the value of the goods or services you received on your tax return.

- **Deductions:** If you spent money that was necessary to receive amounts listed in the income section or you spent money on medical expenses, mortgage interest, taxes, or donations to charity, that money might count as a tax deduction. If you suffered a casualty or were the victim of a theft or vandalism, the amount of your loss might count as a tax deduction.

- **Paperwork:** Save any paperwork or other evidence that supports the amounts compiled in the income and deductions sections.

There you have it: 70,000 pages of details and exceptions explained in a few paragraphs.

# Avoiding an Audit

You save paperwork so you can substantiate the numbers on your tax return in case you're audited. Following are several tips to stay on the straight and narrow and keep out of the target range of the IRS's audit crew:

- Don't forget to list all the income reported to you on forms, including amounts from W-2 forms, 1099 forms, and K-1 forms.

✔ If you're not preparing your tax return yourself, choose a reputable tax preparer. Look for a preparer who is licensed, such as a CPA, an Enrolled Agent, or someone registered with the IRS who has passed the preparer guidelines set out by the IRS. Any reputable preparer should be happy to tell you his or her credentials. Choose someone who has been in business for awhile and specializes in preparing tax returns for people in your profession.

✔ Make sure your tax return is neat and legible. If the IRS can't make out the numbers among the coffee stains, chances are good you'll get to explain your tax return numbers in person.

✔ Beat the IRS to the punch. If something on your tax return is confusing or questionable, write an explanation and attach your statement to the tax return. If your explanation is acceptable, case closed. No need to audit you.

✔ Make sure everything adds up. This sounds like a no-brainer, but check your math! Even if you're using tax preparation software, get out your calculator and recheck your numbers.

✔ File your tax return on time. If you have to be late, file for an extension so that your return will be legally late. Filing late without an extension calls attention to your return.

✔ Sign your return.

# Enjoying Your Refund

We hate tax refunds. If someone receives a tax refund, that person gave the IRS an interest-free loan. The taxpayer could have banked that money and earned some interest, or maybe paid off a loan or credit card early and saved the interest and finance charges.

Many people look at the tax refund system as a means of forced saving, and then count on using that refund money for something special. But why not reduce your withholding and have the money automatically deposited to a savings account during the year? You can earn interest and have a built-in emergency fund.

But enough preaching. If you have a refund on the way, Mint.com sends you an e-mail alert as soon as your refund has been deposited in your bank account. And when you get that refund, you can still put the money away and let it earn its keep. Use the Find Savings tools (see Chapter 3) and search for some nifty alternatives for investing your refund money so that it can grow.

# Exploring New Tax Features

According to Aaron Patzer, Founder & CEO of Mint.com, the following exciting Minty tax toys are right around the corner:

✔ Mint.com will add TaxCaster from TurboTax into the program. TaxCaster is an online calculator that you can use to figure out your expected refund (or tax payment).

✔ Mint.com will have a tax summary feature containing all tax-related tags and tax-related categories (medical expenses, child care, education, and so on) in one convenient tabular form that you can print and give to your accountant or use yourself to determine whether you should take the standard deduction or itemize deductions.

✔ Mint.com is working with TurboTax to coordinate a service whereby you can request that all your 1099 forms can be automatically imported into TurboTax.

# Chapter 22

# Ten Ways to Improve Your Credit Score

· · · · · · · · · · · · · · · · · · · · · · · · · · · · · · · · · · · · · · · · · · · · · · · · · · ·

*In This Chapter*

▶ Reducing credit card balances

▶ Making timely payments

▶ Ignoring grace periods

▶ Keeping multiple credit cards

▶ Correcting credit report errors

▶ Removing old debts

▶ Staying away from credit that is out of reach

▶ Exploring different types of borrowing

▶ Avoiding debt settlements

▶ Adding personal notes to your credit reports

· · · · · · · · · · · · · · · · · · · · · · · · · · · · · · · · · · · · · · · · · · · · · · · · · · ·

*L*enders seem to have only a passing interest in your name, your family members, where you live, and what you do for a living. But everyone wants to know your credit score.

In the 1980s, not long after credit cards started becoming as ubiquitous as television sets and second cars, a company named Fair Isaac Corporation (FICO) developed a method of evaluating credit based on historical performance of borrowing and repaying money and a number of other formulas that to this day remain a secret.

The FICO score helps lenders determine whether they want to loan money to you and at what rate of interest. The score is sometimes used when evaluating people who are being considered for a job. Insurance companies also use FICO scores to help them determine what rates to charge for auto and homeowner's insurance. People with low FICO scores are deemed more likely to file claims and are thus charged higher premiums. It's possible that some people request a FICO score before getting engaged, but that's just speculation.

In this chapter, you discover ten tips for improving your FICO score. These tips are helpful no matter how high or low your score is now.

# Reduce Credit Card Balances

One of the confusing issues about increasing your credit score is the catch-22 that you have to have credit to get credit. You build a credit history and thus a credit score by showing that you can obtain and manage credit.

The easiest way to start building a credit history is to get a credit card. You can apply for a card at your bank, a department store, or a gas station. You might also get offers in the mail for a credit card. Or you can click Ways to Save in Mint.com and see a list of credit cards selected for you based on their low rates and high rewards programs.

## Checking your credit score

When you go to the bank or credit union to try to borrow money, the lender looks at your FICO score. A high FICO score not only makes you more likely to get a loan but also means you pay a lower rate of interest. A high FICO score also makes you more likely to be considered for better rates on credit cards.

The FICO score ranges from 200–850. The scores break down as follows:

- 700–850: Excellent. You get your loan and the best interest rates
- 680–699: Good.
- 629–679: Okay.
- 580–619: Low.
- 500–579: Bad.
- 499 and under: Unlikely you will get a loan.

The three credit bureaus that monitor personal credit are Experian, TransUnion, and Equifax.

Each lender has a favorite company, and each of the companies produce its own credit score. These scores will be similar to but not exactly the same as the FICO score. The actual FICO score is available only from Fair Isaac Corporation.

If you're considering applying for a loan or a new credit card, first examine your credit reports and make sure there are no errors or omissions. You can obtain all three of your credit reports at no charge, once a year, from Central Source LLC at www.AnnualCreditReport.com or by calling 877-322-8228. At the same time, you can purchase a copy of your credit score for $7.95 from one of the credit bureaus at the Central Source Web site. Alternatively, at any time, you can purchase a copy of your credit score from www.myfico.com for $15.95. Here's a tip for getting your credit score for free: Your lender requests your credit score when you apply for credit, so just ask the lender for a copy of the score.

The trick to raising your credit score with credit cards is to use only a small portion of your credit limit. Experts suggest that you should owe no more than 20 percent of your total available credit card credit. For example, if you have a credit card with a credit limit of $2,000, you should have an outstanding balance of no more than $400 on that credit card.

People with a bad credit score because of their history of not making payments on time might have trouble getting a credit card. If you're in this category, don't give up. You can start rebuilding your credit with a secured credit card. Do a quick Internet search for *secured credit cards* to find companies willing to let you deposit money in an account and then use a credit card to make charges against that account balance. Then make payments on time and build a successful credit history, which translates into a higher credit score.

By keeping your credit card balances relatively low, you demonstrate that you can manage your credit well, making you a good risk to lenders and increasing your credit score.

# Make Timely Payments

Late payments show up on your credit report, so potential lenders can see, month-by-month, how frequently you missed your payment and how late your payment was made. Following are four tips for making your credit card payments on time:

- ✔ **Set up automatic electronic payments.** Make sure your payment schedule is such that you make your payment a few days before the due date to accommodate potential nonbusiness days such as holidays and weekends. Not only does this timeliness help ensure that your payment is made on time, but it prevents extra charges for late payments.

- ✔ **Pay your account in full as soon as you make a charge.** If you want to be ultra-safe, you can use your credit card for convenient shopping, and then scurry home, go to the credit card's online site, and make a payment as soon as your charge activity is posted.

- ✔ **Mail payment as soon as you receive your statement.** Don't wait until the due date and risk not getting your payment in on time. See the statement; pay the bill.

- ✔ **Write the due date on the payment envelope.** Even if you don't have the funds available to pay your credit card bill when it arrives, go ahead and write a check and put the check in the envelope. Put the envelope in a place where you won't lose it, and write on the back of the envelope the date when you want to put the payment in the mail. The date serves as a reminder to not miss the payment. If this method sounds too old-school to you, you can get reminders in other ways. Set a payment reminder for yourself on your PDA or smartphone or in your e-mail program. And don't forget that Mint.com can send you an alert, too, as described in Chapter 6.

# Ignore Grace Periods

Many credit and loan programs allow you a window of opportunity to make your payment later than the due date without applying a penalty. Don't be tempted by the grace period! Paying during the grace period can result in higher interest overall on a loan, where interest or finance charges are calculated based on the number of days between payments,

Another problem with using the grace period is that you might find yourself in a situation where last month's charges still show on the current month's bill, and that previous charge gets reported to the credit bureaus as the amount you owe. By leaving a balance on the books into the next month, it looks like you're charging more than you really are, which might affect your credit score negatively.

# Keep Multiple Credit Cards

Surprisingly, your credit score can increase if you use more credit cards. The more credit cards you have, the more available credit you have. As long as you continue to keep your credit card usage low, ideally to 20 percent or less of the available credit on each card, your credit score will improve.

Here's another tip: Older cards are better. Rather than acquiring a lot of new cards, keep older cards alive and use them from time to time. The older your credit cards, the longer your credit history and the higher your credit score.

Some experts suggest that consumers own an average of ten cards, but three or four cards are more than enough to manage in terms of making payments and keeping track of due dates. If you need more credit, consider asking your credit card companies for an increase in your credit limit before exploring the alternative of signing on for a new card. Fair Isaac Corporation doesn't publish information about how many cards represents an ideal number, and it's likely that the ideal number of credit cards is different for different people.

The key is keeping the balances low and the cards old. Owning more cards won't necessarily hurt your credit score, but high ratios of borrowing to credit limits will lower your score, as will applying for and acquiring lots of new credit cards.

# Remove Old Debt

The credit report rules require that old debts settled more than seven years ago be removed from your credit report. The exception is if you were involved in a personal bankruptcy, in which case that information can stay on your credit report for ten years.

Maybe you made a series of late payments years ago, and that information is still lurking in the dark corners of your credit report. Contact the credit bureau reporting the old debt and ask that it be removed. That's all you need to do.

Be sure you examine all three credit reports from Experian, TransUnion, and Equifax. Sometimes information appears on one or two reports but not all three. Any reports affected by the old outdated information should be corrected so that it is current.

Making this correction can boost your credit score, so don't delay!

## Correct Errors

When you look at your credit reports from the three credit bureaus (Experian, TransUnion, and Equifax), don't be surprised if you see incorrect information. Many credit reports contain errors.

Sometimes errors occur when a person divorces and information from the ex-spouse still remains on the report or when two people in the same family have the same name. Sometimes payments that were made are not recorded properly by the receiving company, and that company reports incorrect information to the credit bureaus.

Make a point of reading each credit report in its entirety and making sure you understand every item on the report, paying special attention to any items that are designated as negative or adverse.

Each of the credit companies provides you with opportunities to dispute information on the reports and request a change when an error appears on the report. The credit bureau will tell you what it needs to change the report.

If a company has provided incorrect information to a credit bureau, the company is required by law to correct the inaccurate or incorrect information.

Contact the credit bureaus by telephone, in writing, or on their Web sites to begin the process of making a correction:

Equifax
P.O. Box 740256
Atlanta, GA 30374
800-685-1111
www.equifax.com

Experian
P.O. Box 2002
Allen, TX 75013
888-0397-3742
www.experian.com

TransUnion
P.O. Box 2000
Chester, PA 19022
800-888-4213
www.transunion.com

# Stay Away from Out-of-Reach Credit

When you apply for a credit card or a loan and are rejected, your credit score is lowered, making it even more difficult to borrow from someone else. Avoid being rejected by not applying for a loan you can't get. For example, if you've been turned down for a mortgage, don't keep applying for the mortgage at other lending institutions. Or if you apply for a credit card and get rejected, let at least six months pass and make sure your credit score is higher before you apply for another credit card.

While you're waiting to reapply, work on improving your credit score by lowering your existing debt, making sure every payment is made on time or early, and making sure your credit reports contain no errors.

If you're thinking about borrowing money, talk to a banker. Bring a copy of your credit reports with you to the bank and ask the banker to take a look at them. See whether the banker would be willing to lend to you and at what rate. This way, you can get a sense of the likelihood of success at getting a loan before a report is made to the credit companies that you're considering borrowing. If the banker says it's unlikely the bank will lend to you at this time, find out what changes the bank needs to see in your credit report before they will be willing to make the loan. You can also save time and frustration by asking a lender to preapprove you for a loan before you begin shopping for a house or car. That way, you know in advance how much you can borrow.

# Explore Other Types of Borrowing

One path to a higher credit score involves combining several types of borrowing. If your only borrowing history is one credit card from your favorite department store, the credit bureaus don't have much to go on when assessing your creditworthiness.

Financial experts recommend that you engage in different types of borrowing to improve your credit score. A well-rounded credit history includes bank credit cards, store credit cards, a home mortgage, and a personal loan such as an automobile loan.

Again, you might find yourself faced with a catch-22 situation: To get a loan, you need to demonstrate some credit history, but to develop a credit history, you need to get a loan.

You might get turned down for a loan because of a low credit score or lack of a lengthy credit history. That doesn't mean you have to give up on getting a loan. Here are some different types of loans that might be available to you:

- ✔ **Cosigned loan:** Someone who has a good credit history, perhaps a parent or other family member, agrees to cosign your loan and commits to making the payments if you default. The bank is happy because it can lend to someone who presents less of a risk than you do. As long as your payments are made on time, your credit history improves and your credit score ultimately increases.

- ✔ **Secured loan:** A *secured loan* is collateralized by tangible property. For example, a home mortgage is backed by the house, and a car loan is secured with the car as collateral. If you can't make your payments, the lending institution is protected from loss because it has the right to take the property. Some banks and credit units will make loans secured by the balance in a savings account or other monetary investment. This is another way to build credit if your credit history isn't good, and the rates are more favorable than they are for a secured credit card.

- ✔ **Unsecured loan:** When there is no collateral, the loan is considered *unsecured.* Banks are not averse to making unsecured loans because they can charge a higher interest rate than on a secured loan.

- ✔ **Personal loan:** If a bank won't help you out, you might be able to borrow from someone you know. Personal loans between individuals should be structured with a legal, signed promissory note; and interest should be charged to the borrower. This type of loan won't appear on your credit report but might be a viable alternative if you need money.

- ✔ **Store loans:** Many stores let you make purchases and pay for the item over time. This is similar to using a store credit card, but the credit is extended for a particular purchase instead of indefinitely.

Be wary of offers for 0 percent interest loans unless you're certain that you can make every payment. Often these attractive offers backfire if you miss one payment — all the interest you would have paid if it weren't for the 0 percent offer suddenly becomes due. Read the fine print carefully on any promotion that sounds too good to be true.

# Avoid Debt Settlements

It sounds like such a good opportunity: You can consolidate all your debts into one low monthly payment that is less than you're currently paying on all your debts. Furthermore, you get to settle with the creditors for less than the total amount owed because they will at least get something, even if it's not the full amount you owe.

Does this sound too good to be true? Debt settlement programs abound, and you should try your best to avoid them if you want to maintain a good credit score.

When you enter into a debt settlement agreement, that agreement appears on your credit report. If a creditor agrees to accept a payment from you that is lower than the total amount owing, your credit score is lowered, and the information remains on your credit report for any potential lenders to see.

Some people argue that settling a debt and taking a hit to your credit score is better than missing payments or making late payments and also taking a hit to the score. Although it is true that missed payments and late payments negatively affect your credit score, settlement of a debt for less than the total amount of the debt is at least as detrimental, if not more so, to your credit score.

Bankers prefer to see you successfully pay off a debt in full than reach a settlement, and this makes sense. Would you want to loan to someone who has a history of repaying less than the total amount due?

If you're having trouble making your credit card payments, consider transferring your credit card balances to a new card with a lower interest rate. Click Ways to Save at the top of the Mint.com screen to look at credit card options, including balance transfer options. If you apply for a new credit card account, your credit score drops immediately. But the benefit of being able to afford your credit card payments due to a lower interest rate on the new card will soon offset the temporary decrease that occurred in your credit score.

# Add a Note to Your Credit Report

Dear Mom: I'm having a great time at camp this summer. No, wait, that's not the type of personal note you want to put on your credit report.

When you read through your credit report, you might notice some incorrect or outdated information. Maybe you've tried to no avail to correct this information, or you're in the process of getting the documentation you need to straighten out a problem. All three credit bureaus enable you to add a personal statement on your credit report explaining something that appears on the report.

Maybe a past due amount on the report belongs to a debt your ex promised to pay as part of your divorce agreement. Maybe you paid a doctor bill, but the doctor's office lost track of your payment and reported it as unpaid. Perhaps you're waiting for an insurance settlement to cover costs from an accident, but the bills are coming in and you can't pay them.

If you can explain any unfavorable item on your credit report, by all means add your comment to the reports. The note won't change your credit score, but a lender who is considering giving you a loan will see the statement and can take it into consideration.

# Chapter 23

# Ten Tips to Becoming a Mint.com Wiz

*A*re you wondering whether you've overlooked any of Mint.com's bells and whistles? Perhaps you've skipped to this section to see whether Mint.com has any secret features. Or maybe you just can't get enough of Mint.com. You've come to the right place. In this chapter, you find some tricks and tips that will help you get the most out of the program. Mint. com has hidden gems that even the most experienced users might miss. If you scan through the techniques in this chapter, you're bound to find a few things that could make Mint.com work better or faster for you.

# Adding a Secondary E-mail Address

Mint.com can be your financial conscience, nudging you along a financial path by sending information about how much money you have and how much you owe. Mint.com also e-mails you a weekly summary of all the financial accounts in your Mint.com account to give you a report card of how you're doing. You can review how alerts and weekly e-mails work in Chapter 6, which also explains how you can add an e-mail address to Mint.com.

But what you might not have realized is that you can add a second e-mail address to the program. All alerts and e-mails are then sent to both e-mail addresses. Adding a second e-mail can be a handy feature if you and someone else want to use the same Mint.com account, or if you have e-mail access on your computer and, say, a smartphone or other mobile device.

To enter a second e-mail address, follow these steps:

1. **On the Overview tab, click the Your Profile link.**

2. **Click the Email & Alerts tab.**

3. **Click the Add One link, which is to the right of the Secondary Address link.**

   The window shown in Figure 23-1 appears.

**Figure 23-1:**
Have your alerts sent to a second e-mail address.

4. **In the Also Send Email To field, type the other e-mail address where you'd like to receive messages.**

5. **Click the Close button.**

# Accessing Mint.com with a "Dumb" Cell Phone

Mint.com works best when you're sitting in front of a computer (with its big screen) connected to the Internet. However, you can also download a free Mint.com program called an *application,* or *app,* that works on a mobile device. To download Mint.com for smartphones running the Android operating system, go to www.mint.com/features/android. For the iPhone, go to www.mint.com/features/iphone.

But what if you want to access your Mint.com account from a regular cell phone? You're in luck — as long as your cell phone supports *Short Message System*, or *SMS,* which just about every current cell phone does. (SMS allows you to send and receive very short text messages from a cell phone.)

Mint.com provides the SMS service for free, but your cell phone carrier may charge you to receive and send messages.

To access Mint.com using a standard cell phone, do the following:

1. **Log in to Mint.com.**

2. **Click the Your Profile link.**

3. **Click the Email & Alerts tab.**

    The screen shown in Figure 23-2 appears, so you can add details about yourself, including your cell phone number.

**Figure 23-2:**
View your financial information on a standard cell phone.

4. **In the Enter Your Mobile number field, type your cell phone number.**

5. **Click the Send button.**

   A Confirm Your Activation Code prompt appears on the Email & Alerts page. Leave the Email & Alerts page open and fill in the code when it arrives on your cell phone.

6. **Wait to receive an activation code on your cell phone.**

   In a few seconds, Mint.com sends an SMS message to your cell phone. The SMS message contains a code you can use to link your cell phone to your Mint.com account.

7. **In the Confirm Your Activation Code field on the Mint.com Web page, enter the activation code.**

8. **Click the Finish button.**

To get your financial information using your cell phone, send a text message containing the word *BAL* to MYMINT or 696468 (the corresponding numbers on your keypad). Mint.com will then send your account balances to your cell phone.

If you want to turn off Mint.com's SMS feature, click the Deactivate button on the Email & Alerts tab of the My Profile screen. You can also send the word *Stop* to 696468 from your cell phone.

# Hiding Accounts to Get a Clear View of Your Money

The more financial accounts you add to your Mint.com account, the more useful the program because you get a more complete picture of your financial situation. Sometimes, however, a financial account might muck up your true financial standing. For instance, if you go on a business trip and take a client to a baseball game and dinner, Mint.com might think you've blown your entertainment budget. But that's not true because the expenses are being *reimbursed*, or paid back to you, by your company. The game and dinner were work costs, not personal expenses.

It's easy to tell Mint.com which accounts to ignore when it comes to tracking your expenses. Just do the following:

1. **Log in to your account.**

2. **Click the Your Profile link.**

3. **Click the Hide tab.**

   The screen shown in Figure 23-3 appears.

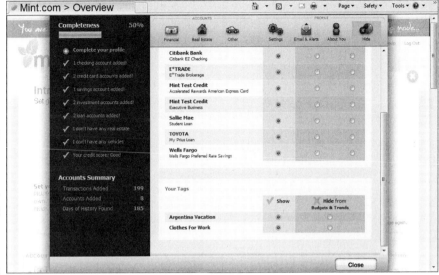

**Figure 23-3:**
Ignore
certain
accounts or
tags to get
accurate
spending
info.

4. **Make a selection in the Hide From column:**

   • Click the Budgets & Trends option. If you have a corporate credit card that you use for work, hide the account from the Budgets & Trends features. You'll still see the corporate card balance on the Overview tab.

   • Click the All of Mint.com option. This option hides the corporate credit card account throughout Mint.com.

5. **Click the Close button.**

You can hide transactions also according to their tags. To do this, follow these steps:

1. **Log into your account and then click the Your Profile link.**

2. **Click the Hide tab.**

3. **Click the Hide from Budgets & Trends option next to the tag you want to hide.**

   You may need to scroll down quite a bit to see the option to hide tags. You can hide any tagged transactions. One good use of this feature is to hide transactions tagged as reimbursed transactions.

# Making Mint.com a Family Affair

When you first set up Mint.com, you most likely added your own accounts first. But why stop there? You can add the financial accounts of a spouse or

other family member to your Mint.com account. In that way, you can understand where the household's money is going, without the hassle of setting
up a joint checking account. You need your family members' permission first
because they will need to provide their user IDs and passwords to you.

# Customizing Categories

Mint.com gets much of its power from *categories*, or groups that classify your
financial transactions. For instance, if you charge $5 at McDonald's, Mint.com
places the transaction into the Fast Food subcategory of the Food & Dining
category.

If Mint.com's preset categories aren't adequate, you can add your own.
Here's how:

1. **Find the transaction that needs a new category.**

   On the Transactions tab, look through the list of your transactions until
   you find the one for which you'd like to create a category.

2. **Select the Category field.**

   Click the down arrow to the right of the entry in the Category column. A
   list of all Mint.com's categories appears.

3. **Click the Add/Edit Categories link, which appears when you hover
   your mouse pointer over any category.**

   The link is at the bottom of all default categories. The Manage Your
   Categories screen appears, as shown in Figure 23-4.

4. **On the left side of the screen, click the general category that best
   describes the expense for which you want to create a custom
   subcategory.**

5. **Click the Add a New Category button.**

6. **Type the name of the subcategory you want to add.**

   As you type, you see the names of subcategories that other Mint.com
   users have added. You might get a chuckle out of seeing what other
   users are tracking. For instance, click the Entertainment category and
   then type **mari** to see what some people are doing in their free time.

7. **Click the Save It button.**

**Figure 23-4:**
Create a
category for
a particular
expense.

# Grouping Your Transactions Correctly

When Mint.com downloads your transactions from your banks and credit card companies, it takes a good stab at which category to put the transaction in. Mint.com will also try to clean up the gobbledygook way many credit card companies display descriptions of transactions. For instance, if you buy something from Amazon.com, you credit card statement probably describes the transaction as something like AMAZON AMZN.COM. Mint.com changes that to Amazon.

Sometimes, though, Mint.com needs your help. For instance, if you buy a basketball from Nike, Mint.com may place the purchase in the clothing category because it doesn't know that you actually bought a basketball, not shoes.

You can change how Mint.com describes transactions and categories in the future:

1. **Click the Transactions tab.**

2. **Click the transaction you want to modify and then click Edit Details.**

3. **Type a new name for the description, or change the category, or both, as shown in Figure 23-5.**

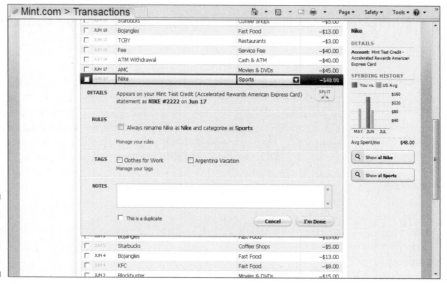

**Figure 23-5:**
Change the
description
or category.

# Editing a Handful of Transactions at Once

You could go through all your transactions and create rules for each of them, as described in the preceding tip. Or if you have a number of similar transactions, you can edit them all at the same time.

Let's say you just got back from a vacation and racked up all sorts of charges. You'd like to tag, or group, all the expenses connected with your trip as vacation costs so you can see the total amount you spent. From the Transactions tab, click the check box to the left of all vacation expenses. Next, click the Edit Multiple button, which is at the upper left, just below the account's value, or *balance*. You can now tag all those transactions as vacation costs at one time. Don't forget to click the I'm Done button when you're finished.

# Backing Up Your Financial Data by Exporting

When you use Mint.com, you're storing all your financial transactions on computers operated by Mint.com and its parent company, Intuit. None of the information is stored on your own computer.

If you've been using Mint.com for awhile, you might have accumulated enough financial data that you'll want to have a copy on your computer's hard drive. Mint.com allows you to save a copy of your data by exporting, or downloading, all your data to your computer.

To export your financial data, click the Transactions tab and scroll all the way to the bottom of the page. Below the last transaction in the list is a small link that says, Export All *x* Transactions, where *x* is the number of transactions. Click that link and you'll be prompted to save your transactions on your computer. The file is saved as a *comma-separated values*, or *CSV*, file, which can be read by most spreadsheet software, including Microsoft Excel. Several free online spreadsheets, such as Microsoft Windows Live Office (`http://office.live.com`) and Google Docs (`http://docs.google.com`) can also read CSV files.

You can export all your transactions, including checking and savings accounts as well as brokerage accounts and loans.

# Budgeting for Expenses That Aren't Monthly

Each month you get a bunch of bills. Utilities, cell phone, and rent or mortgage are settled monthly. Some bills, though, don't hit each month. Property taxes, auto insurance, and homeowner's insurance are a few examples of bills that usually come due every six months or every year. These infrequent bills can be easy to forget and not budget for, which is dangerous because these bills tend to be significant.

Mint.com can help you budget for these nonmonthly bills. Just follow these steps:

1. **Click the Budgets tab.**

2. **Click the Create a Budget button at the upper-left corner.**

   The screen shown in Figure 23-6 appears.

3. **In the Choose a Category drop-down list, choose the category for the bill.**

   For example, you might select Auto & Transport and then Auto Insurance.

4. **For the When Will This Happen? option, select Every Few Months.**

5. **Enter the amount of the bill and how often it's due.**

Figure 23-6:
Budget for
bills that
come up a
few times a
year.

6. **Enter the when the next bill is due.**

   Mint.com will remind you how much money you should be setting aside monthly so you have enough money when the bill is due.

# Comparing Your Spending

Are you spending too much on clothing? Are you pampering your pet too much? How much you should spend on different categories is a personal decision and is based on how much you earn and your financial goals.

But another useful guide to help you gauge your spending is seeing how your spending compares with other people. Rather than keeping up with the Joneses, you might want to know how you can spend less than the Joneses. Mint.com will let you see how much other Mint.com users are spending on major categories so you can size up your spending.

You can access this information in several ways. One convenient method is to see how other people are spending on categories. Follow these steps:

1. **Sign in to your Mint.com account.**

2. **Click the Trends tab.**

3. **Select a time frame.**

   You can select just one month to analyze or click one month and drag to cover several additional months.

**4. Choose Spending⇨By Category.**

**5. In the Compare To drop-down list, choose your comparison.**

You can compare your spending in the category to other Mint.com users in a particular city, a particular state, or the entire United States. You see a chart like the one in Figure 23-7.

**6. Move your cursor over the bars to see how much you're spending versus the average spending.**

**Figure 23-7:**
See how your spending in different categories measures up.

You can use the same screen on the Trends tab to compare your spending from different merchants. Instead of choosing By Category, choose By Merchant. Similarly, you can compare how much you're spending on specific tags by selecting the By Tag option.

# Index

• *C* •

## Apple & Macs

iPad For Dummies
978-0-470-58027-1

iPhone For Dummies,
4th Edition
978-0-470-87870-5

MacBook For Dummies, 3rd
Edition
978-0-470-76918-8

Mac OS X Snow Leopard For
Dummies
978-0-470-43543-4

## Business

Bookkeeping For Dummies
978-0-7645-9848-7

Job Interviews
For Dummies,
3rd Edition
978-0-470-17748-8

Resumes For Dummies,
5th Edition
978-0-470-08037-5

Starting an
Online Business
For Dummies,
5th Edition
978-0-470-60210-2

Stock Investing
For Dummies,
3rd Edition
978-0-470-40114-9

Successful
Time Management
For Dummies
978-0-470-29034-7

## Computer Hardware

BlackBerry
For Dummies,
4th Edition
978-0-470-60700-8

Computers For Seniors
For Dummies,
2nd Edition
978-0-470-53483-0

PCs For Dummies,
Windows
7 Edition
978-0-470-46542-4

Laptops For Dummies,
4th Edition
978-0-470-57829-2

## Cooking & Entertaining

Cooking Basics
For Dummies,
3rd Edition
978-0-7645-7206-7

Wine For Dummies,
4th Edition
978-0-470-04579-4

## Diet & Nutrition

Dieting For Dummies,
2nd Edition
978-0-7645-4149-0

Nutrition For Dummies,
4th Edition
978-0-471-79868-2

Weight Training
For Dummies,
3rd Edition
978-0-471-76845-6

## Digital Photography

Digital SLR Cameras &
Photography For Dummies,
3rd Edition
978-0-470-46606-3

Photoshop Elements 8
For Dummies
978-0-470-52967-6

## Gardening

Gardening Basics
For Dummies
978-0-470-03749-2

Organic Gardening
For Dummies,
2nd Edition
978-0-470-43067-5

## Green/Sustainable

Raising Chickens
For Dummies
978-0-470-46544-8

Green Cleaning
For Dummies
978-0-470-39106-8

## Health

Diabetes For Dummies,
3rd Edition
978-0-470-27086-8

Food Allergies
For Dummies
978-0-470-09584-3

Living Gluten-Free
For Dummies,
2nd Edition
978-0-470-58589-4

## Hobbies/General

Chess For Dummies,
2nd Edition
978-0-7645-8404-6

Drawing
Cartoons & Comics
For Dummies
978-0-470-42683-8

Knitting For Dummies,
2nd Edition
978-0-470-28747-7

Organizing
For Dummies
978-0-7645-5300-4

Su Doku For Dummies
978-0-470-01892-7

## Home Improvement

Home Maintenance
For Dummies,
2nd Edition
978-0-470-43063-7

Home Theater
For Dummies,
3rd Edition
978-0-470-41189-6

Living the
Country Lifestyle
All-in-One
For Dummies
978-0-470-43061-3

Solar Power Your Home
For Dummies,
2nd Edition
978-0-470-59678-4

## Internet

Blogging For Dummies,
3rd Edition
978-0-470-61996-4

eBay For Dummies,
6th Edition
978-0-470-49741-8

Facebook For Dummies,
3rd Edition
978-0-470-87804-0

Web Marketing
For Dummies,
2nd Edition
978-0-470-37181-7

WordPress
For Dummies,
3rd Edition
978-0-470-59274-8

## Language & Foreign Language

French For Dummies
978-0-7645-5193-2

Italian Phrases
For Dummies
978-0-7645-7203-6

Spanish For Dummies,
2nd Edition
978-0-470-87855-2

Spanish
For Dummies,
Audio Set
978-0-470-09585-0

## Math & Science

Algebra I
For Dummies,
2nd Edition
978-0-470-55964-2

Biology For Dummies,
2nd Edition
978-0-470-59875-7

Calculus For Dummies
978-0-7645-2498-1

Chemistry For Dummies
978-0-7645-5430-8

## Microsoft Office

Excel 2010 For Dummies
978-0-470-48953-6

Office 2010 All-in-One
For Dummies
978-0-470-49748-7

Office 2010 For Dummies,
Book + DVD Bundle
978-0-470-62698-6

Word 2010 For Dummies
978-0-470-48772-3

## Music

Guitar For Dummies,
2nd Edition
978-0-7645-9904-0

iPod & iTunes For
Dummies, 8th Edition
978-0-470-87871-2

Piano Exercises
For Dummies
978-0-470-38765-8

## Parenting & Education

Parenting For Dummies,
2nd Edition
978-0-7645-5418-6

Type 1 Diabetes
For Dummies
978-0-470-17811-9

## Pets

Cats For Dummies,
2nd Edition
978-0-7645-5275-5

Dog Training For Dummies,
3rd Edition
978-0-470-60029-0

Puppies For Dummies,
2nd Edition
978-0-470-03717-1

## Religion & Inspiration

The Bible For Dummies
978-0-7645-5296-0

Catholicism For Dummies
978-0-7645-5391-2

Women in the Bible
For Dummies
978-0-7645-8475-6

## Self-Help & Relationship

Anger Management
For Dummies
978-0-470-03715-7

Overcoming Anxiety
For Dummies,
2nd Edition
978-0-470-57441-6

## Sports

Baseball
For Dummies,
3rd Edition
978-0-7645-7537-2

Basketball
For Dummies,
2nd Edition
978-0-7645-5248-9

Golf For Dummies,
3rd Edition
978-0-471-76871-5

## Web Development

Web Design
All-in-One
For Dummies
978-0-470-41796-6

Web Sites
Do-It-Yourself
For Dummies,
2nd Edition
978-0-470-56520-9

## Windows 7

Windows 7
For Dummies
978-0-470-49743-2

Windows 7
For Dummies,
Book + DVD Bundle
978-0-470-52398-8

Windows 7 All-in-One
For Dummies
978-0-470-48763-1

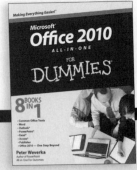

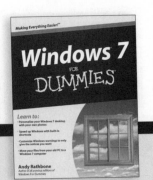

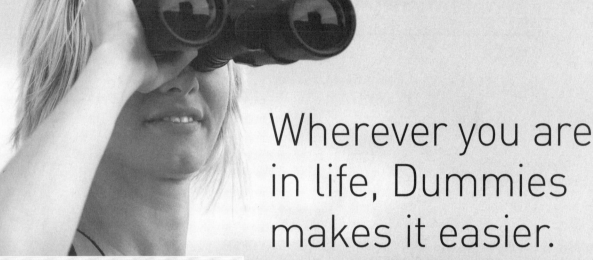